LELOOSKA

The Life of a Northwest Coast Artist

Puffin Rock

TO DR. WILLIAM
SAXE WIHR

FROM
YOUR FRIEND AND
GOOD STUDENT
NANA ARA]
SEP 16'05

LELOOSKA

The Life of a Northwest Coast Artist

CHRIS FRIDAY

UNIVERSITY OF WASHINGTON PRESS

Seattle and London

Library of Congress Cataloging-in-Publication Data
can be found at the back of this book.

Title page illustration: Kolus with Sisiutł
Frontispiece, title page, this page, and page 1 illustrations courtesy of Ralph Norris

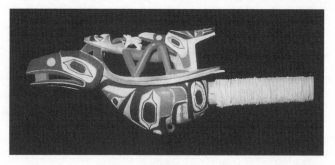

Raven Rattle

CONTENTS

PREFACE

OVER THE SPAN OF FOUR DECADES, from the 1950s to the 1990s, Don "Lelooska" Smith emerged as a superb storyteller, performer, and Northwest Coast Indian artist. His family's daytime educational programs and evening shows of Northwest Coast Indian and other Indian stories and dances exposed literally tens of thousands of people to the diversity and complexity of American Indian lives past and present. His own Northwest Coast carvings earned him a national and international reputation among a generation of carvers that included luminaries such as Bill Reid, Robert Davidson, Douglas E. Cranmer, Henry Hunt, and Bill Holm. That generation helped propel Northwest Coast carvings into the realm of art.

Lelooska's life story was by no means simple and uncomplicated. Born of mixed ancestry, Lelooska grew up with significant Cherokee influences from his mother and her father. In addition, his family's deep friendships with Indians from Oklahoma, the northern Plains, and Eastern Oregon and Washington created multiple layers of identity for Lelooska as a Cherokee, a "breed," and an "Indian." The associations he developed in his adult years added formal and informal ties to tribes and families along the Northwest Coast. In spite of these unusual experiences and his own charisma, skills, and artistic abilities, Lelooska's story also reveals much that is central to understanding twentieth-century Indian lives. When Lelooska and I started this project, his unique capabilities stood out, but as I learned more about his life and experiences I began to realize how much his life story reflects common themes. I hope that readers keep in mind his exceptionalism and the larger picture he represents.

When we began taping Lelooska's life narrative, neither of us was absolutely clear about the end result of our collaborative effort. We were driven by a sense of urgency. Doctors had discovered cancer in Lelooska and the prognosis was not good. At the prime of his life as an artist, this was a devastating blow to Lelooska, his family, and those who knew him. Before we started the interviews, we agreed on two basic goals: that his narrative should be recorded for the younger generations in his family and that it should be made available for a broad audience.

Over the course of nearly two years we taped multiple interviews, and I began creating a verbatim transcript and then editing that for this volume. I had the good fortune of hiring Lelooska's niece Mariah Stoll-Smith (now Reese) to assist with the initial transcription. As she laboriously transferred each word, phrase, pause, and chuckle from tape to paper, Lelooska and I began to pass the narrative on to the younger generation in his family. When I handed the final transcript to Lelooska and his family just before his health went into rapid decline, we took another step toward that goal.

Attaining the second goal took longer. Lelooska agreed that the interviews should be placed in an archive so that they would be available to interested parties. I also had tentative thoughts of some kind of publication, but was not sure what kind of collaborative narrative we might produce any more than I could predict how this information might be disseminated. It eventually appeared in several forums and formats ranging from public talks, elementary school presentations, and collegiate-level classroom lectures to academic conference papers and a volume of scholarly essays in progress about twentieth-century Indian cultural and social history. Lelooska and I have understood these efforts to be a continuation of his long-standing commitment to educational endeavors and his love of performances.

This volume is a collaborative narrative of Don "Lelooska" Smith's life. It is largely the story that Lelooska chose to tell, though it is influenced by the questions I asked him during the many hours of taped interviews and less formal, untaped conversations we had between sessions. My questions were guided by more than a quarter-century association with Lelooska and his family as well as by my training as a historian. Knowing Lelooska and his family long before I became a historian, combined with later work in that discipline, allowed me to look at his life in a unique context.

As a boy, I spent many hours with the Lelooska family. I ate many meals and saw movies there. At the regular, entertaining, and spontaneous black-powder musket shoots, Don, his younger brothers Dick and Smitty, his nephew Jay, and my father, Harlow, and I blazed away in smoky glee at any number of targets. These occasions were always as full of stories as they were lead shot. Fishing with Dick for most of one summer was too. My teenage antics with Jay only sometimes got us in trouble with our families. (They were *very* tolerant of us.) As well as just being around the Lelooska family on a regular basis, I worked at evening shows and sanded carvings for Smitty, all of which has had a deep and lasting impact on the way in which I see the world.

Through all of those years, I was no ethnographer taking field notes; I was a typical teenager focused on my own universe. Because of that teenage vision, during the interviews and editing I turned to my parents, Anna and Harlow Friday, to help me overcome the gaps in my knowledge and perspective about those years. They know the Lelooska family well. Over the years, my mother has served as a bookkeeper, booking agent, jewelry-making assistant, housekeeper, and dancer in the shows. My father helped with construction projects and played an extra in the fur-trade and other workshops, but most often he could be found in the back room watching videos and eating popcorn with Don. Their experiences with the family and insights on this project make them, at least indirectly, part of this collaborative narrative.

My family's close association with the Lelooskas forces me to admit that those same advantages create problems. I cannot be dispassionate and indifferent about Lelooska. I have great respect for him as an artist and a student of history and culture. I am in awe of his abilities to hold large crowds or small groups spellbound for hours with equal ease. I have obligations to him and his family to represent his life story as he chose to tell it that have only been strengthened by doing the interviews. Others who might have conducted such a series of interviews with Lelooska may have chosen to ask different questions, broach different topics, cast the narrative in a different form, or be more of an advocate or critic than I.

Still, no others came forward in the final months of Lelooska's life or in the many decades before that to listen to and record his life story. I have spent several years preparing this narrative for Lelooska's family, for my own, and for the many people who knew Lelooska through his art or his family's educational programs. This narrative is also for those who never had the opportunity to consider the circumstances of Lelooska's remarkable life.

For this project, I returned to the Lelooska family as a friend—and as an academic, which is no less problematic. Scholars have an often deserved reputation for reworking personal narratives at the time of the interviews and during the editing phase to fit their own conceptions rather than those of the people they interview. I am not wholly immune to those tendencies, and this narrative is after all collaborative. I started each interview with a set of questions, but I quickly found that those were only the starting points of the discussions. Don often took control of the conversation, and with his skills as an orator and storyteller he created the narrative structure and plot lines as he recounted his life. For example, I began the first interview by asking him about his early life, but almost immediately he went back to earlier relationships of family and acquaintances that connected to a deep vein of indigenous cultures of North America. He was not going to tie himself to the narrative structure that I envisioned. That has been a powerful lesson for me.

Not every interview session ran so smoothly as that first. Sometimes the interviews were disjointed as we revisited topics or re-engaged those that came up in informal conversations during other visits. I recall one incident when I had driven the 250-odd miles from Bellingham, Washington, to Ariel, Washington, near Mount St. Helens to tape Don, but he was pushing to finish a mask. He was in good spirits and voice, so we chatted for several hours while he carved. I did not tape the discussion, because that would have disrupted his carving; our idle conversation did not. When I returned three days later, Don and I tried to recapture some of what we had covered, with only limited success. Most of the other interview sessions went smoothly, mirroring the roles he and I assumed in the first.

Don was a spectacular orator, which meant that he had significant control over the narrative as it emerged. This complicated my role as a collaborator, and my "voice" is not consistently evident. I am there in the interviews with Don as the "you" against which he measured his "I." I am there, asking questions, guiding the discussion at times, along for the ride at most others. Because of that activity and presence, I should neither claim full authorship nor stand aloof as the all-seeing, invisible ethnographer/biographer so common in many earlier as-told-to texts. To overcome this dilemma, some recent anthropologists include the "voice" of the ethnographer as a consistent and obvious part of the narrative or take more explicit control of the narrative to create an analytical biography.[1] Taking the first approach would have inserted me into Don's life in ways that would not reflect my actual involvement in it. Taking the second option would have meant that I would violate an understanding Don and I had from the outset of this project: to record a series of conversations in which Don spoke about his life and to put those conversations forward for his family and a broader public. Thus, I made a conscious decision to limit explicit exchanges between Don and me to brief passages in the section and chapter introductions, and to those places that require some bridge to span gaps in Don's narrative. Those curious about the differences between the edited version and the full verbatim transcript may consult the copy I have placed in the Center for Pacific Northwest Studies at Western Washington University in Bellingham, Washington.

The narrative proper begins with Chapter 2. Chapter 1 offers readers an introduction to Lelooska's life, and places it in the context of contemporary debates about ethnic and racial identities, twentieth-century Native American history, and Native American art history. The Conclusion revisits those same points. The beginning of the remaining chapters as well as sections within the chapters give added historical background, a brief introduction to critical scholarly debates, and a sense of what that chapter reveals about Lelooska's life. The short passages that accompany most of the sections often afford an understanding of the context in which the interviews were conducted and represent a nod toward the collaborative nature of this narrative.

ACKNOWLEDGMENTS

THIS VOLUME REPRESENTS more than collaboration between Lelooska and me. Behind it are the influences of our respective families and networks of associations. For my part, my wife, Katie Walker, has been an indispensable friend and critic. She kept me on task, offered encouragement and support, and, as usual, went over many different drafts. From the beginning, she was convinced of the merits of this project, for she knows how much Lelooska has meant to our three children—Anya, Becca, and Miles. Without the input of my parents, Anna and Harlow Friday, I could not have filled the gaps in my own knowledge about the Lelooska family. My brother-in-law Joe Walker and his wife, Rachel Belcher, deserve thanks as readers, ad hoc research assistants, and patient friends in awaiting the completion of the project.

My colleagues at various universities provided critical intellectual stimuli and support. John Purdy, Peter Iverson, Steve Haycox, and Andrew Fisher generously gave wonderful guidance on many aspects of Native American studies. Alan Gallay, Kevin Leonard, Beth Joffrion, Diana Shenk, and Midori Takagi provided good conversation about this project, paid careful attention to my writing, and offered helpful critiques. Valerie Matsumoto deserves a special commendation as a consistent booster of this project. Phone conversations with her invariably left me with renewed confidence; early in my work she pointed to other collaborative narratives and started me on an important path.

Western Washington University has been helpful, too, in seeing this work through to completion. Work-study funds paid for the rough transcription of the tapes. A Bureau for Faculty Research summer research grant allowed me to explore Makah history and Native American literary criticism. Western also granted a leave of absence for the 1995–1996 academic year so that I might spend time at Washington State University's Northwest Center for Comparative American Cultures and Race Relations, funded by a Rockefeller Humanities Grant for an unrelated project. That time and my colleagues there—Paul Wong, Rory Ong, Shelli Fowler, the late Collin Beckles, William Willard, Paul Hirt, Sue Armitage, T. V. Reed, and Noel Sturgeon—gave me new insights into the fields of ethnic and Native American studies. Most recently, a yearlong sabbatical from Western afforded the opportunity to finalize this study and work on a second, related book. The students in my history courses at Western Washington University gave me a chance to place Lelooska's life in historical context and have been positive about what I shared with them.

Many others have lent their aid to this project. Gilbert A. Giles, Edward Malin, and Ralph and Karen Norris shared their photographs and time, which were invaluable. Lita Tarver and Pat Soden at the University of Washington Press demonstrated faith in Don's narrative. I am grateful for their ongoing support. They also selected reviewers whose comments proved most helpful and challenging. I am in their debt. I thank Xavier Callahan for shepherding the manuscript through its final stages at the press and Kris Fulsaas for her watchful (and helpful) copyeditor's "eye."

In the end, none of this would have been possible without Don. Thank you.

CHRIS FRIDAY
Bellingham, Washington

NOTE TO THE READER

THROUGHOUT THIS VOLUME, I refer to Don "Lelooska" Smith as "Lelooska" or "Don" rather than as "Smith," for two reasons. First, the public knew him as Lelooska or Chief Lelooska, and his family and close friends knew him as Don. Second, this is a personal narrative to which I am closely connected. It would be absurd for me to pretend to be objective by referring to him as "Smith." There is more to be gained from understanding Don's life on a personal level than from some supposedly objective, abstract, and impersonal academic level. No disrespect to Don is intended by not employing this more formal usage.

Translating the spoken word to the written is not an easy task. Aside from the differences between informal and formal usage, capturing the nuances of tone and cadence of a speaker is nearly impossible. This narrative of Don "Lelooska" Smith's life is no exception. It is not a strictly verbatim transcript of the interviews I conducted with Lelooska. I have edited the transcripts for clarity and have done some limited rearranging of certain sections. I have dropped only those portions of the transcripts that Don indicated he did not want to be public, that might take readers off onto unrelated tangents, or that were repetitive. I do not believe that this editing has undermined the original narrative Lelooska and I created during the many hours of taped interviews. In an effort to help readers get a feeling for his speech patterns, I use punctuation in specific ways. I have employed an exclamation mark whenever he laughed. Readers will note many such points in the text. They are signs that the two of us enjoyed the conversations. Words that Lelooska emphasized are in italics. Contemplative pauses are indicated by ellipses (. . .). These were unusual and significant moments, for Lelooska seldom lacked words. In no instance does the presence of ellipses indicate that some portion of the text has been cut. Again, the curious may refer to the verbatim transcripts for comparison; I have placed a copy in the Center for Pacific Northwest Studies at Western Washington University in Bellingham, Washington.

Competing orthographies make translating Native languages difficult, and dealing with numerous tribes in a single volume only compounds the problem. The ways individuals write their names, which sometimes shifts over the years, also presents a dilemma. Most specialists will have some familiarity with the orthographies, but general readers will find it almost impossible to use some. Because this volume is intended for both audiences, on this count I have favored general readers and attempt to render words in forms that can be pronounced. For the names of individuals, I use the forms they most often employed in their own lifetimes. In many instances, I offer alternate spellings in the footnotes. Although a mishmash of orthographies results, I believe the end product remains comprehensible to specialists and general readers alike.

Native North American politics and history are fields tied to present concerns and issues, part of which revolve around names and naming. I have used the terms "Native Americans," "Indians," and "Native" or "Indigenous peoples" interchangeably. When possible, I have used a tribal designation. Like the orthography, even that is tricky. A modern tribe is a product of many interactions, including relations with other Indian bands, with European American colonizers, and eventually with the U.S. and Canadian governments.[1] Those tribes have asserted themselves, often by choosing names more reflective of indigenous languages. One prime example are the Kwakwaka'wakw (meaning "the speakers of Kwak'wala") of coastal southern British Columbia and northeastern Vancouver Island, with whom Don had significant interaction. Commonly referred to as the Kwakiutl (though with significant spelling variations) in the anthropological and historical literature, the term *Kwakwaka'wakw* better reflects the political and social relations of the many bands that make up the "tribe" and is used as the official label today. The Kwakiutl are in fact one of those bands or tribes that make up the larger group.[2] Don knew of this and other changes in designations but, like many people, tended to stick with those terms he had known for decades. I have indicated such "newer" labels in notes and have not made changes in the text of Don's narrative. I believe this allows readers the opportunity to find familiar "old" terms but to match them up with more recent names. Therefore the Nuu-chah-nulth appear in the text as Nootka, the Kwak-waka'wakw as Kwakiutl, and so on. Don frequently used band and clan associations alongside such broader labels, which I have tried to explain in the notes.

Don knew a great many people, had contacts with many different groups, and was a voracious student of history and culture. Because of the specificity of his references and their wide variety, I have used the endnotes to provide explanations in addition to the usual expounding on academic debates and references to sources. In passages where references need immediate elucidation, brief explanations are given in footnotes or brackets.

LELOOSKA

The Life of a Northwest Coast Artist

Large Cormorant Bowl

Eagle Box

1 / A Life (Un)Masked

PLACING PERSONAL NARRATIVE

I n the fading gray light of a rain-soaked April day in 1996, carloads of people began to arrive at the Lelooska family complex of two coast-houses,* a museum, and an art gallery in Ariel, Washington. They came to see the evening program of Northwest Coast Indian dances, songs, and stories that have awed and inspired children and adults for more than three decades. Most made the forty-five-minute drive north from the Portland-Vancouver area. Anxious for the show to begin but curious about the items on display in the museum and the gallery, they ventured among the trees and bushes to find those buildings. Off to one side of the path that connects the museum and gallery, they could just make out a cramped one-story structure almost buried in the trees, then home to Don "Lelooska" Smith and his mother, Mary. In the past, his grandmother Lady Elizabeth Hinkle, father Fearon, brother Fearon Jr. ("Smitty"), and sister Patty Fawn had lived there, too. Most of the visitors never ventured into that space, though Lelooska hosted many guests after shows amid the swirling sea of loud, neurotic dachshunds that always inhabited it.

---

*The wide cedar-plank houses are one of the key architectural features of the Northwest Coast culture area, which extends from coastal northern California to Yakutat Bay, Alaska. Until the early twentieth century, these were primarily living quarters with significant cosmological meanings inherent in their design and doubled as ceremonial halls. Since the 1950s, coasthouses have taken on more singular ceremonial roles.

The dressing room in the coasthouse at Ariel in the spring of 1996, with the order of the program taped to the mirror and various masks, rattles, costume parts, and clothes scattered about. Photo by the author.

As darkness closed in, a line began to form in front of the newer of the two coasthouses. A few guests—family friends, relatives, and special customers—filed in through the back door before the front doors opened to the general public. On the way to the main performance area, they passed through the cramped room where the dancers changed. In the center of the room sat a worn portable electric heater that dancers used to warm their numbed bare feet between performances. Benches atop a piece of plywood laid directly on the dirt and many pegs in the walls for parts of various costumes as well as coats and sweaters made the room seem even smaller than it was. A large mirror hanging on one wall would have made the room feel bigger, but an oversize piece of paper with the order of the evening's dances and stories boldly scrawled across it had been taped over much of the mirror. The room, disheveled as it was, revealed none of the chaos it would soon hold. The dancers were still down at Don and Mary's house, amid the cedar and alder shavings, tortilla chips, and Pepsi.

Just before the program started, they would tumble into the back room in a rush. Someone would warn them that Don insisted *this* time they keep quiet, but scarcely a performance went by in which that happened.

Passing through the room, the group of honored guests went behind the large painted cedar screen that separated the staging area from the main room of the coasthouse, with its dirt dance floor and plywood-and-plank benches. Behind the screen, masks lay scattered in apparent disorder. Some seemed deflated, even lifeless. Tsonoquah,[1] Wild Woman of the Woods, emanated none of the fearsome power she exhibited when her mask was danced. She casually sat atop a pile of fur, now just a mask staring at the ceiling. Others, carved in the dramatic style of the Kwakiutl,* feigned sleep. Huxwhukw,[2] one of the great cannibal birds and part of the Hamatsa dances, reclined on the floor with its slender six-foot-long beak resting on a bench, almost touching Tsonoquah; its small carving of a human skull dangled almost to the floor.[3] Crooked Beak of Heaven, another of the great cannibal birds, rested on a stool, its jute fringe hanging to the floor. In some cases the fringe is cedar bark, but for the day-in, day-out performances, jute lasts better and in the dim firelight it gives off the same warm red glow of cedar. Above Crooked Beak and next to Tsonoquah slumbered Numas, Old Man, with his oversize head, great white mane, and bushy white eyebrows. His blanket was draped over the bench as if he was there on his haunches with his back against the wall. Antlered Deer sat high on the shelf, nervously hiding from the power of the others below her. Ducking under the blanket stretched between the performance-area wall and the great painted screen, the early guests took their places on the hard benches. Regulars chose their favorite spots to see the masks as they were danced and to watch Lelooska as he told stories.

Within a few minutes, the front doors to the coasthouse opened to the remaining guests. Some had been standing in the rain for quite a time outside, lining up nearly as soon as they had arrived in order to get a good seat. The best were high along the sides against the walls, but there the

* Kawkiutl, or more accurately the Kwakwaka'wakw (meaning "the speakers of Kwak'wala"), live primarily along coastal southern British Columbia and northeastern Vancouver Island. They are particularly well known for their elaborate ceremonies and powerful masks.

small horizontal pole stabilizing the wide cedar planks that made up the walls of the house invariably hit heads, necks, or shoulders in precisely the wrong places. Experienced members of the audience brought blankets with them, but even those were not quite sufficient to keep out the moist chill or to act as padding on the hard benches. As the audience settled in, children bounced excitedly on the benches close to the dance floor, busied themselves with digging holes in the dirt, and repeatedly asked the adults with them, "When will it start?"

Everybody waited and the benches only seemed to get harder and harder. The rain was visible through the rectangular opening in the ceiling meant as a smoke hole and the large double doors that served as the main entrance to the building. The raw cold radiating from the dirt floor conducted a deep chill into the bones of all but the most active children. The layer of dust ground into the benches by countless others who had seen the shows over the years helped conduct the chill. The stack of split wood far away in the center of the room tauntingly sat in the fire pit unlit, and many longed for the eye-watering, smoke-filled feeble heat it promised.

At last the front doors closed. Suddenly a tall, thin woman appeared before the crowd wearing a dark wool button blanket* with a red-flannel appliqué of Supernatural Waterbird and an apron with Salmon stitched on it. Her cedar-bark head ring was trimmed with ermine and festooned with a large abalone square worn at the forehead.[4] She clutched the Tsimshian†-style Moon rattle as if it were a club meant to fend off the crowd. She need not have done so. She cut an imposing figure, at least for the adults, whose conversations quickly ceased. The children continued to scuffle for position, flick dirt at each other, and extend their earthwork projects in the house floor. Parents grabbed shoulders and issued commands to hush, and order slowly settled over the house. In a school auditorium voice, the woman in the button blanket announced that the

---

* The indigenous peoples of the Northwest Coast quickly adapted European-introduced blankets to their own ends, decorating them with buttons, shells, and appliqués, and using them as symbols of power and lineage at ceremonies.

† Tsimshian is the name generally used for the clans and bands in coastal British Columbia just south of the southernmost tip of southeast Alaska in the area between Portland Inlet and Milbanke Sound and including the lower Skeena and Naas Rivers.

program would soon begin. She warned, to little avail, that the children were *not* to dig holes in the house floor or to stick out their feet during the performance because it endangered the dancers, who sometimes cannot see out of the masks. For those same reasons, neither were the adults to use flash photography.

Just as suddenly as she had arrived, she turned and disappeared behind the carved screen. As she left, the feeble electric lights went dead, leaving only a single red bulb glowing dimly. Everyone became a shadow. Behind the screen, spirit whistles wailed, drums sounded, and a song began. The audience unconsciously turned toward the noise, and just as it stopped, a huge figure emerged from behind the screen. *This* was who they had come to see—Lelooska. As he began another song, the entire audience flinched when a wild, disheveled figure exploded from the blanketed entrance with a skin-tingling screech. The masked shaman, draped in his blanket with rattle in hand, circled the room and used his powers to coax flames out of the cold fire pit. He danced in his crouching way around the room once more, then disappeared back behind the screen. Lelooska finished the song, put down his drum, and took up an elaborate speaking staff. Stepping in front of an eight-foot-long, double-headed Sisiutł* drum, he slammed the staff into the floor with such force that even those along the walls felt the impact. "Klahowa tillicum six," he thundered to the assembled crowd in Chinook Jargon.[5] "Welcome, friends," he said, more softly in English. Within seconds, the audience knew that this man was a master orator able to send his voice to every corner of the house. He could take on the high-pitched squeak of Mouse's voice or the timid sound of Deer as easily as the gruff growl of Bear or the menacing howl of Wolf. Those in the house that night did not just hear the stories and history, they became participants in the performance of them. "Welcome to our house," Lelooska continued, pulling them in with his majestic voice.

On one side of the house, the larger-than-life Welcoming Figure† with

---

* Sisiutł, the double-headed serpent, is a powerful symbol representing a mythical sea monster. Don had created a long, low, benchlike drum with that design, behind which he sat during the shows.

† This large, humanlike carving typically was placed outside a house to greet guests arriving for some special event; Lelooska kept this one inside the coasthouse.

its huge hands held up to either side of its mouth yelled a welcome and blew a huge puff of white down onto the people seated before it, much to the delight of the children there. For the next several hours the audience watched with awe, listened intently, laughed, and shouted aloud as Lelooska took them through the night's performance. The adults lost track of their aches and pains and the chill. The children watched, rapt in the dances and stories.

That April show was one of Don's last performances. The cancer that had struck him four years earlier and gone into remission was back. Few in the audience knew of his health problems. Nothing in the performance that night indicated that anything out of the ordinary was taking place. It was a show like countless others before it, and was the way in which the vast majority of people came to know Don ("Lelooska") Smith, or "Chief Lelooska," as most of the visitors thought of him. These family performances at Ariel started in 1963 and grew over the years. Buoyed by the success of those programs, Lelooska and his family regularly added buildings. A second, larger coasthouse followed the first. Then the family put up a large A-frame museum for Don's private collection of artifacts from nearly every culture area in North America as well as items from the fur-trade and Wild West shows. Ultimately, the family established a gallery to display and sell their works of art. It eventually became a showroom for a broad range of Native artists. The growing family complex only added to the huge success of the programs. In the 1980s and into the 1990s, annual attendance at the daytime school programs and evening family shows reached as high as 30,000.[6] Those programs at Ariel introduced children and adults to the variety, complexity, and beauty of Northwest Coast peoples. The present-day performance of Northwest Coast, especially Kwakiutl, dances and songs took viewers beyond the simple images of feathered Plains Indians on horseback, beyond the notion that Indians were of a past era. Although Lelooska produced significant pieces of art, these programs may well stand as his greatest legacy.

Who was Don Smith? How did he come to do Northwest Coast art and these performance programs? How had he negotiated the difficult waters of being a "mixed-blood" Cherokee? How had his art evolved over the years? Over the decades, journalists and photographers have tried to capture Don's life story.[7] While informative, these materials fall short on at least three counts. First, the purposes and brevity of those studies do not provide space for Don's voice to emerge, for him to tell his story. Second, they reveal little about what it means to be Indian in the twentieth century. Finally, they offer only glossy overviews of what it may mean to be deeply engaged in producing Indian art.

This narrative, which brings Don's voice forward in ways not done in previous accounts, is based on a series of interview sessions conducted between 1993 and 1996. The transcripts of those interviews and this edited narrative represent Don's life as he viewed it from the perspective of his sixth decade and facing his own mortality; a diagnosis of colon cancer gave Don and me the impetus to undertake this project. The tapes resulted in a "collaborative text" generated in a dialogue between us.

For more than two decades, ethnohistorians (anthropologists and historians) have recognized that as-told-to (auto)biographies and oral histories are not objective retellings of lives so much as "texts" or constructed "metaphors of self" created at a given moment between the interviewer and the interviewee.[8] This recognition came with a move away from "salvage ethnography" efforts to reclaim an "authentic," primitive, precontact past before it passed away under assault from assimilative, modern forces.[9] While some work of that nature persists, ethnographers have moved into explorations of cultures as flexible, changeable, and diverse systems. They have also begun to examine the choices and limitations involved in the creation of individual and group "identities." They have begun to examine the "mediative" role that individuals, especially "mixed-bloods," play in cultural formations and the mobilization or performance of "culture" for political purposes (such as treaty rights, land claims, or position within a broader "racialized" state).[10] These more recent considerations provide the underpinnings of my writings about Don and my attempts to come to terms with Don's complex life.

Scholars have also come to argue that collaborative works have a number of intended audiences beyond those present at the taping and editing stages.[11] In this case, Don had at least three audiences in mind. I was one, albeit in the somewhat contradictory position of family friend and academic. His family* constituted another, for I had promised to give to the family a copy of the transcripts and any publications that might result from the tapes. The broader public formed the third, including those who had attended the shows and purchased pieces of art, as well as academics and other artists. Don knew from the beginning that the sessions we taped would appear before these audiences in one form or another. The tapes thus reveal what Don chose to tell me in those interviews and what he wanted the others to hear about his life. They also reflect what I asked him at the time and my thoughts during the editing phases that stretched several years beyond the interviews. What emerges from the narrative is not only the story of one exceptional individual, but also one that illustrates many of the larger issues central to the lives of Native Americans in the twentieth century, especially that of identity formation.

Don Smith was born in 1933 in Sonoma, California. His mother, Mary, was three-fourths Cherokee, from Oklahoma; his father, Fearon, was born near the Flathead Reservation in Montana. Although they were around other Indians on a regular basis, neither Mary nor Fearon lived on reservations nor did they seek formal, official affiliation with any single tribe. According to Don, his maternal grandfather, Enoch Fountain Hinkle, "didn't see any future for his grandchildren on a reservation, never wanted them to go to Indian school. He was just adamant about that."[12]

Grandfather Hinkle kept the family away from life on a reservation, but that did not mean that the family severed ties to reservations and Indians. Hinkle kept in contact with people he knew from his days with Buffalo Bill's Wild West Show and made sure to introduce Don to them. Don's exposure to this world grounded him in the cultural patterns of many different tribes. It also let him see how Indian cultures, even if as caricatures, might be performed and consumed by non-Indian audiences but not lose their relevance to Native Americans, either individuals or groups. The stories that Don learned at his grandfather's knees and Don's own actions later in life help clarify Native American lives in the twen-

---

* Don included the members of the Sewid family, who are prominent in the Kwakiutl tribe in British Columbia and who formally adopted him in the 1960s, as part of an extended clan to which he belonged and owed a great debt. See chapter 6, "Openings to New Worlds," for details.

tieth century. One of the most important is how identities are forged through choices people make and the experiences they carry with them. Indians have refused to be glassed-in museum-case models of culture but instead have taken the forms of expression available to them and have made them their own.

The connections and friendships Don's grandfather, father, and mother had with many different Indian people—reservation and nonreservation Indians—also reveal that Indians do not live in isolation from each other or the "non-Indian" world. Don's life illustrates how he and others like him created pan-Indian identities through contacts like these and how those identities were not necessarily in conflict with tribal and family identities. Lelooska's life represents the significant multitribal and multi-ethnic heritage of many Indians today.

As Don's life suggests, however, legal and political definitions of who Indians are do make a difference and may not reflect multiple generations of cultural influences. For much of his adult life, Don struggled against allegations that he was "not Indian" or not the right kind of Indian. Sometimes these were simply narrow, jealous jibes by supposed (non-Indian) experts that a Cherokee should only do "Cherokee art." At other times, the fact that Don was not enrolled with a particular tribe left him vulnerable to charges that he was not officially an "Indian." Many twentieth-century Native Americans have faced similar dilemmas. Don's experiences show how at least one person negotiated them.

In addition to offering a window on twentieth-century Indian identity, Don's life also connects with the rise of the mass-produced Indian "curio" trade and the transformation in artistic circles of perceptions of Native American artifacts from utilitarian craft to high art. For Don and many others like him, the first introductions to the curio trade came through women in their families. While grandfather Hinkle bounced from war to war and job to job, and Don's father, Fearon, started and restarted a series of automobile-related small businesses, Don's mother, Mary, provided a regular cash income for the family through her craft work, especially small carvings of animals and people.

In the 1880s, Indian women across North America entered into the cash and wage-labor economy through the production of items ranging from baskets, weavings, and moccasins to "Indian" and "Western" figurines.[13] Before that time, trade with tourists was irregular and promised unpredictable returns. After about 1880, traders on reservations and then off-reservation mail-order "trading houses" emerged as middlemen in the exchange. This left Indian producers of the goods with less control of the market as well as the production, for the traders tried to get Indians to make specific items. A greater regularity and predictability of income from the enterprise offset the loss of control, however, and Indian women especially became the primary producers of the curios. Most in the art world looked askance at what they perceived to be the low quality of these mass-produced items and refused to consider any utilitarian items as "art."

By the 1930s, though, private and federal patronage of Indian art fostered a new sense of what might be artistic, even if whites frequently determined what was "authentic Indian art."[14] The possibility that some items produced by Indians were high-priced art promised greater returns to certain individuals. Increasingly, though not exclusively, producing "art" fell to men. Ironically, the demand for high art strengthened the curio trade, as did the mid-twentieth-century imagery associated with Indians that offered many Americans a way to distinguish the uniqueness of the American experience from war-torn Europe. Regardless of the motivations, the growth of consumer capitalism in the United States served to expand the demand for Indian curios, and women continued to mass-produce cheaper items for the trade.

Mary Smith's participation in this sector of the economy not only was typical of many Indian and "mixed-blood" women, but also provided an important role model for Don. From her example, he realized that he could make money and even a living in the curio trade. Like the Wild West shows, making curios was not simply playing to white ideas of what authentic Indians were. Neither was it a purely mercenary activity. Grandfather Hinkle's habit of carving animal figures as he told their stories instilled in Don the realization that these arts had a multiplicity of meanings ranging from a commodity to be sold to symbols and metaphors of deep cultural significance. The two activities were not mutually exclusive. Following that line of thought and frustrated with what he was being told in his schools about savage Indians, in his midteens Don abandoned school and took to craft production for his livelihood.

In the late 1940s, Don began to come into his own as a craftsman and artist. Increased interest in Indian curios made some of this possible, for Don and Mary found outlets for their work not only at the familiar trading houses but also at their own roadside shop and at a booth they rented at the Oregon State Fair. In the late 1940s and throughout the 1950s, Don carved a multitude of figurines and animals and did feather and beadwork for tourists and gawkers who yearned for "Western" and "Indian" crafts.

The curio trade did not rest solely on non-Indian demands. Don's customers also included individuals from Oregon Indian tribes who wanted ceremonial regalia or commemorative sculptures. This customer base emerged from a particular set of circumstances. Native American populations, which hit a low about 1890, were on the rise in the 1940s. With their greater numbers, Indians increasingly participated in rodeos, pow-wows, and state fairs on a variety of levels, but often that participation depended upon them "being Indian."[15] This, in turn, fostered a demand for beaded clothes and feathered bonnets. Through his family contacts, Don had learned these skills and had become adept at meeting his customers' demands.

Where Don lived made a tremendous difference in his ability to take advantage of his skills, the booming curio trade, and the emerging demand for modern, or at least newly produced, Indian art. By the 1930s Don and his family had moved to Hubbard, Oregon, just outside Salem. Federal Indian policies and the 1958 flooding of Celilo Falls on the Columbia River required numerous meetings in Salem and Portland between delegations of Indians and government officials, often funneling them past the shop.[16] Many also traveled the road to and from Chemawa Indian School,* where Native American children from as far away as Alaska boarded. Those movements complemented the steady stream of Indians already traveling along the road on seasonal work cycles, on trips to participate in fairs and rodeos, or on their way to visit friends and family throughout the state. Whether they knew it or not, Don and his family

---

* Established in 1880 at Forest Grove, Oregon, as the Training School for Indian Youth, but later moved near Salem and renamed the Chemawa Indian School, the institution is the longest-operating Indian boarding school in the United States.

had settled in one of the best places in the state to meet Indians from virtually every group in central and eastern Oregon.

The shop became a way station where people stopped for visits as brief as a few minutes to as long as several weeks. This was an "Indian" shop, and Native Americans patronized it regularly. This common identification was a ground-level pan-Indianism[17] foreshadowing and accompanying the emerging political strategy adopted by many tribes and individuals when they began pushing for treaty rights and sovereignty. That common "Indian-ness" as well as the individual visitors had a tremendous influence on Don's life.

Although the curios at the Smiths' shop and the regular presence of traveling Indians were noticed by non-Indians, Don's flair for public performances drew many people to him. He was always willing to talk about the items for sale or his growing collection of objects he had gained through trade or as gifts. As he started carving, that too became part of what people came to see. By the late 1950s, schoolteachers began bringing their students to the shop. The informal talks developed quickly into regular performances in which Don drew upon his childhood and early adult experiences of listening to the stories and histories from earlier generations of Plains and Plateau peoples. While Don sang songs, his siblings sometimes performed dances. In his continued contact with Native American reservations and participation in the Pendleton Round-Up and the Oregon State Fair, Don built his repertoire; through his experiences, he explored the cultural space between those who were consumers of Indian cultures and those who were Indian. He did so in ways strikingly similar to Indian participation in the Wild West shows of his grandfather's day or the rodeo and powwow circuits that were emerging in Don's own time. Performance was always very much a part of Don's life.

In the shows at the shop in Hubbard, Oregon, Don began to supplement the Plains and Plateau stories and dances with materials from the Northwest Coast. This began a journey that he followed for the remainder of his life. Don found himself attracted to Northwest Coast art from his first moments of dabbling in the stories and carvings. At this time in his twenties, Don began copying masks and figures from the handful of books and museum catalogues then available, as well as from the pieces in museums. This was a strategy employed by a great many doing North-west Coast arts at the time.[18]

Call it forethought, intuition, or accident, but there is no denying the amazing timing of Don's transition to Northwest Coast art. Northwest Coast Native American art, along with that of the Southwest, was among the first that critics and aficionados recognized as "high art." The sculptural forms of Northwest Coast art, scholars suggest, fit easily into the critics' conception of what art was, much as the pottery and painting of the Southwest similarly fit such norms. This accounts for the relatively early recognition of Northwest Coast Native American art and the delayed acceptance of Plains beadwork as anything more than utilitarian. While Northwest Coast carvings gained recognition as art in the 1940s, most collectors paid attention to older pieces. Not until the mid-1960s did newly produced works become accepted as marketable Indian art.[19] Don's timing allowed him to build upon his carving skills and improve his reproductions at a time when the pressures to meet high artistic standards were only just forming.

Don was fortunate. His early carvings were, by his own admission, rough imitations of the old masters and paled in comparison to some of the work then being produced in British Columbia and Alaska. He threw himself into carving, bringing to the effort every bit of his faculties, intelligence, and skill. In the process, he became one of several important figures who drove Northwest Coast art out of the realm of artifacts to be salvaged and into modern art and contemporary use. Don's reputation opened many doors, and the 1960s federal patronage he received allowed him to connect his artistic productions with a group's heritage as well as inform the culture and politics of several tribes.[20]

Don's artistic reputation and reach expanded from the mid-1960s to his death in 1996. Part of his success came from within as he experimented with the artform and developed his own particular style. The continued growth of the popularity of Native American arts in those decades helped him attain acclaim. In spite of his achievements, questions of identity so common for Indians in the twentieth century continued to affect him. While I was conducting the research for this narrative, on three occasions I found how significant these issues were. In the first, at a 1997 historical conference I had just delivered a paper regarding Don's experiences with a federally sponsored arts demonstration project, in which I broached the issue of "Indian" and "tribal" identities. Afterward, a person who works for a state historical society approached me and said: "I found your paper *very* interesting. You know, we never really thought he was *Indian.*"

The second incident happened a year later at an archive. I had requested clippings files for Chief Clarence Burke, Chief Tommy Thompson and Flora Thompson, and Lelooska, just as the card catalogue had listed them.[21] The person behind the desk handed me the clippings files and felt compelled to add, "Wouldn't you know it, the one who is *not* Indian has the thickest file!" The person apologized upon realizing I was working on a study of Lelooska's life, but followed the apology with the comment, "But he wasn't really from around here, was he? Wasn't he Cherokee or something?" Those phrases—"not from around here" and "Cherokee"—meant, for all practical purposes, non-Indian, fake, and inauthentic.[22]

Those incidents are emblematic of the notions that too many people hold. Too often "being Indian" and "being tribal" get reduced to some "essential" and unchanging set of cultural markers. People hinge the definition of Indian identity solely on enrollment in a federally recognized tribe* or calculate it on the pseudoscience of blood quantum.[23] For all of the discussion in academic circles about the changing and shifting boundaries of individual identities and group ethnicities, about the relational nature of self- and group identification, variations of these insinuations abound. The irony of that situation has not escaped scholars, who have issued calls to engage complicated interpretive frameworks.[24] Sometimes the academic jargon common to those writers alienates popular audiences and fails to reach the very people the authors had hoped to pull into the debates. This narrative seeks to engage general readers and scholars in a historical discussion of twentieth-century Indian identities through Lelooska's life. It demonstrates that Don was "Indian," that he was not a mere interloper in a world of "authentic culture" to which he

---

* Most, though not all, federally recognized tribes operate under treaties ratified by the U.S. Senate. Many tribes negotiated treaties, but the Senate did not ratify all of them. Members of unrecognized groups can still be "Indian" but receive none of the "benefits" accorded to members of federally recognized tribes.

did not "belong," and that "mixed-blood" people not only are cultural creators but can be directly involved in critical tribal politics.

The third incident happened at the 1997 historical conference mentioned above. There, in commenting on the paper I presented, John Purdy astutely linked Don's life to that of D'arcy McNickle and helped me realize that Don's life story was more typical than I had at first thought. Purdy also offered an observation of Lakota writer and scholar Elizabeth Cook Lynn: "We've always known who was Indian and who was not."[25] Don never doubted that he was "Indian," though it was clear to both of us that what that meant changed over time and in different contexts. Don's life speaks to these critical issues and engages an ongoing dialogue in Native American studies as well as in the broadest categories of racial and ethnic studies about the tensions between agency and attribution, about choices and boundaries, about the dynamics, contingencies, and power relationships in making those determinations.[26]

At the performance in Ariel, Washington, that April in 1996, attendants escorted Tsonoquah, Wild Woman of the Woods, into the coasthouse from the depths of the cold, damp woods outside the door. The light of the small fire flickering in the center of the building made her huge, hairy form all the more fearsome. Her white eyes, brightened by the green background of her sockets, burned into those sitting in the house. A band of white on her cheeks highlighted her pursed red lips. Her pendulant breasts and the basket on her back stood out from her black face and body. The basket served as a reminder of the children she had seized and carried away; her lips signaled supernatural power. Tsonoquah represented not only a being of immense power, but also one of Don's family crests, acquired when James Sewid adopted Don into his lineage.[27] She was also one of the pieces that inspired Don when he first began looking at Northwest Coast museum pieces for ideas as he made the transition from a craftsman to an artist, from a person engaged in the curio trade to one consumed by Northwest Coast art.

Tsonoquah danced, as she did so many times at the coasthouse in Ariel, in sync to a slow, soothing song. She lumbered around the house fire helped by attendants who not only guided her but also helped control

Tsonoquah (Wild Woman of the Woods), the three-way transformation mask used for decades by the Lelooska family in its programs at Ariel. This mask opens first side to side, to reveal one inner mask, which then opens up and down to reveal yet another, innermost mask. Chief James Sewid of the Kwakiutl in British Columbia granted rights and privileges to use Tsonoquah to Don "Lelooska" Smith and his family. Photo courtesy of Ralph Norris.

her power. She finished a circuit around the fire, stopped, threw back her head, and howled her mournful cry, "oooh, hum, hum, hum." Then her face exploded, not once, but twice—first to the sides, revealing an inner mask of the human form of the being who saved the world from a flood, then again, up and down, showing the audience the innermost Spirit

Ancestor mask.* Just as suddenly, the masks slammed shut in reverse order and Tsonoquah was back, moving around the house in her rolling gait.

That mask is significant not only because it represents Don's lineage and "performed ethnography,"[28] but also because it suggests how we "see" peoples' lives, particularly through autobiography and biography. As a person is paraded before readers, his or her general outline of personality and experiences becomes evident. For fleeting moments, readers get glimpses into an inner life, but all too quickly the masks slam shut, leaving only the outer shell visible, that form we expect to see. We know there is more behind the mask once we have glimpsed it, but it is difficult, even impossible, to truly *know* all of a story or to present it as *the* story.† Other authors might construct different masks covering the spirit inside and be equally as "true" to Don as I. Yet my association with Don and his family provide me with insights into the inner masks that Don himself created. I acknowledge the uncertainty of entirely knowing a person or people, but Don's story reflects the importance and complexity of Native American lives as a *part* of the twentieth century, not as exotic addenda to it.

---

* Transformation masks may have a variety of beings represented by their inner masks, depending on the needs of those using the mask and the ideas of the carver. Don liked that contrast because one was fearsome, the other more benign. Don also chose Spirit Ancestor to represent and honor his connection to James Sewid's lineage.

† Kwakiutl viewers of the masks would most likely recognize the figures represented with each transformation, but even they would be left to interpret the meaning intended by the carver and the person displaying the mask.

2 / Growing Up Indian

S trong ties to places, distinctive memories, and personal associations
are at the core of Native American self-representations. The many
autobiographies, as-told-to narratives, and biographies of Native
peoples reveal that one's family position, an identification to a "tribe"
(or tribes), and a more amorphous but nonetheless palpable sense of being
Indian are layered one on top of another.[1] Drawing on all these identifiers,
Indians create a collective, though not unified, memory. Deep connections to places stand as one of its most important components. How this
is accomplished can vary widely. Creation narratives that link Indian lives
to the origins of humankind at a particular and known place provide
important avenues. For many individuals and families, reservations offer
another potent set of ties to "home," even though the boundaries are
defined by an outside power and in spite of rampant economic poverty
often found on reservations. Even off-reservation and non–federally recognized Native Americans link a sense of self to a tribal identity rooted
in a place.[2]

These attachments to place are not unique in a worldwide perspective.
They can be found among aboriginal populations around the globe as
well as among later migrants to, or cultures in, particular areas. Certainly
Buddhism, Christianity, and Islam retain the centrality of place in terms

of origins and sites of significant events. Indeed, wars continue to be fought over control of and claims to ownership of many of those places. In North America, though, aboriginal peoples have a significant cultural connection to their origins as "people" that most of the continent's later arrivals cannot claim, all legalities aside.[3] Even theories of ice-age migrations across a land bridge are not enough to remove the sense that Native Americans have occupied North America since time immemorial.

In spite of first occupation of North America by Indians, other people did come to this continent. They not only attempted to colonize territories and claim the wealth of the lands, but they also brought with them diseases that swept through Native populations, killing by some estimates as much as 90 percent within the first century of "contact."[4] Handed down across the generations, memories of those struggles and their continuation inform Indian identities significantly. Native American oral histories, told through families and networks of association, tell a markedly different story from that of the standard textbooks, which even to this day tend to treat Indians as a historical era, not as peoples. Those oral histories reveal sites of resistance to the imposition of a standard story or dominant narrative that marginalizes and ignores Native peoples. At the same time, Indian oral histories yield no uniform, single story. They reveal few pure heroes and villains. Instead, they suggest the importance of giving heed to many voices, to the range of experiences among various peoples and within individuals. They indicate what scholars and the general populace have been far too slow to recognize: the shifting and complex weave that makes up the fabric of Indian peoples' lives.[5]

Don "Lelooska" Smith's recounting of his childhood experiences is cut from that same cloth, offering glimpses into how he developed his voice, his sense of self, and his identity as "Indian." In that process, childhood influences were critical.[6] Born off reservation in 1933 in Sonoma, California, as a "mixed-blood" child whose parents and grandparents did not maintain or seek enrollment with a federally recognized tribe, Don came of age in the tumultuous era between the 1934 Indian Reorganization Act (IRA) and the postwar years of relocation and termination.[7] The IRA fostered a new tribalism even though at base it was still assimilationist in terms of forcing a rigid political hierarchy on reservation governments.

Native peoples either bent it to their own ends or mobilized in resistance to it. In either case, the IRA resulted in a new context in which Indian cultural and political leaders moved openly and directly to challenge their colonization.[8] A grassroots pan-Indian identity was also emerging to match the one prompted by federal Indian policy.

The people in Don's family and a far-flung network of family associations helped him appreciate the many layers of identity. They also gave him a sense of competing histories and the very real consequences of the colonization of North America. He recalls, for example, learning at an early age of U.S. attempts to eradicate Indians and efforts to control the historical memory of those events through public schooling and even in Hollywood's manipulation of popular culture. He also recounts how resilient people could be, and through his family he came to know people who survived the "campaigns to assimilate the Indians."[9]

BALANCING THE HISTORIES

Like putting an overlay on a map to find the coordinates.

In his back room, Don sat in his chair while I set up the tape recorder next to me on the couch and put a small microphone on the cluttered corner table between the two of us. For nearly forty-five minutes before we started taping, I had explained the details of what I intended to do with the tapes and transcripts, making certain we both agreed on what we were about to do. I also spent much time discussing the intricacies of and reasons for oral-history agreements—those documents that assign copyright for intellectual property to the interviewer but that also spell out the rights of the interviewee—which are essential in the litigious world of the present day. That discussion added to my nervousness about how the session and the entire project might proceed. Don did not seem nervous, though the legalistic details of oral-history agreements made our conversation stilted.

I started the tape recorder and Don immediately took control of the session. He began to talk about memory and how people remember. He spoke about his family, friends, how he learned to be an ethnographer as a child. Don also traveled across time, folding his story back over itself like a blanket. Although his cancer medications may have contributed to that temporal construction, it is also a particular feature of Indian senses of time, of the relationships between the past, present, and future. That first taping session set the tone for those that followed.

Lots of tribes had what they called remembrancers. It was a very important position, and of course they would try to pick somebody and teach them the little memory tricks and things to do it. The memories of the old, old people are really remarkable. You can have a conversation with some of the old people, and then the next time they run into you they pick up the conversation where it left off. I mean, you're scrambling for what they told you last! They're going to expect you to remember this. And they love to see if you really remember it.

I was so interested. I suppose my granddad* is responsible for that because he gave me so much respect for these things. And some of Grandpa's old friends were pretty raunchy old coots. Some of the old Sioux and Cheyenne and one old Pawnee in particular were right out of a time warp almost. Well, they kind of followed my grandpa. They would come out and visit. You'd get a call from the bus station or the train station: "Well, I didn't have anything to do so I thought I'd come and see you." They might be there two days, they might be there two months, we might have them three years. Because I was the grandson of their dear friend, they seemed to think it was incumbent upon them to educate me when they were there. So I would listen to their life histories, the things they had been involved in, the people they had killed, and things like that.

Grandpa got acquainted with a lot of them when he got out of the service after his first hitch.† There was a guy hiring expert riders with good character credentials. He snatched Grandpa up pretty quickly because his discharge had across the top "Character Excellent." Those old discharges had that if you had really pleased your superiors. The discharge listed all of his service and a little character thing. It was quite a document.

Grandpa signed on with the guy, even though he didn't know what the

---

* Don's maternal grandfather, Enoch Fountain Hinkle, and his wife, Lady Elizabeth Hinkle, lived for lengthy periods of time with their daughter, Mary, and her husband, Fearon Smith, Don's parents.

† Enoch Hinkle served in Troop A of the Fifth Cavalry, first in the Philippines shortly after U.S. occupation and increased Filipino resistance, which became significant by about 1903.

heck he was signing up for. It was travel and it was fun. He was young; why not? He had been around horses, which is what he loved I think almost as much as his own family. It turned out it was with the Buffalo Bill Cody Show.* Part of the performances Grandpa got to be an Indian, other parts of the performances he was a cowboy, sometimes he was a soldier and he got scalped, and sometimes he helped out with the Indian end of it if somebody was sick.

The old Cherokee chiefs who were a part of Grandpa's background at that time wore these grim broadcloth suits and white shirts, and they were just about as far from Grandpa's image of a glorious Indian persona as you could get. He saw the Sioux, the old Cheyenne, Arapaho, and Pawnee and, boy, those were the "*real* Indians," as Grandpa used to refer to them! No "Civilized Tribes" in those.†

Well, he got acquainted with a lot of them and at that time [1910s and 1920s], when he was young, there were still a lot of the old guys around who had participated in the big Indian battles and the wars on the Plains. So he just learned everything he could. He got very good in Lakota. He was a master sign talker. Of course he picked a lot of that up in Oklahoma because they put so many tribes there that sign language really spread to tribes that hadn't used it a lot before. But he made some very, very fast friendships. They were lonesome. Here was somebody who was young and could read and write—in my grandfather's case, marginally. He went from one culture to another very, very comfortably.

So he set out to learn their side of the thing. When he was in the military, he got the military version of the Indian wars but in the show were the old guys from the opposition. Their stories interested him, and then he got involved in their religion and their mythology. He would have made a

---

* The Buffalo Bill Show toured the United States and Europe between 1879 and 1917, and was among the most famous of a number of such shows.

† The Five Civilized Tribes are the Cherokee, Choctaw, Creek, Chickasaw, and Seminole, whose towns, farms, and political structures earned them the title of "civilized" in common parlance of the nineteenth century. Many ended up in Oklahoma because of removal and relocation. Sioux, Cheyenne, and Arapaho migrated to the Plains by the time of European American arrival there; the Pawnee were much earlier residents. The federal government eventually relocated the Southern Cheyenne, Arapaho, and Pawnee to Oklahoma reservations, and assigned the Northern Cheyenne to a Montana reservation and the Northern Arapaho to one in Wyoming. Other Plains peoples ended up in Wyoming, Montana, and the Dakotas.

Enoch Fountain Hinkle ("Plenty Stripes") and Don in Plateau/Plains regalia. Don's mater-nal grandfather was a tremendous influence on Don. Photo courtesy of the Lelooska family.

great anthropologist or linguist. He could just sop up languages so quickly. And he really enjoyed people, especially interesting people. But "*real* Indians" really got to be his passion. So after all those years, these old guys still loved him and would come and visit, and sometimes he would go back there.

I got to make a couple of trips with him to Oklahoma and the Plains when I was young [1930s]. It was pretty remarkable. Grandpa would sit down in the evening and say, "Well, my friend is going to tell you about the fight that his people were in. My cousins were on the other side." Well, when he said "the cousins," he meant the Osage[10] shirttail relatives. For instance, in that Winter Campaign[11] when Custer made that terrible strike against the Cheyenne and the Arapaho, he deserted a lot of his wounded to withdraw while he had a victory, and it could've got a lot tougher if everybody got together, at least the Indians felt so. But some of the Osage's version was different because they scouted for Custer. So Grandpa had heard all of the details from the Pawnee and the Osage: that made it rather glorious. He got to talking to some of the old Cheyenne and they began to tell their version of the thing, and then he would prompt them, and they told me what it was like to be in the camp, settled in for the winter. It had a promise that you were safe, more or less, from Army problems if you didn't do anything you shouldn't, like running off horses or doing away with some of the wasichu [whites] if you happened to find out where they were vulnerable!

All this was in very, very frank terms. I saw my grandmother wince many times. One of Grandpa's old buddies was a Pawnee guy whose name rendered into English meant something like Wolf-Walking-in-Silence. He isn't walking silently, but in a supernatural kind of envelope where there is no sound, nothing makes a sound, and this Wolf is traveling through this void of silence. When the old guy sits down and really explains to you what his name meant and having had this come as a vision, it was a very powerful, spiritual experience. It was something. He was the only Pawnee Grandpa was *really* close to. He thought a lot of them were kind of sellouts.

The Pawnee, like the Osage cousins, as Grandpa called them, also served the Army. The North Scouts were Pawnee, and old Wolf was one of them as a very, very young guy. He got off on scalping. He even described the whole process. He talked about how it made him sick, and sometimes young fellows, first time they took a scalp, would throw up. The old warriors would kid them about that for a long time, so then they would have to *really* be bold, take lots of scalps, too, so they wouldn't be kidded anymore. He described the whole process so vividly, even to the sound it makes—that popping, sucking sound as it is pulled off from the head!

I took that to my first-grade teacher. You were to tell a true story! And so I said, "Well, there was a Pawnee warrior and he was sixteen years old and he killed a Cheyenne. He shot him off his horse and then he went up and he cut his throat. And he rolled him over and where the hair was braided, he ran his knife around it.* He stuck the tip of the knife under it and pried it up a little and then he just peeled it off like, like tape, and when it comes off it goes . . ." and I made the same sucking, popping noises. Here was this *horrified teacher* getting all the gruesome details of the correct Pawnee style of removing the hair!

She said, "Uh, did someone read this to you, Donald?"

So then in the second grade, I'm sitting in the class—Mrs. Woodard, nice lady, very civilized—and all of a sudden I see all the kids are looking in the back of the room. Very quietly, Grandpa had come into the room and along with Grandpa is this *really* tall Indian. I remember him taller than he really was, but I would guess six-two, maybe even more. Very erect, looked like he was cast in bronze. He was standing there and he had these holes all around his ears from multiple earrings. He wasn't wearing them, but you could see the holes very easily, and his hair was done in the old Pawnee fashion—it was old Wolf. Mentally he still was a warrior and here he is wearing nice moccasins, but a nice suit. Always wore a silk neckerchief tied up, lot of rings on his fingers. So they stood there and of course class just came to an immediate stop, and Grandpa grins—he was very charming—and says, "Well, don't let us disrupt anything. I need my grandson." He got me and goes and talks to the principal. He says, "I'd like my grandson to take some time off from school and his grades are good. I know that." He says, "What you can teach him, he can always learn. What my friends and I want him to learn, there is only a short time because a lot of these people are very old." And, by golly, he talked Mrs. Ray, the principal, into it and I walked

* "It was a place about this big around," Don indicated, making a circle with the index fingers and thumbs of both hands.

for a week. I had to make it all up! I got off for a week so I could hang out with Grandpa's old buddy.

Well, we went on beyond the first time Wolf came to visit and the scalping story that so appalled my first-grade teacher. He told me how Pawnee youngsters grew up: Pawnee mythology, Pawnee religion, seeking a vision, how they interpreted visions, what you told people, what you kept to yourself to preserve the power of what was in the vision, and a lot of things. He made me a nice little bow, about two feet long. He showed me how to fletch arrows and the best places to shoot animals and people to get the maximum effect. The Pawnee bow is pretty short. It was pretty powerful, too. Especially the ones like mine made out of elk antler layered like a car spring and then bound with a sinew and faced off with a rattlesnake skin over that. All of it was laminated with hide glue. It had about a ninety-pound pull.* It was quite a powerful little weapon and because it was short, why of course it was easy to handle on horseback, where a longer bow wouldn't have been.

Well, he told me all of those little nuances, and things like why the Pawnee hated the Cheyenne and why they fought against them even though they weren't that fond of the whites. Wolf was respected. It was like meeting not quite a god, but something pretty close. This was somebody who had been there. It wasn't a story. It wasn't a movie. All this stuff I learned—how to do a lot of these things, how to start fires with a fire drill and all that. Grandpa loved all that stuff too. We were three kids there. Of course, Grandma was not at all sure that this was wholesome and healthy!

Now, I go back to school and it was "Dick and Jane" and "see Spot run." Laugh, baby, laugh. School was school, but the Indian thing was something else. I mean, it was separate. They were two different things. It was like you walk through a wall in time. I've gone through the veil of a long-gone time and it was great stuff. I had no idea the real significance of it, whether my grandpa valued me and the information enough to go to some considerable lengths to see that I was exposed to it. It never gave me any conflicts. When I was in school and with the kids, I was a kid. I did kid things and I learned kid things. The time I spent with my grandfather or around the old

---

* The force required to draw the bowstring. Ninety pounds is difficult to pull.

people was learning, too, but it was just so fascinating. It just swallowed me up. Those were the *best* times.

I was bored with school, really. I think I had an IQ of 160–170 or something like that. The teachers went nuts over that. It had to be a fluke, they thought! I liked the other kids and we played and things, but the magnet was always back to what I had learned about another world, another era, and there were still people alive who lived it. I prized this stuff more and more as time went on, especially as these old people began to drop off.

I hoarded it in my mind and then I got to reading. You read the books and then you think back on it: "Is that the way old Wolf said this? The old Sioux, would they approve of this? Is this how it was?" It is like putting an overlay on a map to find the coordinates. Well, it got to be like that— written history, oral history. It kind of happened without any real effort. I had two versions of these things: one was written on the pages about "the savage Sioux" and how "they destroyed the valiant Custer and his command at the Little Bighorn," and on the other hand I had a smiling, gentle, almost pious image of one of Grandpa's old Lakota friends.[12] I mean, he was a *very* sacred person in his religion and all. I could no more think of him as being a savage as I could my Grandma! So I began to question a lot of the stuff that was in the books. There were so many of those old people that came and went through my life.

Grandpa knew an old fellow whose white-man name was Dewey Beard, I guess after Dewey at Manila Bay and all that.* He was just a kid at the time of the Indian wars. But he remembered a lot and he had been at the Little Bighorn, I guess, on the day of the battle. I always remember him. He had this very spiritual quality about him, like a lot of the older people, and there was such a gentleness. I mean, here you have these wrinkled old people; I suppose a lot of kids would've been scared of them. They were pretty formidable-looking people, with their long hair and earrings and things like that. But there was such a gentleness, really, and such a . . . feeling of loss and longing for something that he would never be again. They were so matter-of-fact about much of this stuff.

---

* Admiral George Dewey (1837–1917) sailed into Manila Bay, the Philippines, in 1898 and claimed the Philippines as U.S. territory during the Spanish American War.

I used to listen to and look at the old guys' and old ladies' eyes and think, "Gee, they're still really very sad, they're still wounded in their hearts." That came to me pretty early as a kid. I could see and feel that when I talked to the old people. I think that was how my granddad set my feet on wherever I'm going, a long, long time ago, he and his old friends, and the old guys that I would meet as I got more and more interested, involved with this tribe and that tribe!

Old women would tell me folk tales. You see, in most tribal societies there was a division of labor in the old times, a division of the kinds of things they taught.[13] There were only certain things a woman was allowed to teach a boy. So a lot of this had to come from the men and the women were encroaching. It just wasn't proper for them to do some things. But folk tales were great from women. And of course they were willing to explain how they did certain things. You flatten quills with your teeth, and what you do for dyes and medicinal plants and things like that. Matters of character, war, histories, and things like that were kind of the man's department. Well, they weren't allowed, on a lot of reservations, to pass this stuff along to their own grandchildren.* I mean, there wasn't anybody to hear this. The old people were full, full up to the top of their heads with knowledge and things that they wanted to pass on to somebody, and to have a young pair of ears presented. It may have given some of them the sense that there might be a continuance in passing it on to somebody.

Very, very early on I learned with the older people that you never asked a direct question. You had to push your ignorance out like a checker piece, and if you framed your question as just an ignorant statement, then they would comment. Inquiry kind of got to be a habit. You didn't ask out-and-out questions. You would make a statement and then they would come out with the information. It was kind of standard. Your asking them is considered a little boorish.

One of Grandpa's friends had survived the Wounded Knee fight.[14] (His name will come back to me. Since I've been tired from these medications, I have to wait for a lot of little things to come back.) His mother had been wounded mortally when he was a baby-in-arms. She ran off down the coulee

---

* Indian agents appointed by the federal government often discouraged "traditional" Indian cultural practices, especially among the children, and promoted assimilationist policies.

to get away from where the killing was going on, and the blizzard came in just about that time—big, big blizzard. Just snow. You couldn't see through it. Like a wall. The old people used to talk about that blizzard like that—a whiteout, I suppose.

But in the coulee, finally, she just found a little sheltered place and curled up with the baby as close to her as she could get, and she died. Apparently her body heat sustained the baby under the snow until some guys came out and found the baby.[15] So you could say, "Well, where your mother was killed and they found you alive after the battle, what was that like?" But that was not how it was done. I got into it by saying, "Yes, in that big storm, probably no one could've survived, especially a little child. No one could have survived that." He had, but it would've been impolite to ask him that, or to press it.

He said, "Yes, there was maybe one, maybe two survivors. One was a baby and Grandpa told me about him."

Oh, boy, here we go! I said, "Oh, a baby?"

He says, "Little baby."

I said, "Uh, feeding from his mother?"

Then he talked about having been taken in and raised. Always, they told him how his mother had saved his life, how they dug him out of the snow. So he always felt that there had to be some purpose in all this when there was so much death. For the little frail baby to survive, there surely had to be something that he had to do. Things didn't happen without reason, in his estimation. So you would kind of ease, ease into those things. Sometimes you really had to display ignorance.

THE FABRIC OF TIME AND LIVES

You can't pull it out a thread at a time.

Don was a little taken aback when I asked him, "When did you first think of yourself as 'Indian'?" His reply to me indicated that he and his family had never been anything else. Don's family may not have lived on a reservation or been officially recognized by the federal government as Indians, but the values his family and its circle of friends instilled in him gave him a sense of connection to the past and continuity into the present.

From a young age, Don actively pursued these connections, and his grandfather first taught him how to be his own ethnographer. Don took to that style and found that learning one thing led to another. He discovered paths into a broad range of knowledge stored in the generations before him. His connections with those "elders"—those storehouses of knowledge—stand as a reminder that in spite of tremendous blows dealt to Native peoples by colonization and mortal diseases introduced from outside North America, Indians survived, persisted, and adapted.

For Don, learning came not just from his family and the elders, but also from his childhood acquaintances. No matter where Don found himself, there was always something more to learn. His inquisitiveness, his abilities to absorb and contextualize information, and his intuitive skills at developing friendships that he acquired as a child served him well in later years.

I don't think I ever . . . thought, really, about *not* being Indian. It always surprised me when people say, "Oh, you're Indian? You can't be Indian." It was always there, ever since I was born: the way I was raised with Mom, her leanings are entirely in that direction, with my granddad. I never really thought of it in any other way. I never had to make a conscious decision that I can recall. It just was like becoming a craftsman or artist or whatever I am, which grew out of the family. You see, a lot of full-blood women and the Métis* in Canada who are mixed-blood got involved in cottage industries based on traditional crafts.[16] Well, just like them, Mom painted, drew, carved, and made dolls. It was traditional Indian art, and some of it was falling off on the side of Western art because she grew up on ranches around horses and loved it.

It got to the point where I needed some money. My parents were great believers in *earning* the old-fashioned way! So when I needed some money, I whittled something and, by golly, it sold. Well, it was kind of neat. I enjoyed making it and, son-of-a-gun, this would take care of a couple Saturdays of movies and popcorn. I just kind of grew into it.

And then the more I learned, the more I began to appreciate the old

* In Canada, unlike in the United States, a specific, if ambiguous, legal category—Métis—exists for the people of mixed Indian, French, and English ancestry. Since the 1960s, that definition has broadened to include people of mixed Indian and non-Indian ancestry.

arts. I wanted to know how they were done, how they were made, and the purposes behind them. It is a fabric. You can't pull it out a thread at a time, because when you pull one, you get another and another and then it just swallows you up. If you have curiosity, why, you just pursue it.

A lot of people look at a painted rawhide parfleche, those big painted envelopes that the Yakama called *shatkati,* and most people are content to look at it as a big envelope made out of some kind of skin and painted with something. I wanted to know what it was for. I wanted to know where the paints came from. I wanted to know how they were put on. With brushes? Uh-oh, no. They were done with the porous nasal bones of buffalo, which is kind of neat. You would mix your mineral paint, dip your buffalo paint-brush into it, and it would kind of suck that paint up into it; and then when your bone paintbrush made contact with the rawhide, it would flow out, kind of like a felt-tip pen, you might say, in a very crude sense.

So it leads you in a lot of directions. Okay, how do you get the hair off an elk hide or a buffalo hide—an even bigger project? Well, all right, the recipe from an old Walla Walla/Nez Perce lady was that she would take it down in the creek and she would tie it to a stick. Annie Moxmox* taught me more about making that stuff than anybody I ever ran into. She was very, very good. She told me the current would make it flap up and down in the water and the sun makes the water in the little creek warm in the summer. She used to say, "And pretty soon all that hair just gets loose and goes away. Then I go down and I pull it out and I stretch it. It is nice and white." Okay, you got the hair off. Now you have to flesh the underside and get all that so it is nice and even. Ladies had very, very strict rules for dressing hides. Of course, as a young guy interested in learning this stuff, I had to be very careful because this isn't a man's stuff; you're crossing the line into a woman's department. So you have to approach it from the idea that "I want to know, somebody needs to know because someday you may quit doing this and somebody ought to be able to tell people how this is made because they don't know what a big job it is."

---

* Annie Moxmox Johnson (1885–1973) married Thomas Moxmox Johnson (1888–1964), who was a descendant of Peopeomoxmox. (Peopeomoxmox—Yellow Bird or Yellow Serpent—tried to contend with the growing population of European Americans in the Oregon Country. In 1855, territorial militia troops seized him and brutally executed him.) The Johnson (Moxmox) family is Cayuse, and many live on the Umatilla Reservation.

They think about it, then they say, "Well, maybe you're right. Okay, I'll tell you all about it." So that was how I would get into it, but you're crossing a line in a lot of these cases to learn some of this stuff. So, okay, I had to learn about preparing rawhides, how to get the hair off. You could also bury it in a pit with wood ashes, and the lye from the ashes will also cause the hair to slip. That was another recipe, though.

Mineral paints came from the Yellowstone Park area, from that part that the Park Service now calls the Paint Pots. For hundreds and hundreds, maybe thousands, of years, different tribes traveling those trails through the Yellowstone would collect that and the women would make it into little cakes, dry the little cakes, and they would trade them when they could. Still, I'll bet you could go to Crow Fair,* where they have their big do, or you could go up to Browning, Montana, and I bet you could find those little cakes of mineral paint still being offered for trade.

So you had to know how to get that and the people who had it if you didn't go and get it yourself. You knew the particular groups who would have this stuff. Then you had to learn how to pulverize it, get it very, very fine, finer than flour if you're really going to do a good job. Then you have to use buffalo fat, but it is better to have something that is a little more penetrating. Bear grease will penetrate better than others. Then you get into the matter of a young bear being better than an old bear for that, because an old bear's fat will turn yellow. You go on and on and on and on. And then the paint will stick better if you paint it on with the transparent glue. Well, there are two kinds of glue. One is better than the other. One is made from the scraping of the inside of hides when you're preparing for tanning, and then you cook that down into a soup, down into a goo and a mix. That is one way. The best comes from the glutinous material you get from beaver tails—beaver-tail glue. You size the rawhide with that and paint over that. That is why there is seemingly a white line around fine old parfleches. It is because the rawhide got dirty but the part that was under the glue didn't absorb the dust and the dirt as easily. So you could see all this design in your mind's eye, and you're painting it in something that is as transparent as clear soup.

---

* Crow Fair is an annual combination powwow, rodeo, and fair held southeast of Billings at Crow Agency, Montana, the third week in August since about 1907.

Laying your design out, that was an accomplishment. I mean, those ladies knew what they were doing. They were laying it out with finger measurements. Some had little sticks they used. But you could see how you've gone beyond just saying, "Well, that is an Indian suitcase, that is a parfleche." It has carried you into hide preparation, how to prepare paints, how to prepare the surface to be painted and all. You've just opened up a whole can of worms. Then you get into the different kinds of parfleches: the big envelope types; then there were the square ones, which were used to hold sacred objects. There were the little cylindrical ones Annie Moxmox made.

She was a darling, just a darling. They would come to the Oregon State Fair every year in Salem. Dick [Richard Smith, Don's younger brother] used to like to go over to their big teepee. He would go over there early. Just as soon as we would get there, he was gone. He would make a beeline over to their teepee because that was about the time she was starting to fix breakfast. She could flip flapjacks in a little iron skillet. She could just turn them clear over. She would be there with her little cookstove. She would flip them up and catch them in the skillet. Boy, he thought that was so neat. He would zip over there as much for the show as the hotcakes, which were pretty darn good!

When I was a kid, Dad owned a tire shop. Rex Cooper, while he was around, worked for Dad. Good old Cherokee, tall, slim, and his wife, Retha, was white, Scandinavian maybe. He had two daughters. They were about a year, year and a half apart—Patty and Donna. They were my bosom buddies. They were beautiful girls. Gee whiz, they grew up to be gorgeous women. And then Joe Shaw lived next door. Joe, I think, was a Ponca.[17] He was an engineer when they built the runways on the air bases at Fairbanks and Nome.[18] Underneath the runways, it was all plumbed with steam heat so they could have it all season. The Aleutians weren't far away, and the Japanese were island hopping into the Aleutians.* He was really a prize package as far as the government was concerned. He got shipped off up there to Alaska.

Fern, his wife, stayed with us. Fern used to run a roadhouse in Oklahoma.

---

* In 1942, the Japanese bombed Dutch Harbor, Alaska, and occupied several Aleutian Islands as a distraction from Midway, the primary military objective. The United States sent troops to Alaska and used that attack to increase support for the war on the home front.

I always thought maybe that Belle Starr[19] might have looked something like her. She knew the Bible frontward and backward—drank about three-quarters of a case of beer every day. When it wasn't beer, it was black, black, black coffee. Turned out that Joe came back from Alaska with an Eskimo girl about my age, named Colleen. Colleen's dad I guess was Irish; her mother was an expert furrier. They brought her mother down a few years later and got her a job at a furrier in Salem. Man, she could do anything with fur, new skins and things. Didn't speak a whole lot of English.

Those three girls and I—Patty, Donna, and Colleen—were just great, great, great, great buddies. Of course, Colleen had been raised very Eskimo. I learned a lot from Colleen, too. She really used to set Grandma's teeth on edge. We were babysitting Fern's dog because Fern had gone back to Alaska with Joe. So we had Colleen and Tubby. Tubby was a little black dog about the size of a dachshund, only he had a short tail and woolly black fur. Colleen would sit with Tubby on her lap and she would pick the fleas off and crack them with her teeth. That would just set my grandmother crazy. Colleen was a thoroughgoing Eskimo. She had never seen a tree till she hit Seattle.

Intelligent, gee whiz. Colleen could play the piano like a darn . . . yes sir, she knew a lot! Yeah, I never told Mom about some of that either! She eventually got herself through high school, got herself a couple years of college. I think she married a doctor. Last time I saw her, she was about seventeen, eighteen. She was just as pretty as a picture, just a beautiful girl. She had the loveliest skin; it was just a light copper color.

Colleen, Pat, and Donna—I think the four of us could have licked our weight in wildcats. I probably would have stood back and let them take care of it, actually. They could be pretty savage! We were pretty close in doing kids' stuff. We could get ourselves into a lot of little stuff. Of course we made it to the movies fairly often. They could consume mass quantities of popcorn, I'll tell you.

3 / Family across the Generations

Many cultures point to family relationships and understandings as a key, even a defining feature. It is basic. The role models provided for children by family and friends profoundly affect how they grow up. One's identity is formed, at least in part, out of these early learned experiences. Children develop patterns in which they operate for years to come. While this is by no means unique for Native American families, the particular sets of understandings are. In many cases, connections to places, to long histories of struggles, to the pain wrought by European conquest of the continent are passed down across generations. Increasingly in the twentieth century, these family narratives came together to foster a broader "Indian" (or pan-Indian) identity alongside those of family and tribe. But Native peoples do not live in a vacuum. Their lives and ways of understanding the world have been inexorably altered by centuries of association with the many migrants who came to North America from around the world and even by Indian exposures to life in other countries.

Such was the case for Don. He grew up hearing stories of his family, of the lives of their many friends that connected him to a past experienced by many different Indian peoples. He also gained appreciation for many other cultural traditions, including the "Western canon." His ability to negotiate those different influences, to chart a safe course amid them illustrates his own tenacity, the security of self that his family provided, and the importance of understanding lives across generations.

DAD

He never understood art, but he was always supportive.

Don's father, Fearon Smith, was born in 1906 in Montana. He worked a variety of jobs there and in eastern Oregon. While he never identified as "Indian," he came into close association with many Native peoples in the region. In some respects Don inherited those networks that his father had established, though he extended them significantly. The major breadwinner for the family early in Don's childhood, Fearon lost his business near the end of World War II, leaving Mary and Don as the main income earners in the family. Beginning in the 1950s, Fearon increasingly moved into a supporting role for those two, which continued until his death in 1987. Most visitors to the family complex at Ariel, Washington, overlooked him, a man of few words and little desire to be in the public eye, and instead focused on Don, his siblings, his niece, his nephew, and Mary. Most purchasers of Don's art did the same, not realizing that Fearon was a vital part of the entire process as procurer of wood, sander of carvings, and builder of crates for shipments. Indeed, his efforts made the entire family's artistic production inestimably greater. While Fearon received little praise for his efforts, Don and the family clearly recognized his contributions. In his quiet, reserved way, Fearon taught Don much about life.

Most of the years I was growing up, through the [Second World] War period and everything, why, he was involved in tires and recapping, tire sales, and all. I remember I was very small and I used to go out to the logging camps with him. I would usually end up over in the cook shack getting fed. That was always something I looked forward to. He would take in a load of tires and take out a load to be recapped. He got himself appointed a deputy sheriff, which helped with collecting because loggers were not the easiest people in the world to collect from. First of all, they were hard to get to and when you bearded them in their own den, why, they could be a little difficult! Dad usually had a flask in his hip pocket along with his star—his credentials. It went from sociability to legality.

*Fearon Smith Sr.,
Don's father, in the
1950s. Photo cour-
tesy of the Lelooska
family.*

Salem is where I started school. We lived on a road there that was way, way up above on the hill. You could see the airport from there. I remember there were the blackouts during World War II. Camp Adaire, which became a big military base for training troops, was on over a far, far distance. The Timberwolf Division was trained there. My grandpa Enoch Fountain Hinkle was the guard and security for a while there, and some of Dad's friends were, too. They worked on the base and then every Saturday and Sunday, they would usually have some of the guys who were out on leave for the weekend on a pass to dinner. They would go to the USO [United Service Organization] and they would pick up these guys, take them home, and give them a home-cooked meal.

After he sold the tire shop in Salem, Dad had a service station. I'm not sure how many years he ran it. It was toward the close of the war, just afterward for a few years. My uncle got out of the service and Dad hired him. He had a couple of Italians from New York that he hired who wanted to stay in the Northwest. They had taken their basic training at Camp Adaire. Boy, they were a pair of characters, Joe DeFilipi and Artero Miola! They were Italians, right out of a comic book! Hanging around them and knowing all the Italian jokes, something of their sense of humor and values, I think probably made it possible to have really excellent relationships later in my life.

Dad was always very busy earning a living. Oh, we went hunting and fishing. I used to go to the logging camps with him. That was a big deal. Of course, for a little boy loggers are colorful characters. Like old cowboys and old Indians—a little larger than life. First man I ever saw killed, I saw killed in a logging camp when I was a little kid.

Dad was a *great* role model. He was very macho, a real character. He and my grandfather got along very well, but they were from two different points of view, I guess you might say. Dad was not much into art or things like that. He never understood art, but he was always supportive. It was hard not to be; I earned a third of the family income at that time!

He was always very proud. I remember my last year in school, ninth grade—I was out of school by the time we moved to Hubbard—I was elected student body president of the junior high school. That was a very big deal for Dad. Any time you won any prizes, got awards or things like that, Dad could understand that. But he didn't understand, sometimes, how precious, how important to me some of the honors and friendships that I had among the old people were. I loved my dad and he'll always be a major player in my heart and part of me, but he was not part of the driving force in my life.

Dad grew up in Yellowstone Park. His father, C. M., was a drayman and a teamster. He had all this horse-drawn road-building equipment. Dad was a *pretty* good horseman. He had the imprint of a pair of pliers on his behind, where he had been thrown off a horse in Montana on the frozen ground and somehow the pliers kind of imbedded themselves! I remember my Uncle Bob [Robert Dean Hinkle, Don's maternal uncle] used to kid him about that. He would say, "Show them your pliers, Smitty!"

But Dad's concerns and my concerns were different so, you know, there wasn't that camaraderie. I loved my dad. God, I miss him. I miss his wry humor and his ability to be so frank you feel like you've been scoured with a blowtorch. Dad had an awful lot of wisdom. He had done a lot of living and a lot of mistakes, and he was a very good judge of people. And he was tough. He always knocked his thumb back when he got tough and whacked somebody out! He would take his thumb and pull it and pop it back in. He never backed down from anybody that I can remember.

I remember once, some big, young fellows came into the service station.

Fearon and his paranoid dachshund, Phaffner, in 1983. During this stage of his life, Fearon sanded all Don's carvings, packed and shipped all the items for patrons and art shows, and kept the grounds and buildings at Ariel in good shape. By late afternoon, one could usually find him in this position, in his portion of the family work area. Photo courtesy of Anna and Harlow Friday.

They were going to rob the place. Well, Uncle Bob scooped me up, one hand on the back of my neck and the other in my belt, and tossed me into a pile of tires. I guess he grabbed a tire iron then. There was this awful scuffle. By the time I scrambled back out of the tires, the whole darn thing was over, blood all over the place. Bob had cracked one of them over the head with the tire iron and Dad had knocked his thumb back good from thumping on the other one.

Grandma thought my dad could do no wrong for a long time. But Grandma and Mom bought a beautiful little place on Capon Road about a quarter of a mile from Chemawa Indian School. They paid for it with Mom's hard work and her miniature saddle business. Then Mom let Dad mortgage it when he went into business in the service station. He lost that and, after that, I think Grandma probably got a little more critical where Dad was concerned. When Dad lost his business, it was hard on him, but he pulled himself together. Part of that, I think, was the strength of my mother and my grandmother, too. It kind of helped him pull his britches up and get going.

But when you're a kid, you miss a lot of those things, especially when you're gone quite a bit of the time, off here and there.

I discovered a lot about my dad from the old guys when we began to go up to Pendleton regularly when we were doing publicity and public relations for the Round-Up. A lot of the older Indians would say, "Oh, your father is Smitty?" I would say, "Yeah." Then they would say, "I knew him years ago," and out would come one of these stories! I learned a lot about my dad. He had been a wild young man, and he knew lots and lots of the Indians. Of course, Dad's dad was part Indian and built some of the early roads in Yellowstone Park. Dad was born on the Flathead Reservation and kind of grew up around the construction camps and things like that, learned to drive teams and stuff.

Somehow he found his way to the Pendleton area when he was just a teenager and worked there for years. He knew all the old Indians. I already knew quite a few because they would come through and stop, and I had made war bonnets and dance regalia and stuff for a lot of the families. But all of a sudden, "Oh, yes, your father. Oh, we got drunk a lot of times together. He was a good man! Good man." I would hear all these neat stories about my dad. One of his old buddies was nicknamed Snoose. He was an old cowboy, a good old boy, a little busted up. That was when I began to really learn about my dad. I remember Snoose once said to Dad, "Well, what are you doing, Smitty, how're you making a living?"

He says, "I'm a cottage manager at the state reformatory." This was after the service station.

Snoose said, "Hell, Smitty, you're the biggest juvenile delinquent we ever had up here."

That was when he was a cottage manager for ten years at McClaren School for Boys, the reform school. He was one of their real good cottage managers. He ended up with most of the Indian kids when the administration found out that his family was all thoroughly Indian. Why, the Indian kids would come in, a lot of them wouldn't eat and they would just sit there, look at the same page in the book at school and wouldn't communicate at all. So he would take them over and he knew how to communicate with them: how to read things that the other people who hadn't been around Indians all their lives wouldn't think about. He had an awful lot of Indian kids. It didn't take a whole hell of a lot for an Indian kid to get thrown in the reform school.

Some of the old Indians knew him and really loved him. Well, Dad's first wife was Walla Walla* and I had a half-brother, Cecil. Cecil was a great guy. He had had TB of the spine and they collapsed his spine, so he was kind of a hunchback, otherwise he would have been a big, big guy. I loved old Cecil. The idea of a half-brother is ridiculous, I mean, he was my brother, period. But Dad, through his bootlegging activities, couldn't get custody of Cecil, and Mom and he tried for years; finally when Cecil was a man, why, he came and stayed with the family for quite a while. I really got to know him. Those people there at the Round-Up would tell me things about my dad.

Sometimes Dad would tell me things that he wasn't too proud of, but that were kind of funny. See, my dad, in his youth, was a rascal. He was a bootlegger in the days when bootleggers were not really thought of as useful to the community! Dad, having grown up around Indians over around Bozeman, Montana, and being part Indian, got along very, very well. He knew all the little games to play. So he did very well bootlegging and a lot of his customers were Indians and remembered him. He laughed about one great big, huge Umatilla guy—really big guy. He came up to Dad's room and he wanted a bottle.

Dad said, "Yeah, have you got the money?"

He said, "No, I haven't got any money, but I got a brand-new suit I just bought and I'll leave the suit with you, then I'll come and I'll get it. It is brand-new."

Dad said, "Well, okay." He was pretty liberal. I think that was why the old guys remembered him rather fondly. So Dad took the suit. One week went by, two weeks, three weeks, about a month, and the guy hadn't come back for it. So Dad gets out the suit and he looks at it. Dad, at that time, was pretty slim and pretty fit. He was a cowboy and he was working for a ranch and driving those big twenty-mule teams they used to have on their threshing equipment.[1] He looks at the suit and it has got possibilities. It is a nice color. He takes it down to the Chinaman[2] and has it cut down to fit

---

* Walla Walla are a Columbia River Plateau people with a presence on the Umatilla Reservation today.

him.[3] No sooner does he get it back in the room, when there is this knock on the door. He opens it up and it is this great big huge Umatilla guy. He says, "I want my suit, here is your money."

Dad says, "Just a minute, I'll get it." And he takes the money, goes in, puts the suit in the box, takes it out and hands it to him. "See you, good-bye." Closes the door! Dad said, "I never saw him after that, but I bet he really thought he had put on a lot of weight when he tried that suit on." And he would laugh!

He also told me about bringing horses in, sticking 'em in the pound until they cooled off, and then buy them out of the pound. That made every-thing legal. You had a bill of sale. Dad got one of Old Charlie Whirlwind's horses, and every time he would see Dad he would say, "Hey, you got my horse." Years later, his son comes up to him in Pendleton and he says, "I remember you. You and my dad were friends."

Dad says, "More or less."

"Yeah," he says, "you got my horse!" Talk about memory. This is one generation to the next. "You got my horse."

Mom hates the racial slur words for Indians—buck and squaw, words like that. Well, Dad, being of cowboy mentality, used those quite often. He used to rather set Mom's teeth on edge. Sitting there one day, kind of in the shade of the teepees at the Pendleton Round-Up, he says, "Son, because of one Umatilla squaw you might not have ever been born."

I said, "Oh?"

He says, "Yeah, I was hauling a load of wood for Naomi Eat-No-Meat." Now, part of the deal was the wheat farmers and the ranchers who rented the land[4] would get in the winter's wood for the Indians they were renting from. So he was bringing in this big load of wood in two wagons, started across this wooden bridge, I guess it was the Umatilla River. He gets the team well up on the bridge, and mules don't like Indians anyway and they don't like wooden bridges just about as much. The team is really kind of itchy and he gets all this right out onto the bridge, no place to turn off, no place to back up, and this Umatilla woman pops out of a sweat lodge that was kind of under the bridge. She jumps into the river stark naked and lets out this unearthly scream. You've never really heard a scream until you hear somebody hit the water coming out of a sweat lodge. The mules just went berserk. He said they scattered the wagons, the wood, and the harness over two quarter-sections of land! And he said, "Son, I could've been killed and you'd never have been born." Of course, here are all these old cowboys and the old Indians. They're all sitting around laughing. "Yeah, boy," they said, "you might never have been born!"

A little while later that same fall, same thing again. He takes the wood; this time he is lucky. He gets out there with a load of wood and it is dark by the time he gets in there. Old Naomi Eat-No-Meat comes out around the corner of her little cabin and she has got a lantern. She holds up the lantern and walks past the mule team and they panic again. She had just come out to see who was there. I can just see her. "Who is out there? Oh, you got my wood. Oh, my goodness, look at them mules." They scattered wood all over, tore the fences down. Of course, he had to go back and fix it when all was said and done.

Dad's brother Carl flew a SPAD [a French-built biplane] in World War I. Flew through the whole mess. Almost all of his squadron was killed in those canvas coffins. The day the armistice was signed, he was in Paris. He started across the street and a drunk woman ran over him with a Dusenberg and killed him. Then Dad's mother died pretty early on. Mom always sort of put some of Dad's little faults aside to me as a kid by saying, "Well, he never really had a mother. She died when he was quite young." Then later, his father married Ma Brigham. We called her Ma Brigham because she had been his wife. When he died, she married this Welsh tinker, Old Man Brigham. They lived out on the Santiam River [a tributary of the Willamette River near Salem].

Ma Brigham knew all the stuff on the family. She told Mom the story: "You know, Fearon's father was a wood colt." That was an old, old expression meaning he never knew who his daddy was! So that was a big thing. We don't know what the name might have been, but Smith is what we ended up with. Apparently his mother had left the country pregnant, with her black serving gal. Came from Tennessee to Bozeman, Montana. Settled in there and ended up starting the lying-in hospital, I guess they called it, for women who were pregnant and unwed mothers. She founded that, all by herself. She had to have a lot of grit or she never would have made it.

Dad had worked at a lot of things. He had been a muleskinner [a driver of mule teams]. He had been a cowboy. He had been a bootlegger. He had been a lineman on the high-tension lines. He had done enough carpentry and electrical stuff that he knew how to pretty much keep things running around the place. He could plumb a little. I mean, he wasn't a finish carpenter or cabinetmaker but, boy, if something needed fixing he could do it. He built a big log house when we lived at Hubbard.

I was really woefully deficient as a carpenter, probably because my mind was always someplace else. I would undertake to help Dad. Oh, God, it always ended up pretty disastrously. Once, he was putting in some pipe or wiring under the floor, before they started up with the logs. Dad had crawled under there to work. I'm laying the shiplap subfloor and I'm banging away. Boy, I was doing good, too. I was just hammering away. I was laying those and I finally got the floor finished. Looked back down that floor of a fifty-foot-long, twenty-four-foot-wide building, and I hear this muffled noise. I had nailed my father under the floor! Man, I tell you, you should have seen me tearing those boards off! Dad had a little bit of a temper! He came out of there wringing wet with sweat. He was suppressing his anger. I could tell because the veins were kind of standing out on his temple. Boy, he looked at me, he had his hammer in his hand and I thought, "Oh, Lord, let that first one be a good one!" He says, "Son, why don't you go and carve and I'll take care of this." I remember his voice was real thin and kind of shaky! I hear about that from Mom once in a while, nailing my dad under the floor.

Once Grandpa, Dad, Uncle Bob, and I went fishing up at Suttle Lake. We were out in the boat. There were these rowdy slobs who had been camped next to us. They had gone over to what they call the Red Slide. They had these great big gallon bottles of beer. They had them just sitting about half in the cold water of the lake near where they were fishing from the bank and had their boat tied up. I had a pellet gun, one of those good old Benjamin pumps. You could pump one of those up to where it would shoot about like a .22. So I pumped the thing up, and I was just kind of popping away at floating sticks and things, and my dad looked at my grandfather, my grandfather looked at me, and he says, "Son, hand me your pop gun." Grandpa looked over there. He put the thing under his arm to hide the gun from view. How the world he ever did it, I'll never know. He looked over there, and he looked back at my dad, and my dad has got a big grin. *Pop. Pooey.* There goes one of their big gallon jugs of beer. He says, "Pump it up again, boy." I pumped it up again, rather surreptitiously this time,

Don as a boy on the pony his father gave him. Photo courtesy of the Lelooska family.

because I didn't want to get any blame attached to me. Dad was looking, just grinning, and Bob was just shaking with hysterics. I handed it to my grandpa. Grandpa puts it under his arm again. *Pop.* Another one, *pooey.* Boy, now they're running around like crazy. Their beer is popping and they can't figure it out. They look out at the boat. Nothing going on there! He got three of them in a row! We decided it was time to pull up anchor and go over to the Black Slide.

At one point, Dad bought me a Cayuse pony. She was a bay, name was Dot. He bought her from Mel Lambert, our good friend Kenny's relative; Mel was just getting into his rodeo announcing career at that point. Dot was just a typical Cayuse pony, bigger than a Welsh by quite a bit and indestructible. I enjoyed riding her. She taught me a lot. Whenever I really got careless, she would unload me—unload me real good. It was a matter of honor: get up and get back on. That was the rule. Boy, if you weren't totally unconscious, you were expected to get up and get back on. I had a lot of fun with her and I also had all the responsibility. Shoveling it out and unloading the pickup and keeping the hay and the feed in there. It was real good training. It was up close and personal. I still love the smell of horses. But she sure had an ornery streak. She would just wait and when I would get care-less, *bang!*

I used to ride her down between the two tracks of Southern Pacific down to the train station at Chemawa Indian School. One time I get down there, see how some of the kids down there I knew were doing. Whoops! She unloaded me, but I was smart enough that time that I grabbed hold of the saddlehorn. She didn't throw me. It probably would have killed me, land-ing on the rails and the rocks. She just sort of unloaded me. She dumped me between the two tracks. I've still got hold of the reins and here comes the train. Boy, they moved then. The war was on and those trains didn't stop for nothing. So somehow I got my darn spur down under my heel and couldn't walk. I'm trying to get back on! She is going around and around in circles! The train is coming! The train is whistling. She is going around in circles. Here is this little fat kid trying to get up on the horse! You talk about your life flashing in front of you! The only thing I could think was, "By golly, if that train hits me, it is damn well going to hit her, too!" Finally I pushed her over into the other set of rails. Boy, I swear that train passed within about three feet. I'll tell you, old steam engines are hot and have all that stuff flying off of the cars, the dust and dirt and grit and the smoke and the wind! Yes sir, I was pretty careful about my riding down the railroad after that. Never told Mom about it. No sense worrying her! A horse will teach you an awful lot about life.

MARY AND OLD MARY

It is in my mom's character.

Mary Smith, also known as Shona-Hah (Gray Dove), produced Western and Indian crafts and curios throughout Don's childhood and his adult years. In doing so, she took a common path for women, especially Indian and "mixed-blood" women, who struggled to support their families. Not particularly concerning herself with the debates about art versus craft, about tradition versus consumer goods, she fashioned leather goods, carved small figures and dolls, and did other craft work that she sold in the family's combination museum and curio shop, to traders, and at fairs and rodeos. Her experiences gave Don options and experiences that bore him well in his teenage years and beyond.

Born in 1912 to Enoch Fountain Hinkle and Lady Elizabeth Hinkle, Mary grew to adulthood in circumstances that would have tried a more fragile soul. Her father's repeated failures at ranching, his long periods away from the family for military and related service, and his inability to deal with a life-threatening accident to Lady Elizabeth forced Mary to take on adult responsibilities quite early. Mary's adventurousness and force of will, perhaps modeled after that of her father, must have helped her cope. To many casual observers, these were not at first apparent under the grandmotherly guise she donned during the last three decades of her life, but they were there nonetheless. Indeed, the stories about her abound. Those that are most revealing have to do with her ability to rein in a crowd. At the Pendleton Round-Up, the family hosted a dinner in which the "cowboys" and "Indians" literally sat on opposite sides of the table. When arguments boiled up into what promised to become an all-out brawl, Mary nearly beat the crowd into submission with her stew ladle. On another occasion, she reportedly bared her chest for movie actor Slim Pickens to autograph.

Yet even before she married and had children, Mary took care of herself. Just a year or two before her death, her granddaughter Lee Ann had returned from an art show in Santa Fe with a photo reproduction of late-1920s rodeo women. In recounting the trip to her grandmother, Lee Ann pulled the postcard out and Mary immediately said, "How did you know that was me?" Lee Ann had not realized that Mary was one of the women. Mary did not talk about herself much, but that was not for lack of character or history. Don's recounting of several stories about her gave a sense of her personality, her family life, and how much of an influence she was on him.

In the context of his mother, Don also spoke about his maternal great-grandmother, Old Mary, whom he never met but knew through family stories. Her presence in Don's life, which was evident even during his illness, illustrates the power of family narrative in shaping people's understandings of the past and the present. She also gave Don a very personal sense of connection to a Cherokee past.

When I was young, Dad usually worked nights at McClaren [School for Boys near Salem, Oregon]. Nighttime was when they usually had most of their trouble because during the day they were supposed to be at school or working and all that. This one little varmint broke out of there; he headed to our place and knocked on the door. He said his car had broken down or something.

Well, Mom knew where he was from immediately by the hickory shirts that they always wore. She told him "no" and slammed the door, then she reached up over the door and took down the rifle. I was sitting there doing something at the table, and I thought to myself, "Well, maybe there is something out there and she is suspicious." Outside she went; I got up and I just kind of went along behind her. By this time the little varmint out there is trying to hotwire our car. She couldn't see his head, so she shot under the car and she shot him in the ankle! He flopped over screaming. The state cops finally came and they carted him off—complimented her on her shooting! Things were different then. About two years after that, he got out of the school again and killed his grandmother in The Dalles with a hammer and burned down the house on top of her. Mom heard that from Dad. She said, "I wish I could've seen his head; he'd never have lived to do that!"

Another time, they were having a big riot at the school. Ten of them busted out and headed across the fields. They were going to come and steal a car at our place. At least that was what one kid told Dad. So Dad called up and he says, "You're going to have some company." He says, "I'll tell the cops, but the boys might be there beforehand."

No sooner had we hung up the phone and looked out across the field when, boy, here came all those great big sixteen-, seventeen-year-old kids— big, big guys. This time I was going to do a Western movie on them. Again, Mom beat me to the gun. She was always quicker than I was at that. I suppose I should be ashamed of that. She stepped out in the yard. She laid the gun over the fence and she said: "Stop right there, boys," and they stopped. Then she shot over their heads and they turned around. I have never seen human beings run so fast. They took off across that field. One of them hit the barbed-wire fence and bounced off. He must have bounced ten feet from running into the fence, and he got up and went limping off. A couple hours later, the cops had the whole bunch of them. The deputy knew Dad and Mom, and he stopped by later.

He said: "My, my, you *certainly* did civilize those little monsters! They were almost glad to see us when we got them down there in Canby! They kept saying some woman here was going to kill them. I knew right away what woman."

"Well, those guys," she said, "I just shot over their heads."

He said, "Well, there wouldn't be any particular laws against that, but there might be some questioning!"

Cherokee women, especially elder women, were extremely important. They owned the land. They had the power of nomination and veto. They could depose a so-called chief.[5] They got themselves together, they sat in the seven-sided council house—seven sides for the seven clans—and they voted with their moccasin, as the old expression goes. They sat behind their menfolk, and they let them know their opinions when things were being discussed or voted on. They didn't get out there and strut around like the guys did. They would just reach out with the toe of their moccasin and punch him in the kidney to let him know what their vote was. He wanted to get fed or anything, why, he better listen to the little prodding foot. They were immensely powerful. And it is in Mom's character. It sure as heck was in her grandmother's character.

I know her grandmother, Old Mary, only through the stories. I was a very, very small child when she died. She broke her hip and she wouldn't have a white doctor. She died rather than let one touch her. Part of the reason for that was that she was an herb healer, which is a pretty sacred occupation. Mom remembers her little old cabin was just filled with stuff hanging and drying, and jugs of this and jars of that. People would come from miles and miles to get her remedies or to come and get her and then she would go and stay with somebody who was really sick or injured. She was really little and she smoked a pipe. She and her daughter-in-law, my grandma, Lady Elizabeth Hinkle, never quite jelled because she was really from another time. Grandma had all of these refinements of a good education and was a teacher and fairly removed from things Indian. Old Mary— Mom is named for her—would chew up Mom's food when she was a baby and Grandpa used to laugh about that, because that was how they made baby food in the old days. Grandmother could just hardly stand that.

Old Mary was a terror. Well, I'll give you an example: Her son Enoch, my grandpa Hinkle, ran away with a friend of his, a young boy. He was always running away someplace. They were going to hop a train and go some-where. His friend slipped and fell under the wheels. It just made sushi out of him. So Grandpa immediately went back home. This was a terrible, ter-rible thing. His best friend had been horribly killed right in front of him. So he stayed around a couple of days, then he got his suitcase and took off. He got to where he was going that night and opened up his old beat-up suitcase, and here were all these bloody rocks that she had gone down and picked up at the railroad and put in his suitcase. Boy, he came back home and he stayed *quite* a while after that. She operated a lot like that.

One of his aunts was another terror. Old Aunt Nancy was very, very wealthy by the standards of those times, lots of cattle, lots of horses. Some of the whites around were getting the cattle from mixed-blood Cherokees who were starting ranches. They started a big scare about hoof and mouth disease. They were going around to round up the cattle and supposedly shoot them. Old Aunt Nancy informed them when they came to her gate that if there was any shooting done, the sheriff would be the first one. She might get two or three more before they got her. They turned around and left and they never bothered her cattle.

She had everything on the place under lock and key. She had this big block of keys that she wore on a man's wide leather belt around her waist, and she used to get lots of her help from the poor farm! That didn't set too well with Grandma. Grandpa's wife, Lady Elizabeth Hinkle, was another one of those very, very strong hit-you-right-between-the-eyes type of people.

Do you know what happened during the Civil War? I had forgotten it till one morning when I had started eating breakfast again after the doc-tors said I had to build myself up. Mom was in there; I'm going through the paper and I said, "My God, there is another rape." I shouldn't really read the paper. The guy had been let out of jail and stuck right back into the neighborhood, which is the thing that really *bugged* me.

Mom said, "Yeah, well, my grandmother knew how to deal with people like that." When the men all went off to the Civil War, a lot of bad guys, whites, drifters, deserters from both armies ended up in the Indian Terri-tory. And in the Cherokee communities there it was just old men and boys, young boys, because, I mean, if you were thirteen years old, you had picked a side at that point. One of these guys came in and he sort of terrorized the

Don's mother, Mary "Shona-Hah"
Smith, at the age of sixty-five. The fam-
ily matriarch, she was a noted artist in
her own right. Photo courtesy of Anna
and Harlow Friday.

little community where Mom's grandma lived—Old Mary, the one who was the herb doctor—and he raped a girl. Because he carried a gun and was considered dangerous and he had shot a couple of people, nobody was willing to tackle him or felt that they could.

Well, Old Mary said, "We'll take care of him. When our men are not here and the older boys aren't here, the old men will only get themselves killed. We'll take care of him. We're going to get him drunk; when he passes out, leave him to me."

Well, they gave him enough liquor that he passed out. She and a couple of the other women, probably kin—you usually call on your family in situations like this—tied him to a tree and castrated him. When he came to, they tied him astride a horse with his hands tied behind his back and they ran the horse out of the country! After that, they didn't have much trouble with drifters stopping in that particular little community.

That was what Old Mary did. Mom is so proud of that. The pride in her voice when she was talking to me. That was part of the family tradition. Cherokee women were wonderfully resourceful. She took great glee in telling me that over my breakfast.

LADY ELIZABETH

She was just like blue steel.

Lady Elizabeth Hinkle brought a very different sensibility to Don and the family. She had years of experience as a ranch- and farmwife, and she had a formal education that she shared with Don and the other children.

My grandmother and her brother were orphaned when they were very, very small. Her brother had gone to one family and she went to a fairly wealthy Southern family who had clear reminiscences of the Civil War and what they had lost and all that. The family that adopted her named her Lady Elizabeth! She took the name of the Southern family, Hodges. That side of that family goes back to something like 1310; they're supposed to be descended from a noble family, the Heffners. Grandma rather liked that except we kept kidding her, "Yeah, Uncle Hugh." Every time we mentioned Hugh Hefner [publisher of *Playboy* Magazine], we would call him "Uncle Hugh!" "Oh, those Heffners, yeah!"

My grandmother was raised the least Indian of my immediate family— that Southern upbringing that she never quite shook. She had great respect for tradition, information, and history and all. That Southern family educated her. Of course, they had their own point of view as to various races. My grandma was, for her time, quite well educated. Grandma always knew that she was part Indian; probably it was her mother. But that wasn't even discussed in her family! I guess they told her when she finally finished college and was going to Oklahoma to teach that she was adopted and probably had some Indian ancestry.

My grandmother was a schoolteacher and that was what brought her into the Indian Country and to Grandpa, eventually. She could've clobbered the whole Indian thing, but she was much more tolerant than I would've ever expected of her. She did adapt. In fact, it was remarkable that she was so tolerant of a lot of these barbaric things that Grandpa loved so much.

She must've been fifty, sixty years old when her brother finally found her. I think he was the president of the Board of Trade in Saint Louis or Kansas City or something like that—a successful businessman. Bill; he found her. Oh, that was quite an interesting reunion. He called up on the phone and it was a big moment for everybody when they found one another. It was kind of interesting the way they found one another right at the end of their days. Her brother got part of their family history together. He had tried to trace as much as he could find out about the family, but he hadn't found a whole lot. He brushed up the family history and I think rewrote it a little. Grandma always felt that he could've snipped some of the racial stuff out of it—the fact that they were probably both part Indian.

Lady. Some of the Osage relatives would come to visit. "Them Pittses," as Grandpa called them. Grandpa didn't have a lot of respect for Osages because he said they never worked. Well, my God, they didn't have to, because of the oil, they were the Arabs of their time!* Anyway, Ina and Almas came to visit and I remember they called Grandma "Lady," and I thought about that, for she was "Grandma" to me. "Lady, Elizabeth? Well, okay!" Lady Elizabeth. . . .

When she was mad at me, she used to call me a throwback. "You're just a throwback." Usually when I was doing something pretty barbaric like scraping hides, singing in the morning when the sun came up, and things like that—slipping further toward the pagan past! It was not a Southern Baptist sort of thing.

She was *deeply* religious. Not in the way my grandfather was, because he was pretty traditional in that. Actually, they weren't that far apart in their religion when you melted the whole thing down. She was immensely strong, a character; she was just like blue steel. I don't think she was afraid of anything, unless it would've been something happening to a member of the family. She had no "ethnicity" as I recall, other than the family. She was *totally* dedicated to the family and its welfare.

My God, what a strong woman. When Mom was young, they got snowed in up on the ranch there on Fish Creek in Wyoming. Mom said the snow was up to the eaves of the log cabin and Grandma was just getting over diphtheria. Her dog got it from a dead cow he chewed on and she got it from him. This old trapper who was wintering with them helped to nurse her through. Grandma was real sick and expecting. Because she was weak and sick and all, why, the baby was stillborn. Grandpa very lovingly took the little body and wrapped it and put it in an old boot box. That was all

---

* In the Osage oil boom (1912–1928), the Osage managed to establish tribal ownership of the reservation mineral rights, and a few benefited immensely.

they had. Grandpa put it out where they kept the elk meat and the food in storage until spring when the ground would be soft enough they could bury the baby. He buried it on the fence line there at Fish Creek. She came out of that. Talk about pioneer women and living the old, hard, man-against-nature stuff, why, that certainly was.

Later she got burned in a fire. Her dress caught fire and burned her from the waist down, horribly. They didn't think she would ever walk again. First they thought she wasn't going to live and she did. Mom was responsible for her survival and the fact that she did walk, because Mom never let up. I think Mom was probably twelve or thirteen then. She would spend hours soaking the bandages off and exercising her. They had her on morphine because it was an easy way for the doctors to handle the pain and all. Finally, when she was healed, Mom threw all of the drugs out. The shock from the withdrawal, I guess, could've been pretty serious or fatal. But she came out of that and she got to walking and, boy, she could out-walk anybody.

Of course, Grandpa loved her deeply, though they spent a lot of their life apart. He was off here and he was off there. When things got dull or the cattle business wasn't going too well, he would go into the army for a while, then come back.* He got to drinking. Of course, drinking and the cavalry were synonymous in the old days. Well, for as much Indian blood as he had, he held it pretty well. But for a while, he just was totally destroyed by Grandma's burns. He couldn't deal with the fact that she was going through all of that. There just didn't seem to be anything he could do. It wasn't something he could fight; something that he could take hold of or beat it over the head like you beat a horse around his ears with your hat, which is something he loved to do. He loved bad horses and he loved to ride them. But he went through a hell of a time when she was suffering from those burns.

So old Harley, his brother, and his wife, Thelma—an Osage girl; they had ten or twelve kids—helped to get him through. They would sober him up; they would finally get him straightened out. But it was the one time that Grandpa's guts kind of failed him. That was his Achilles' heel, I guess, when

---

* In one way or another, Enoch Hinkle participated in every war effort from the Spanish American War to the Korean War.

the woman he loved so dearly had to go through this. I think he kind of had the idea that there was something that he wasn't doing to make this better. He couldn't find the key. It just killed him, practically. But Mom stuck and stayed. She was another tough, tough, tough lady.

Grandma was so dedicated to the family. She had a stroke. She was coming around pretty good and then the damn fool doctor told her, "Well, you'll never walk again." Bingo. With Grandma, if you weren't doing your job, you weren't going to do. She, who had been raised the least traditional, did the same thing almost that the old Indians do. She told Mom, "Love y'all. You've got to take care of one another. Goodnight." She turned over and that was that. Died. Mom thinks that she just willed herself to die because she felt that she would then be a burden on the family. She was *so* independent, I mean, fanatically so. It doesn't seem strange to me at all that that could happen even though she was mending as far as she probably could've mended. But she wasn't about to be a burden on anybody and I think she just turned over and said, "All right, Lord, here I come." That was that.

She was a civilizing influence on me, I guess. She taught me respect for learning, that knowledge—whether it was book knowledge or the kind my grandpa loved so much and that I loved so much—that the two [kinds of knowledge] could complement and enhance one another. But she insisted you needed good language skills, otherwise people wouldn't respect you. You needed it because you might have to get a job someday and the more you know, why, the better job you could get, at least that was what we told kids then. She was quite a civilizing influence. Her approach was different. Her Southern upbringing taught her to be a little more dead center than Grandpa was about things.

Grandma started being with the family a lot because Grandpa was in and out of the service so often. And when he wasn't, why, it was Wyoming ranching, the horse business, and things like that. She was great at home education. I can remember when I was a little bitty kid, she used to read me the *Odyssey*, Shakespeare's plays, too. I guess she was the one who got me hooked on Shakespeare and the flow of language and all. Grandma, because of the way she was raised as a Southern lady, thought it was very important. She loved the classics.

I can't remember when I wasn't read to, when I went to bed and when

Don with Lady Elizabeth and Enoch Fountain Hinkle, his grandparents; Bob, his uncle; his siblings; and several cousins. Photo courtesy of the Lelooska family.

I was sick, especially. She didn't read *Winnie the Pooh.* All that stuff was a waste of time. I was getting Shakespeare and I was getting some of the Greek classics, Greek mythology, and those kinds of things from Grandma.

I liked *Macbeth.* That was bloody! I still like *Macbeth,* and *Hamlet.* She was very good at illustrating. She would take the words and then she would talk to you about it. She says: "Now, in this part of the story, he is sitting by the grave where this gravedigger is and they're talking to the gravedigger. This skull comes tumbling up with the dirt." She says, "Whose skull was this? Oh, it were some mad fellow. Yoric, the king's jester." Then Hamlet takes the skull and he so loved the old jester and he talks about how he bore Hamlet on his back. Let's see, "How his jibes were wont to set the hall arock with laughter." You see how the darn stuff sticks! So here he is holding the skull. Boy, that is a *real powerful* image. He is remembering this man who he loved from his childhood. *Wow!* Then the big funeral scene: Ophelia has drowned herself and her brother catches her in his arms just one last time—"What ceremony else?" Because she had committed suicide, she couldn't have a blessed burial.

So then that gets us off into religion and religious prejudices and stuff like that. Here I am a *little kid!* But it really grabbed me better than a comic book, a lot of that stuff. Then the last scene, "Here cracks a noble heart." The King is dead. The Queen is dead. The place is littered with bodies. Finally, old Hamlet is croaking. His best friend had "shishkabobbed" daddy behind the tapestry. They were powerful images and they stuck with me. The language, the cadences were like music, and there were all these words that had to be explained to me; I think that is why I had a *terrific* vocabulary when I first started school. The teachers really just couldn't figure that out. Two things: one, the accident of nature, wherein I may or may not have been pretty intelligent, I don't know; that, and the fact that Grandma had put a lot of this stuff in my head. Even Mom never read trash. She was fond of reading me natural history books.

Grandma loved good manners and good taste: wipe your feet and wipe your nose and stand up straight! You know it when she got on your case. Boy, you might just as well give up and change your ways. She always had these good little jibes that she would be getting you with, like if my grades weren't where she expected them to be, which was A, A, A, why, then she would be calling me "dumb head" for weeks! I really had to turn in a performance to get that out of her! I was so bored with school most of the time, there was no challenge there. But she was rather merciless in her expectations and her means of getting them. She was rather ruthless. She would've made a fine Prussian general, Grandpa always said!

Here I've got Grandma on one side trying to make a proper little gentleman out of me. On the other was Grandpa, who was sort of the barbaric side! Grandpa, who *so loved* the old ways that he had to pass it on, to share it, and to expose me to it because he knew the value of it. It could've made a real mess out of me psychologically, but it just seemed to kind of flow along so naturally. I thought *all* kids did this stuff. I thought that all went to movies with old cowboys and old Indians, went off to live in a teepee for weeks at a time, and had old Indians, old cowboys hanging around the house for weeks and weeks and weeks! No, no, it turned out they didn't. It was *really* pretty bizarre. But Gram really was a wonderful lady.

ENOCH FOUNTAIN HINKLE

He wanted me to understand . . .
that this is all one God wearing many masks.

No single individual had a greater influence on Don during his childhood than his grandfather. Born in 1880, Enoch worked as a ranch hand and then joined the U.S. Army to serve in the Philippines. From that tour of duty until his death while working on a troop transport ship in the Korean War, Enoch continually returned to the military, never quite shaking it from his self-definition and sometimes using it as a safe haven from the vicissitudes of life—personal and economic. Still, home for Enoch and Lady Elizabeth from the 1940s on was with their daughter Mary and her family.

When he was with the family, Enoch had a habit of carving small animal figures and telling Don stories about them, thus blurring the distinction between crafts and cultural heritage. That was an important lesson, but perhaps more critical were Enoch's tales of his days with the Buffalo Bill Wild West Show and the many people from that era whom he introduced to Don. By the 1930s and 1940s, those shows were part of the past, but the individuals who had participated in them were not. Don's contact with the people from Enoch's life plunged him into a pan-Indian world. Although each of these individuals came from distinct Native American cultures, they also conveyed to Don the centrality of being Indian beyond the tribal differences. This too was an important lesson, for it allowed Don to extend his horizons rather than limit them to just his family's experiences. He recognized the pain that these earlier generations bore as they suffered the loss of lands and sovereignty. Yet his association with those who had participated in cultural phenomena like the Wild West shows also demonstrated how Native Americans might develop cultural critiques of their representations by non-Indians even as they participated in the making of them. He realized that Indians were no less "Indian" for having taken part in Wild West shows. This lesson he repeatedly saw around him as a child and he carried it with him for the rest of his life.

Enoch also helped Don see how one could learn from these circumstances. He taught Don about the best ways of asking questions, about how to observe behavior. By witnessing his grandfather's relationships, Don established his own. Quite literally at his grandfather's feet, Don learned how to learn in the informal but nonetheless powerful world of stories, as well as how to be a highly effective ethnographer.

Grandpa had learned so much in his life, but getting him to sit down was practically impossible. He always rolled his own cigarettes and paced the floor. He was a pacer! If he wanted to talk and you were going to listen, you had to walk with him, back and forth in the living room if he couldn't get outside. If he could get outside, you might end up miles away. He just had that awful energy.

I suppose my grandfather would have been a little frightening to people. He had been one of the handsomest guys, I guess, from what they tell me, when he was young. He had snapping black eyes, this wonderful manner, the graceful hands you get from being a sign talker so much of your life. But he had had a saber run through his cheek and out by his eye and it got infected. They had taken the eye out and washed it, cleaned it, and put it back. He had this big saber scar on his check and he had another big one through his leg. Well, this wasn't in battles or anything, this happened on the parade grounds. They would do these saber drills for the visiting dignitaries with the crack cavalry guys. You only had to be off about two inches and somebody took a saber through their leg or worse. He was also a boxer, a lightweight. He wasn't a very big man, slight, quick. He was the regimental champion boxer. He had a lot of neat scars and some bullet holes and things!

Grandpa had, from time to time, killed people. He never talked about that. He never talked about the military stuff much, but I happened to meet a guy who had been the commanding officer in the Philippines. He was running a photography studio, making the tinted portrait photography that was popular in the thirties and forties. I would usually go to a movie downtown on Saturdays after I got through working around Dad's service station. I was walking up the street; this guy was standing there on the sidewalk and he says, "You're Enoch Fountain Hinkle's grandson?" I didn't know the guy and I said, "Yes, sir" in my best trooper's manner, because my grandfather would've expected that of me. And this guy says, "Yes, you *certainly* are! Come in, come in. Let's talk." So I spent a lot of Saturdays there after the movies. I would go down there and I would wait at the studio. When he didn't have anything to do, he would say, "Well, let me tell you about your grandfather. I'll tell you the things he won't tell you, and you should know." I heard all about the Philippine campaign, my granddad, and lots and lots of things. My listening was instinctive. Those were the best moments of my day! And to remember it, to go through it over and over again in your head and try to find little pegs to hang the important events on so it would "stick," as the old people would say. Otherwise, as they put it, it just comes and it bounces off, it doesn't go *into* your heart. It just bounces off.

He taught me a lot about my grandfather and I found out how he got some of his scars. I found out he had had malaria and nearly died and they shipped him out. He was a sergeant at that time and an expert shot.

One Sunday this guy said, "Your grandfather'd be very angry if he knew what I'm going to tell you because he would never talk about this to anybody, I don't think." Apparently he was picked as kind of a bodyguard for the families of the American officers in the Philippines. So whenever they went to the marketplace or to church, why, Grandpa went along. Once a man came out of the crowd as the officer's family was headed up the steps of the church. The Moros of Mindanao were Moslems on their pathway to glory: to kill a Christian Filipino or, better yet, one of those damned Americans. He was a *jurmentado,** a guy who had devoted himself to be killed. They would bind him up with rawhide, which I guess reduced the hydrostatic shock of being hit with a bullet and also slowed down the bleeding process. Then they would lace him with hashish, or whatever. He had one of those big, two-handed *barongs,* with the big willow-leaf-shaped blade about two feet long and the handle about a foot more. He just was coming through the crowd lopping off arms and legs and heads, chopping people in two. He was headed up toward where the aliens were, the American military, and he just kept coming. So Grandpa got between him and the officers and their families and pulled out his old .45 long Colt. As the guy came in good pistol range, why, he put one into him. Put another one into him. Guy just kept coming, just flailing away. He kept coming and he started up the steps and he kept coming. You only load a cavalry pistol with five shots

---

* In some parts of the Philippines, a *jurmentado* is a person who may commit murder and suicide under the auspices of religion.

so the hammer always rested on an empty chamber—boy, that was *religious.* The last shot—it sounds like an adventure novel or something—the last shot, the guy finally folded up. Five slugs, none of them missed. It took that much. Forty-five long Colt was a powerful cartridge.

So it was a big deal. They wanted to put Grandpa in for a decoration. He tore up the papers and he refused. The officers called him in. They wanted to know why he was refusing the decoration. This would be good for him and it would be good for them, and he said, "I will not accept any honor for having killed a brave man." Grandpa respected the Moros very much because they were furious, fearless people. A lot of them were pirates out of the Sulu Sea.

This was the struggle. Here again was the alien or white society encroaching upon the culture of another people. Language helped him a lot, his ability to assimilate a usable vocabulary in a short bit of time. He picked up Tagalog quickly. He could communicate. He was one of the ones who went out to look for a patrol that hadn't returned; the Moros had caught them swimming and you couldn't tell who was what or whose parts belonged to the others. They got them all. He had nightmares about that. I can even remember some of his nightmares. He would sit up in bed. Then he got the darn malaria and it lasted for years. He still had it when they went to Wyoming. He would just sweat and shake for a day or two and be just totally debilitated, and then he would bounce back. He would take his quinine and it would go away a while, but for years and years, Grandma said, he had suffered with that.

They brought him back to the army hospital at the old Presidio in San Francisco. You know what happened then? San Francisco fell apart! He was there in the 1906 fire! So they're all in the hospital at the Presidio and the thing is falling apart. He had come back with the wounded and the guys who had malaria. The officer came in and he said, "How many of you men can stand up?" And Grandpa says, "I can, sir." The officer says, "All right, you pick a rifle squad and form them up, we need you."

The looting was terrible. They would find looters, they would just march them into an alley, and they would just shoot them on hand. I know once I heard my grandpa tell my Uncle Bob about catching the guy with his pockets full of fingers with rings on them. His tactic was, he would find the corpses bloating in the street or in the wreckage, and he would fall down like he was weeping over somebody he knew. He had this knife and he would just cut it off at the joint because you couldn't get the rings off of the fingers the way they would swell, and he would chuck them in his pocket. The pockets of his coat were full of fingers with rings on them. I don't think the guy lasted long after he got arrested.

That was why Grandpa went to live with the Osage cousins, this kind of stuff. The family, I guess, knew about some of the problems he was having. I think it was a sister, married into the Osages, that he went to live with. Grandpa always thought the Osages were lazy, cowardly suck-ups to the whites. He tolerated them, but they were not like the Sioux, the Cheyenne, the Arapaho, the Blackfeet, and those people that he loved so much.

He had names from most of the tribes that he had been close to. One Lakota name he had meant Plenty Stripes, from the fact he was a sergeant-major. In Montana, he knew quite a few of the old Blackfeet, some of the Guardipees—old Frank Guardipee, and Yellow Kidney and Wades-in-Water and a lot of them. The Guardipees were from those mixed-blood families. On the Northern Plains, a lot of the mixed-blood families became very prominent because they assimilated white society and yet some of them remained very thoroughgoing Indians. But they spoke well. They weren't quite as ferociously "Indian" in appearance as the others. They got a lot of jobs and politicking in the tribes. They really kind of ran the tribes for a while on the Plains. I spent one, two, nearly three weeks with the Blackfeet. Good people. Old Frank Guardipee was sort of the official greeter and storyteller for the Great Northern Railroad;* very picturesque, very well spoken, handsome old guy and also a remembrancer: myths, folk tales, stories of their battles with the Cree and the Sioux and on.[6] Great guy. They sure were handsome people, the old Blackfeet. I think they are the handsomest of *all* the Plains people.

When I was a kid, I was at the opening of medicine bundles.† It was practically unheard of, but because of the respect they had for my grandfather and the fact that I had learned things, I got to see some things like that when we were staying in Montana with Grandpa's friends. It had been kind

---

* The Great Northern Railroad did much to promote tourist travel and often hired Native Americans as "color" to add to the tourist experience, especially in Glacier National Park.

† Medicine bundles, or thunder bundles, are sacred objects imbued with immense power in and of themselves, and they contain other objects of like power.

of a late coming of summer, but you know when that first great thunder-storm comes across the Plains, not just the little "defriggledies" of weather, but that big, grand demonstration of the powers of nature, that is a time when a man who possesses the thunder bundle has to open it. When they came and got me to go in with the old men and sit in that lodge all that night and watch the whole ceremony, I think that gave me a feeling that somehow I wasn't a little kid anymore. My granddaddy stressed, "This is something very unusual and very, very holy to the Blackfeet people." I think at that time, if it hadn't been all of those *old, respected* people, the old men, it might have been different, but to be allowed in that company, to be offered the pipe—the pipe went around—I wasn't a kid anymore, certainly not much of a kid!

It was in one of those big Blackfeet lodges.[7] They have a liner inside that is also painted. The outside is painted with a painting that belongs: the right to that painting is property, and it comes down from the time when it was received as a vision or it was given by the spirits to an ancestral person, although they had the right to sell it for horses or something and transfer the responsibilities of these great painted lodges. That was pretty impressive.

Well there in Montana, when you get a thunderstorm, you get a *thunderstorm.* We have nothing here to compare. Literally, you can feel the ground just shake like the tread of some awesome powerful thing, then the wind comes, and then the hail and the rain. It was just like when Mount Saint Helens erupted. You begin to realize your true dimensions in the scheme of creation and you're not very big! That was the first time I can remember being in a big lodge when a thunderstorm came up. Of course, the next night was the night that he had to fulfill his responsibilities of opening the bundle, taking out the pipes and blessing the pipes, and singing all the songs. I forget how many songs were associated with it. It took all night and then in the morning as the sun first appeared, why, then there was another thing that had to be done. We had to go outside—the sun was coming up, the darkness was gone—and we thanked the Creator and all of the forces of nature that are really the Creator in his different personalities. You can quit being a kid at that point.

Grandpa knew all kinds of people, especially from the Buffalo Bill Show days, not just Indians. In the town of Salem, Oregon, in the late thirties and early forties there was a Buddhist temple with an abbot.[8] My granddad knew cause in the absence of an available Indian herbalist, which his mother was, he liked Chinese doctors and he liked Chinese. How he got involved with the Chinese community in San Francisco is another story. He liked the Chinese also because he liked to play fantan. In fact he lost a poultry business once. Anyway, he used to take me down to the Buddhist temple and I would sit there in the back and listen and watch these old, old, old Chinese people, not many of the young ones but the old people. I kept thinking, "They're not so different from Indians. Gee, kind of squint your eyes a little bit, they could be Indians!" He exposed me to that. Went to a synagogue with some of his Jewish friends. Been to a Catholic Mass, also Greek Orthodox. But the thing that he wanted me to understand is that this is all one God wearing many masks.

UNCLE BOB

You could talk to Uncle Bob about anything.

Not all of Don's role models were "elders." Among the younger generations, Don looked to individuals like his uncle Robert Dean Hinkle (1925–1980) as a strong male figure. Bob boosted Don's self-esteem in ways that Enoch or other family members could not. Only eight years older than Don, Bob was a confidant to Don and a vigorous young man negotiating the difficult mid-twentieth-century position of being Indian in a broader society that denigrated and trivialized Indianness. Decades later, Don still mused about how his grandfather and uncle could balance the contradictions in their wartime patriotism to the United States with the decades of governmental and societal mistreatment of Native peoples. Even if the men in his family never fully resolved those contradictions, they devised ways of living with them—valuable lessons for any Indian youth.

My maternal uncle, Bob, was one of the major players and that was very, very significant. Cherokees count your bloodline as the mother's. Your maternal uncle has the responsibility of educating you, your spiritual education, training as to whatever you're going to be. Could be a horseman, silversmith, warrior, whatever it was in the old traditional society. So the father is respected very much, but he is one step behind the maternal uncle in *real* responsibility. That is hard for a lot of non-Cherokees to understand, but it is very much the same on the Northwest Coast.

I know when I was little, Bob was really an idol of mine in a more intimate way perhaps than my grandfather, because there wasn't this *towering* respect that I had along with love for my grandfather. Bob was *young.* He wasn't all that much older than I, so he was closer in very personal kinds of things, the things a kid likes to do. He was good at catching frogs. I remember that we used to catch frogs. He loved to fish. He built model airplanes. He *loved* airplanes.

Bob went into the navy to be an aerial gunner during World War II. He was just a marvelous swimmer, a real good athlete. They sent him up to Whidbey Island* and they tested him up there, and then they put him on an underwater demolition team (UDT)—the frogmen. They trained him for that and, I mean, he could kill you with his eyelids when they got through with him.

He got all ready to ship out. He was superpatriotic, as was his father, my grandfather Hinkle. Bob by that time had a revenge thing going. His uncle Harley's son Bob—Harley, my great-uncle, also had a son named Bob—was killed on Iwo Jima. So Bob was about ready to ship out with the UDT and he was going to avenge his cousin Bob's death. I mean, this is a traditional thing to do. Well, they took a bunch more tests. He didn't get to ship out with the UDT guys. They sent him to instrument school. He apparently tested too bright on aptitude for mathematics and things, so they sent him to Chicago for instrument school. Oh God, he was mad. I guess he came pretty close to punching out the powers that be over that! He didn't know that that was going to happen. He had no idea that he would test in that way because he didn't care much for school. He was bright. I know that. But he always thought, "What the hell, why didn't I cheat? I didn't know what the hell I was going to test. I was going to be a gunner and they made me a frogman because of a test." Now here he is, off to instrument school, and he wants to go kill Japs.

Well, he got through instrument school and they shipped out for the Pacific. The war is now waning; the islands are dropping pretty regularly. So

* Whidbey Island, in Puget Sound just north of Seattle, Washington, is the site of a naval air base.

they sent him out to Majaro,* which is centrally located to a lot of the areas where the navy had their planes. They needed servicing and they had all kinds of instrumentation that was developing more rapidly than they had technicians to handle it. So Majaro was to have their best technicians and they would ship the instruments or parts of the planes that had instruments—torpedoes and things like that—to have adjustments. There weren't people on the ships qualified to do that. They would get the planes in there any way they could.

Well, when they got to Majaro, they had just taken the place and a lot of the Japs who were there had killed themselves; they were piled up and bloating, you know how the tropics are. So the only Japs Bob got to do in was with a bulldozer digging trenches and getting them underneath before everybody got sick from the corpses. I remember one letter he wrote, kind of ruefully. I remember Grandma reading it and kind of chuckling. He said, "I must have buried a thousand Japs today, but damn it, I didn't get to kill one of them." I think it bothered him a lot for a long time because he really wanted a scalp!

My uncle Bob was a big, good-looking guy. Kind of a James Garner type, only he was better looking even than James Garner. I think he is the handsomest man I ever knew. But, boy, there was a guy who could beat your ego into shape and pull up your britches and shape you up into a man. That sort of stuff. He was about as macho as a half-dozen John Waynes. He was one of my heroes. I miss him so. You could talk to Uncle Bob about anything. One reason I never got married was his marriages that he worked so hard at. I came pretty close a few times, but I would think about Uncle Bob—it was better than a cold shower! I know a lot of people ask, "Why? Why didn't you ever get married?" I'm married to what I do and married to my family, I suppose you might say. I'm not immune. I've had a lot of, lot of friends over the years, especially when I was younger and goofier but *that's* another story!

Anyway, being a parent is pretty daunting. I don't really know whether I would have made a good father or not—I think a better uncle. Besides, I didn't have time for that. There was always something else to do. You get

---

* Part of the Ratak chain of atolls in the Marshall Islands in the South Pacific at about 171° E and 7° N.

married, why, then half of your life belongs to somebody else and you have half of their life. Making the two match and then accomplishing a lot of the things you would like to is very difficult. I always felt that if I didn't go ahead with my art, I would probably not be a real good companion for anybody in a life's dream! But kids are great.

SIBLINGS AND RESPONSIBILITY

Oh, they put the pebbles in my hand, I can feel them yet.

Don did not grow up alone, though the manner in which he took his position as the eldest son distinguished him from his siblings. Aside from Cecil, Don's half-brother, Dick, the second brother, stood second to Don in the family order. Patty bore the burden of being the only daughter, and Smitty (Tsungani Fearon) occupied the position of "the baby" for many years. Although keeping family relationships together as adults was not always easy, those childhood and young adult years still held an important place in Don's heart.

Don gained much from each family member, but as the eldest child he also had obligations to fulfill for his family. Some of these Don took upon himself, but others his family expected and even imposed upon him. One particular incident resonated through the years. It was that moment when a small ritual began his transformation from a boy to a man.

Very early on I got the message: "Well, you're the oldest, you're the example. You have a responsibility to the younger members of the family." My grandpa was very good at that. In fact, he and my granduncle Harley were taskmasters at giving me a sense of responsibility in that matter. I was real young, about twelve, thirteen, I guess, somewhere in there. We took a long walk, sat down there in the wood lot. They were talking to me about the traditional responsibilities of a Cherokee man. A woman had the house and the land. She looked after the farm. The man's job was to direct the upbringing of male children and to see to the general welfare of the family, to protect the family. I don't know how they ever got to protect anything if all the women were like Mom. The enemies were all dead before you got your gun loaded!

But they have a thing that they do for the eldest child. They take your

Don (right) carving as a teenager in Hubbard, Oregon, with his brother Dick doing bead-work and his sister Patty carving. From infancy, the children were immersed in Indian and Western Americana arts and crafts. Photo courtesy of the Lelooska family.

hand and they put a little pea gravel–size pebble in your hand for each member of the family. It is usually an extended family among the Cherokee. When you have all the pebbles in your hand, it is getting pretty full. Then they take more and put them in there and say, "These are the unborn, so you have responsibility as maternal uncle to them." Then they close your hand up as best you can and they all put their hands over it. They squeeze it down and they say, "Now never let one pebble fall by your carelessness." In other words, let no life that is in your keeping, in your hands, ever slip by, because this is your responsibility. You're the eldest and it goes on clear through your life. You become what in the old days they called a Beloved Man. You're sort of a judge, banker, priest to this little clanlet! That has a *profound* effect on the way you look at things, how you look at your brothers and sisters, your concerns for them. It has never left me.

I suppose if I would have gone off someplace or something, why, it might have been different, but it just kind of grew. I still feel the responsibility. I feel my responsibility to Smitty's children. They are all as important and dear to me as if they were my own daughters, Mariah and Lottie. And now we've got my grandniece Jamie and grandnephew Dustin, Jay's kids, and I have a responsibility to them. Those are the unborn, you see. They've been there all this time. They just hadn't become people yet. But I think that did a lot to change my life. You have a . . . a duty. Oh, they put the pebbles in my hand, I can feel them yet.

Now, the first incident when I really *had* to take that responsibility was when Dad's service station went kerplop and we moved out to Hubbard. That was when my income and Mom's income from our art became a major item in our survival. Dad eventually worked himself into a good position at McClaren, but all those state jobs pay—at that time, at least—very, very little. With the family bills and obligations to take care of, it was a little tough. That was when I really felt that this was my chance, the time had come to do what I had promised to do to keep the family together, to keep it strong, and to help it prosper for everybody's sake. That was the time.

My brother Dick was a lot like Uncle Bob. He had the temper that Bob had—oh boy, Bob had a temper—and a little bit like my grandfather in that he would run terrible risks, just for the fun of doing it. Dick is kind of a mixture. He wrecked three cars in a row! I traded with old Mel Lambert— at that time, he was a pretty-well known rodeo announcer; he is on the board of the Cowboy Hall of Fame now—I traded him a carving of a stage-coach being chased by Indians for a car for Dick, his first car. He wrecked it in about eight hours! Next one, same thing. Next one, same thing! He could've killed himself so easily.

Dick was a real athlete. If he had been motivated or found the sport that he really wanted to dedicate himself to, who knows? He loved horses. He loved bad horses.

So did Kenny Lambert. Kenny is kind of a brother. We raised Kenny. He had a tough home situation. He is Nez Perce on one side. When he was a little kid, the teachers at school voted Kenny the boy most likely to commit

Richard Lee (Dick) Smith at about the age of ten, dressed in a fancy dance outfit, next to the family's museum and curio shop in Hubbard, Oregon. Dick also performed for school programs. Photo courtesy of the Lelooska family.

a homicide. He liked to make bombs and things like that! He almost lost his thumb doing that. If ever I needed a loyal friend, somebody who I knew was going to be there to the last round, it would be Kenny. If I had something life threatening that I had to go into, and I wanted somebody at my back, boy, I tell you, Kenny and my brother Smitty would be unbeatable.

Kenny has kind of an old, traditional style of loyalty that is unquestioning. He is your friend. That is it. There is none of this moralizing, anything like that. Bang! Kenny will do it. He is a wonderful guy. He has been a wonderful father. He just needed to settle down and find out where he was going and who he was. Wonderful wrestler; he was really a savage opponent. He won a lot of prizes. I don't know whether he won the state championship or not. I know he was really close at that time. I really trust old Kenny with anything I've got, including my life.*

My sister Patty has always been herself. Patty is the darnedest people person. She could charm the horns off the Devil, I swear. She just genuinely loves people! I mean, it is no act. She is impetuous and flies into things. Sometimes it requires considerable damage control! Her flight into that thing at Yamhill Market† really caused a big explosion within the family; I tried every way I possibly could to talk her out of it. So did her husband, Michael.‡ She is a little bit bull-headed like my dad was in that she'll go ahead, but that is the same quality that makes things work for her, too.

She is a dear person, a loving person, a caring person. I think she cares too much. I don't think there is much in nature she doesn't love. She is always mothering something: caterpillars to ducklings, dogs and cats, horses and skunks. Her marriage to Michael, a veterinarian, was the Lord's master stroke, I think, in giving her a happy life.

Animals respond to her. Mom and I went through the darnedest thunderstorm you ever saw in your life, the roads were flooded. We went clear over to Newberg, home of the kennels where some of the finest dachshunds in the United States, or anyplace else for that matter, are raised—very, very fine dogs. Mom went in and saw the one she wanted; it was just the way Patty had described the puppy she wanted. She wanted one that was black and tan, and was fun and cute and all that stuff.

Well, out comes Mom with this dog. I hold that dog all the way through the storm. He is wrapped up in my sweater. Cuddling him, trying to keep him warm. We got to the house and he is all cuddled up and snuggled up; we take him in. I put him in Patty's arms. The minute he is in Patty's arms, the little S.O.B. tries to bite me! And that was the way it went. Patty was it. Anybody else, their life was in danger! From that instant, when she touched

---

* Kenny Lambert died suddenly of cancer between the time that Don was first diagnosed with cancer and when he died. Kenny's death was hard on Don; his sudden passing due to cancer and Don's own battles with it made his death particularly difficult for Don and his family.

† About 1980, Patty decided to open a gallery at the Yamhill Market in Portland, at which time the family gallery closed. The Yamhill Market gallery proved too costly to run and it closed. By 1992, Patty and Don made amends and reopened the family gallery at Ariel.

‡ Michael Cook married Patty when her children Jay and Lee Ann were teenagers.

Patty Fawn Smith at about the age of six, in Hubbard, Oregon. She is most likely dressed for one of the early school programs that the family began there. Photo courtesy of the Lelooska family.

him, he was her dog and they were inseparable—Pepsi. And then we got Cola for Smitty, a little brown one. Pepsi and Cola—pair of little savages.

My youngest brother, Smitty, was ill a lot of the time. He was just right on the edge of leukemia for a long time. He had a really bad blood deficiency. When he was born, his navel was torn out and that gave him problems for three, four years. They didn't get that tended to until he had appendicitis. He went in for the appendectomy and the surgeon took care of the navel thing. He knew it was wrong when all those pediatricians had been missing the whole issue. Got that straightened out.

Fearon Tsungani Smith Jr., or "Smitty," as he is known to most, at about the age of three, in Hubbard, Oregon. Photo courtesy of the Lelooska family.

Up to that point, Smitty didn't have much to say. There is an old joke. These people have a child. Kid doesn't say anything. Won't talk. One year, two years, three years old, four years old. Gets to be about five years old. The whole family has been going crazy because the kid doesn't talk. Doctors, everybody has examined him. Won't talk. One day the mother sets the mush down in front of him and the kid tastes the oatmeal and says, "This damned oatmeal is cold." Mom says, "Darling, you can talk. You can really talk." Mom said, "Why haven't you said anything before?" He says, "Up to now, things have been all right." Smitty was kind of like that. He had very little to say. He was very much . . . inside, Smitty.

He was just about the dearest little boy, had these big eyes, beautiful child. At some point we got to doing publicity for the Pendleton Round-Up. We were doing programs, and Smitty took part in them. He was just a tiny little guy. I remember carrying him back from the big prize dance in Pendleton, and into the village where the teepees are, asleep in my arms. . . . Great kid.

He suffered a lot. He had that blood deficiency. It was looking very much like he was sliding into leukemia because he had a real blood deficiency that kept getting worse and worse and worse. Scared us all to death. A Canadian doctor put him on raw liver. You would freeze the raw liver. You would grate it up in V-8 juice and he would drink that. I think maybe it is buttermilk culture or something like that. I remember it came in a little folded-up piece of cheesecloth. Looked like dirty cheesecloth. It came by special messenger from Canada. Kept a jug of it in the refrigerator for him. And we would set it out overnight and it would work on the milk. Then he would drink it. He never complained. Never heard him complain about anything through all that. He just didn't talk a lot. He smiled a lot. He was just the most dear little, little guy. He put him on that, and some other medicines. He came right out of it in about sixteen months.

After that operation, I don't know, it was just like they had thrown the switch on the tape recorder and he began talking, and he has never stopped. Smitty loves to talk. He is like me, I guess. But he talked and he talked and he talked and he talked and he talked and he talked. We couldn't shut him up. He has been that way ever since. He is a real communicator.

Used to spend a lot of time just playing with him and making him things. Made him a whole rodeo of little cutout Brahma bulls, horses, and the cowboys, things he had been seeing at the Pendleton Round-Up. Quite a few cowboys came to the place, some of the rodeo clowns.

Of all of our family, Smitty, I think, is the finest example of a human being. Spiritually, emotionally, he is a rock. When they send me in for my surgery, I'm not going to go until he is back from New York. If there is anybody who can hold Mom together if anything should go wrong, it is Smit. He is great.

4 / Learning from People

I n the 1930s under Commissioner of Indian Affairs John Collier, the federal government sought to strengthen tribal governments on reservations. While this maneuver was meant to assimilate Indians into the political mainstream, it fostered a new tribalism and assisted in the growing legal and political challenges Native Americans mounted to assert treaty rights, especially regarding the use of resources and lands. In 1946, when the federal government established the Indian Claims Commission, it hoped to use this special court to end the disputes over treaty lands within several years. Such was not to be the case, and over the next quarter century, Oregon Indians filed nineteen cases before the commission. This meant frequent travel to Salem and Portland by tribal officials. The 1958 flooding of Celilo Falls on the Columbia River also called for numerous delegations of Indians from the small town there to meet with government officials before, during, and after the falls were flooded.[1] Political activity nourished a common bond among different tribes as they confronted similar issues. Thus, by the 1950s and early 1960s when the federal government adopted policies that threatened to terminate the federally recognized tribes, Native Americans drew upon existing pan-Indian identities and growing political strength to mount an opposition—one of the great ironies of the termination policy itself.

Amid these tribally based mobilizations, supra- or extra-tribal identifications (pan-Indianism) surged forward outside of politics. On social and cultural levels, Native Americans remained connected to one another among the tribes and even off reservation. Some individuals were surely isolated, but Indians as a whole were not. Rodeos, powwows, urban centers, and even urban taverns served as the loci for informal but potent networks of association that affirmed being Indian along with specific tribal identities.

In the latter, Native peoples recognized the cumulative effects of racism directed against them and turned the label "Indian" around, creating out of it a symbol of collective resistance that carried politics into social and cultural realms. Moreover, emergent pan-Indianism provided a means for those who had moved away from reservations, whose families had lost direct contact with the generation of the grandparents, whose "mixed-blood" descent made it difficult to choose between traditions, or whose residence or birth had not put them on tribal rolls to identify with peoples from reservations. Being Indian on or off reservation did not remake uneven power relationships between Native Americans and the U.S. government, or between Indians and whites. Native peoples still faced economic repression and suffered racist treatment. Yet being Indian was a source of pride and strength amid a world that consistently belittled, denigrated, and typecast indigenous peoples.

The location of Mary and Don's shop near Salem helped them tap into this regional pan-Indianism. The manner in which Don and his family engaged that identity was not simple. Don recognized that his craftwork affirmed the inherent worthiness of Indian cultural practices while simultaneously reinforcing white perceptions of what "Indians" were—befeathered relics of a past era to be viewed safely in museum cases or on movie screens. Yet as the stories Don learned, and retold during the interviews, suggest, Native Americans have at the very least put plenty of "brambles" in the messages they sent in spite of whatever "beatings" they suffered.

KLONDIKE KATE

I loved characters. . . . I learned a lot without ever being taught.

If I'm anything, I am the sum total of all the people I've ever known. I guess that is what you finally become in your life. As luck would have it, the people

I've been around and gotten to know through my life have been extraordinary. Nobody would ever believe it. I wouldn't attempt even to tell anybody some of the silly stuff because it is hard for me to believe it, and I lived through it!

Klondike Kate and old W. C. Kelly—I don't know how we got to know them. Well, I know how I met Kelly. Kelly had been the coachman for a well-to-do family in Salem. He was a little Irishman about five-four, maybe five-six; he had been to the Yukon Gold Rush in '98 and he was a veteran of the Boer War. He was a little, old, tough, ornery Irishman with a great shock of white hair. It had been red at some point. God, what a character. He loved the daughter of the family he was working for, but he was only the footman for the family, their horseman, and took care of the carriage. She had a clubfoot, she never married, but he stayed close to her all of his life. I mean, boy, it would have made a great, great love story. But he had been to the Klondike and he had a lot of great tales from the gold rush era. He would talk about Klondike Kate and the Nugget Saloon and Dawson.

We ran into Klondike Kate somewhere and she sort of attached herself as an unofficial grandma or auntie of us kids. She married a lot—Pantages, Matson, a half dozen people. A dancer and, gosh, what a lady. I've got her garter in there with those other things from Skagway, Alaska—1901. She gave me that. I think my brother Dick has the autographed picture that she gave him.

Those are living history books. You can read about Soapy Smith and Frank Reid and the vigilantes. They were going to clean up Skagway. Soapy was a con man, but he sort of elevated himself to the level of racketeer, and he had all kinds of scams and schemes going. So when they tried to clean up the town, why, it ended up he got shot and Reid got shot. But to talk to somebody who said he had been there—I had never any reason to doubt old Kelly—and talking about where he was shot, how long it took him to die, and how he suffered. He could just smell the coal oil lamps and the damp woolen clothes and the room. Well, the Irish, my God, they're gifted with a silvery tongue. He made it awfully real. Kelly and Kate were great to get together. He just worshipped her. Get them talking and then just sit back and listen! You've always got to watch the Irish, though—marvelous, marvelous turn of the phrase. Yeah, I loved characters.

MOVIES WITH THE "OLD GUYS"

I don't know Hollywood, but we're a lot harder to kill than that!

I went to movies with old cowboys and old Indians sometimes on Saturdays and *that* was an experience. It was a wonder that we didn't get thrown out. Somebody was always turning around and shaking their head, or making the sign saying, "Oh, they lie!" To make that sign, you use your index and middle fingers in a "V" like it is coming out of your mouth. If you make it up this way, in front of your face, that is a wolf or a scout. You point it down so it is coming out of your mouth, why, then you're a double speaker. Sign language is a whole thing. I have a speech impediment where sign language is concerned. I'm left handed. Most of the signs come off the right hand. So I really have to think, not so much around today's Indians, but around the old guys, because I was expected to get it right. I was Enoch's grandson. Because they respected him, they felt they had a duty to treat me like a grandchild. And if I didn't get it right, they made sure I did get it right. A lot of the old Indians didn't believe in spanking children or punishing them. They had something more dreadful. I call it "The Look." If you really messed up and you had failed something they had expected of you, they would give you this look. It wasn't angry, it was more . . . disappointment. From these people, boy, that was worse than getting hit with a brick! "The Look!" You wanted to go crawl under something.

So on Saturdays, I liked to go to the movies that had people in them who Grandpa knew or who I had run into through his old buddies. They were always interesting. *The Plainsman* was one old Gary Cooper movie. Then during the war they came out with several really spectacular Indian Western movies. One was *Buffalo Bill.* Old Louie McClare was in that one. I think one of Grandpa's brothers was in that. It was a matter of doing pullovers with horses and herding the horses, and getting actors on and off of horses alive!

The old guys knew pretty well how they shot movies and how they put things together, what stunt men did to make the heroes look good and all that kind of thing. So I came to appreciate movies more for the technical content, I suppose, than the dramatic acting—of which there wasn't a lot in those old "B" Westerns! The old guys would sit there, mumbling: "This guy has shot about twenty Indians when he has never reloaded that six-shooter!" By cavalry standards he only had five shots in it! One old guy from Montana is laughing, poking my grandpa, saying, "Yeah, well, I don't know Hollywood, but we're a lot harder to kill than that!"

Then my grandpa's other two friends, Henry Axtel, a wealthy timber baron from Port Orford, and a movie actor, Edward Everett Horton, teamed up one summer to go and find Black Bart's treasure, which is supposed to be in the caves at Bandon, Oregon. I got to listen to all that stuff. They're bending over the table. Here is this British accent, that tall guy, Edward Everett Horton. You can ask Mom, this is the absolute truth, they were looking for a Spanky for the *Our Gang* comedy at that time. Boy, he just pleaded with Mom and Dad to take me to Hollywood. He thought I would be the perfect Spanky. I might have been. I suppose I was chubby and kind of cute and precocious. I could mock his British accent perfectly. I've always been good with accents. But Mom very wisely vetoed it.

A. M. LUCIER

If I could get her talking . . . I usually could avoid the piano lesson.

I took piano lessons. Yep . . . I wasn't very good . . . but the lady was remarkable. A. M. Lucier, a spinster. Her family had come from Switzerland. They were old settlers in the Willamette Valley. House always smelled of lavender. Lavender, I can smell it now. That old piano and drinking tea: "One lump or two?" All those nice little nuances from another age, actually. She must have been seventy-five or eighty years old.

Good Lord, I was sitting here with my niece Lee Ann one evening watching TV, my emotions are very close to the surface now with the cancer and this medication, but there was one piece of music that really got to me. It was "Star Trek—Next Generation." Captain Picard is playing the little pipe that he got when he was sent back in time and lived his life all over again. That *tune* he is playing is one she tried to teach me on the piano. I heard that and *bang*, I was back there, the lavender was there, she was there with that soft accent that she had—such a gentle, gracious person. Man, it just floored me for a while because of that tune. Isn't it funny what music can do to you? Lee was sitting there, I think she thought

I was a little screwy, the tears are coming down. I said, "I know, I know that song. I know that song." This is a futuristic show, what, 200, 500 years in the future? And that damn song cracks me up! But it shows you the impact she had.

She also taught my sister Patty, who had a recital. She was *better* than I was at that. I wasn't so much interested in the piano, but I was vitally interested in her remembrances from her parents of when the Indians came from the Coast Range across the Willamette Valley to go up into the Santiams* to dig roots and pick berries. Then they would come back through and they would stop off there for a while. Sometimes they would spend the night. These Indians from the coast usually had something to offer. There is a basket in the museum collection at the A-frame that has this little peak on it. It is a funny little basket hat and I think it may be one of the only Calapooya† women's spike-top skullcaps like that around. I've never seen one in a museum collection.

A. M. Lucier's mother liked it and she saw this as something you could hang on the wall and put flowers in. So this old Indian woman was admiring her roses. She offered her a bouquet of roses for her hat. The old woman took off her hat and gave it to her. She took the roses and went off toward the Santiams where they were going to harvest. Well, she came back, early fall. Old Indian woman came: stomp, stomp, stomp, up the path. She stands there looking injured. I don't know whether she spoke Chinook Jargon or how they communicated, but the old woman pulls out the roses and now they're all wilted, they're sticks. She says, "No good. Hat, still good." Her mother didn't want to give up the basket, so she went around to where the clothesline was and she had this red flannel petticoat that was hanging on the line. She took that down and she offered it to the old woman. "Good." Took the petticoat, put it on over her dress, and away she went. Well, that is the story of that basket. That is why the darn museum collection means so much to me, because of those remembrances of early Salem and of course the tribes in the Willamette Valley. There is so little known about them. They perished and disappeared or went into those melting pots at Grande Ronde and Siletz Reservations.[2]

* An area in the central Oregon Cascades with a river and a pass by that name.
† Also Kalapuya. The peoples of the Willamette Valley and Tualatin Plain stretching from the area west of current-day Portland, Oregon, to the area near Yoncalla, Oregon.

But that was A. M. Lucier, music teacher, elegant lady. I had been dealing with the old Indians for a while by that time and I knew if I could get her talking about old Salem and the early settlers out through the Willamette Valley, I usually could avoid the piano lesson. It was very interesting, her oral histories and her remembrances. I never did ask her why she never married and had children. That was something that I really wanted to ask. She *loved* kids and I always wondered why she was a spinster all her life.

HARRY HOBSON

All these things just melt together into your self.

There used to be a totem pole on the old highway where Chemawa Indian School is. It finally rotted and they moved what was left of it down onto the campus. Well, across from there, just as you start up the hill out of the Mobish Bottom, Harry Hobson had a fine big old house and workshop. He was really, really famous and well connected around Salem. He knew everybody. He was a bowier and he held a world's title for flight with a longbow. He made bows not out of fiberglass, but out of wood—yew, lemonwood, all kinds of things. He also made fishing rods and arrows, fine arrows. Taught fly tying in the area. He was quite a historian and a great friend of the Indians. I guess my family got acquainted because my grandmother ran a poultry plant for a packing company. Uncle Bob got to saving the marabou, the fluffy feathers, and the pointers, the wing feathers, from the turkeys, for Harry. He would collect them and wash them up. Then he would sell them to Harry Hobson. Bob was just a kid then.

Harry Hobson's basement, when I was a little kid, was the *most wonderful place in the world.* It was full of Port Orford cedar. You know how that smells? You ever smell an arrow shaft? Well, imagine thousands of arrow shafts seasoning in the sawdust from making them. The basement was full of it. It would just make your eyes water. That is another one of those things that could just about bring the tears out of me: every time I work Port Orford cedar, I'm back down there in the basement again with all the glue and the bows are in the process and everything.

Harry was such a neat old guy; he was always talking about the wood, how to approach the wood and grain, and backing bows, and how the Indians made bows. He knew everything. Indian kids could come from Chemawa over there. He hired a lot of them. Got a lot of them started on their way through life and kept encouraging them. "Finish school. Learn all you can." Got scholarships for some. He was just a great guy.

I spent a lot of time in Harry Hobson's basement. He was a great raconteur, a real, old-time storyteller. He could make things just come *alive*. He would tell all these stories about the pioneers, the Indians, and the people he had known and shooting bow and arrow. He just lived for archery. He and my grandpa used to discuss the difference between Indian bows and longbows, the relative values of these in various sorts of situations, which made great listening for me. That was one of my favorite places. I learned a lot without ever being taught, old Harry just never stopped talking. Kind of like me now, I guess; with my little pills in me, I rattle on.

That place was special. Harry was special. His sister was named Manzanita, and she was great, too. She came to the Oregon Centennial [in 1959]. It was a 100-day celebration and I think she made every one of the 100 days. Because we knew Harry, she got close to us. She was quite a gal, Manzanita.

When the war came, there was a great big Lakota kid, great-looking kid. I mean, he was the classic Plains Indian. He had the nose and he had that dark copper skin, beautiful hair. He was going into the service. He came to see Harry, and I was sitting there in my favorite little chair that he had for me at the bench. I think I was turning the silk on some Calcutta fly rods to help him and while away the time, and then I'm getting all this history out of him while I'm doing that.

So the Lakota kid comes and says, "Well, I'm going."

Harry says, "Oh, you enlisted."

He says, "Yeah, I'm going."

Harry says, "Well, right now the way things are going, they'll send you to the Pacific, I think."

He says, "I hope so."

And Harry says, "Bring me a Jap scalp."

He gave him a big hug, and the kid started up the basement stairs and I remember he turned around and looked at Harry. He had this wonderful deadpan look on his face and he says, "I'll bring you a Jap scalp." Turned around, gone!

Two years later, the kid comes back! He was decorated all over, Guadal-canal, I forget what all. He had all kinds of medals. He was in the papers. Came back a hero. Boy, he sure looked like one to me. He has this little brown paper bag all crumpled up. Harry looks at him; he's got this look on his face. Again, he could get so deadpan. He had a gorgeous, great big grin, full of teeth. He hands it to Harry.

Harry looks at him and he says, "Washte." In Lakota, that means "thank you."

He looks at Harry, he says, "Washte-hilo" ["very good"].

Harry reaches in the bag. "Oh, my God," I said to myself, "it is a Jap officer's scalp!" It had hair about two feet long doused in jasmine perfume. Apparently a lot of the officers did that. Scents seem to do something to my memory. If I smell jasmine, I can see that glossy scalp coming out of that paper bag and the look on Harry's face! He looks at it and he turns it over and I'm thinking, "That, that is a human scalp and it is a Jap scalp. They're enemies. Okay." I knew from Wolf that this was *really* honorable stuff.

Harry says, "I'll keep this always" and he made the sign for "good" for the kid. They go off and they talk a lot. Lying on the workbench there is this scalp with that jasmine perfume, even though you were getting this dead skin smell from it. I don't know what became of it. Harry had that for years and years. Last time I was ever in the workshop as a young man, it was still hanging there. I often wondered what became of it. But you don't want to tell those Lakota to do you a favor because you may get it! Yeah, it was all nicely dressed inside. Kid knew what he was doing. He had been raised right!

Another thing that Harry had that fascinated me, and I could just spend hours holding them and looking at them, were these treasures from Ishi the Yahi Indian.[3] Harry knew him very well. Harry had known Ishi right up to the time that he died of tuberculosis. Ishi made Harry a set of these beautiful Yahi arrow points. I mean, he did them from the ground up. I can remember I would take those very, very carefully out of the big leather quiver that he had. It was a white-man quiver, but it was a good place to store it. I would take those out and lay them all out. I don't think with a magnifying glass you could've told one arrow from the other. They were so perfect. Each one a perfect clone of the other and very meticulous, tiny, smooth; the finish was just incredible. The points were just flaked so fine. They looked almost like satin. I used to spend hours just admiring those and thinking, "Now here is a man they found in a slaughterhouse." He came from being a stone-age Indian, not even "traderized," to working in a museum, and then the white man's diseases finally killed him. I would sit there and I would conjure up all these pictures. One by one, his family is being killed and finally the rest of them were all wiped out by the miners, the whole story, because Harry would just tell the story over and over and over again. Going hunting with Saxton Pope* and Ishi. I remember those arrows. Boy, they impressed me. I've never seen arrows that fine in any museum collection *anywhere.* I mean, they make Plains Indian arrows look crude by comparison. All these things just melt together into your self.

I really suppose I should've turned into a real spoiled brat. I mean, old Harry was always making me a new bow and a new set of arrows. "You got plenty of arrows?" "Oh, yeah, yeah." He wanted me to shoot. I tried a longbow. I didn't like that long English draw with one of them. He says, "Well, let's try your grandpa's method, the little snapshot short bow." Strong, and it has a quick draw and release, very quick. I got good at that. He would throw up bags stuffed with paper. "Yeah, that is pretty good, pretty good. You're not pulling even, that is why you missed that one." Hours! My little blistered fingers!

Then, if you're real good and you swept up the basement or something for old Harry, he would take his old Olympic bow out. He would string her up and take a couple arrows outside. That big totem pole stood right at the crossroads there at the road to Chemawa Indian School. He would rear back with that and he would plink one of those shafts into the top of that totem pole. That thing had arrow shafts sticking all over it sometimes if he had just had a lot of company. He just loved to step out there and just draw back—"swish, thwock." Most beautiful draw on a bow, I mean, it was just flawless. It just flowed and the arrow went and it was so effortless. I would watch that thing disappear, that little flash. Then you would hear that

---

* Saxton Pope was a physician at the University of California hospital when Ishi was at the museum.

"thwock" and you knew he had nailed that totem pole again! I'm surprised the cops didn't come and get him.

JACK WILSON

. . . the first privileges . . . that I ever received.

Jack Wilson taught carpentry down there at Chemawa Indian School. He was a Klaskino.* He was the *last* of his people. They had all died off and he had moved down to the States from up there in British Columbia. He got a job, too. He had been a boat builder. He was tall. Taller than a lot of the people from the west coast of British Columbia. He was probably the last of the noble line of the Klaskino people. There are a lot of scholars, really, who don't know about the Klaskino.[4] Culturally, they stood kind of between the Nootka and the Kwakiutl. They hunted whales and . . . they were wonderful.

That Deer story we tell, about the Wolves and the Deer, is from Jack Wilson and the dance is from him, the song is from him, so is the Bear. Those are the first privileges,† really, that I ever received. "There wasn't anybody else left," he said. "I know you'll do something with them. I hate to think that all my people will be forgotten eventually." He was thoroughly grounded in their mythology and traditions and things like that. He was a good storyteller.

He was also a friend of old Harry Hobson's. I used to go over to see Jack quite a bit because Harry Hobson's place was just a little stroll from Chemawa. Harry's basement was always full of some bunch of people who were interesting like Jack or the kids from over at the school. There were Tsimshians and some Tlingits at Chemawa. They had a bent toward carpentry anyway, so they were very, very good at the school there. At Chemawa, they turned out bakers, carpenters, housemaids, laundresses, and things like that. They did it all with macaroni. God, the kids hated that. Macaroni and cheese about five times a week.

---

* The Klaskino were a band located on the northwest end of Vancouver Island generally associated with the Kwakiutl of British Columbia; by the 1890s they were assumed to have merged with others to form the present-day Nuwitti and Quatsino.

† This refers to specially sanctioned rights to ceremonies, rituals, and histories passed on to individuals as cultural property.

FLORA AND TOMMY THOMPSON

They really taught me to understand.

I don't know when it started. It might've even started with Grandpa or Uncle Bob, or Harry Hobson, maybe Dad, who was around The Dalles–Celilo area. I don't know. I knew Flora and Tommy Thompson so long that it is hard to remember just when it first happened. Some people are in your life so early that you just kind of accept them like family. They really taught me to understand a lot about the Washini Faith and the religion that preceded it, before Smohallah and his Dreamer Religion began to take form.[5] Tommy was 104 when he died back in 1959. His fish-drying house was on Long Pole Island. That was his privileged fishing place. His tribe was the Wanapum, which means "People of the River." Their language is mostly Shahaptian. Apparently his uncle, Stoketkli, met with Lewis and Clark and smoked with them when they came through. He was later killed by some of the Indians on the Deschutes River. They cut off his arms and legs while he was still alive.

Tommy was a very spiritual person. For him, like most old-time Indians, the world was a living place. It wasn't dead rocks or just trees or dirt. For him, everything was alive and had power in varying degrees, depending on where it sat in the scale of creation. Your health and everything depended on your ability to keep these things all in balance and not to offend or commit any crimes against your fellow members of the natural community.

He was also very funny. Had a real sense of humor. Wonderful Chinook Jargon talker. He used to jokingly say, "Long time, long time, four wives. Law no good now, just got one." Of course that would set Flora off. I don't know whether it was the white man's law or whether it was Flora who dispensed with the other wives. Otherwise, a lot of the older guys had multiple wives. They usually had different domiciles for them, but it was still going on until pretty recent times.

Flora was remarkable. When Tommy died, she sort of took over as chief, which I think made some enemies. But she did a lot of good and she had made a lot of friends in the Oregon State Legislature and other places. She would interpret for Tommy because Tommy didn't feel sometimes his English was adequate to the job. I remember she had her handwritten copy of the Treaty of 1855.[6] She always carried it in this beaded bag. God, I don't know what happened to that. I hope it landed at Warm Springs or someplace.

Flora Thompson and Chief Tommy Thompson of Celilo Falls, with Don as a teenager in front of the store at Hubbard, Oregon. Don probably made the wagon that Tommy is holding. Relationships like those that Don forged with the Thompsons were central to his evolving Indian identity and to his growing skills as an ethnographer. Don also established lifelong friendships with many visitors to the family store. Photo courtesy of the Lelooska family.

She would come down to the Oregon Historical Society annual meeting. Nothing daunted her. They were always trying to get that copy of the treaty away from her. "Well, maybe someday," she would say!

She had the most beautiful walk, that wonderful straight back. Only those old women who have grown up wearing moccasins, I think, have that kind of carriage, what Mom calls a sashay. I'll tell you, if I had ever found a girl who had Flora's walk, I think I would have been a dead duck! I can see her yet, walking. Oh, Grandma Flora, she was sort of our self-appointed grandma. That was what she wanted to be called, Grandma Flora.

PUBLIC SCHOOL

I just never seemed to get back to going to school.

Many scholarly works have dealt with the trials and tribulations caused by the placement of Indian children in federal boarding schools between the 1880s and the 1930s. A second body of literature takes up the dramatic and forceful changes in education demanded by Native Americans in the 1960s and 1970s.[7] While such foci are justifiable, they have underemphasized the dramatic impact of the forced integration of Indian children in public schools between the 1930s and the 1960s. Don's educational history was not typical. He was bright, and he learned the value of different "canons" from his grandmother and grandfather. Some of his teachers believed him intelligent enough to succeed in the "white" world. He even had a strong Indian role model in a student teacher in his classroom. Yet Don's decision to drop out of school by the ninth grade was a common one, for few Indians made it much beyond the elementary grades in public schools. His stories indicate the bright as well as troubled spots in mid-twentieth-century public education for Indian children, and suggest that more needs to be known about this time frame to better understand its impact on Indians. His experiences also shed light on current issues of understanding cultural differences within the educational system.

The teachers always took quite an interest in me; I suppose it was because of those darn IQ tests, which must have been a mistake! Anyway, they always wanted me to look into becoming a doctor or a lawyer or something like that. The first test was when I was in the second grade. Then they took another one when I was in the third grade, I remember. Right on through school you were tested about every other year. The superintendent of schools there near Salem got to be kind of a friend of the family. I think how we got acquainted with her was that she just came out to visit us. She just kind of wanted, I think, to see where the hell I came from! That pretty well startled the rats out of her because we've always been pretty unconventional.

But it made a big difference. It opened a lot of doors, I suppose. But frankly, if I could change anything, I don't think I would.

In all the years that I went to school, I did have one doozy of a teacher, in my last year in school. Her name—are you ready for this?—was Miss White. Miss White hated naked barbaric savages, which was one of her favorite ways of referring to Indians. She and I didn't really see eye to eye. I got along great with all of my other teachers, but she taught social studies and she was unabashedly a *bigot.*

They had started this student teacher thing where they would send out the new teachers, who would serve an apprenticeship for a semester, then they would get them into the system. They needed teachers really badly. Well, lo and behold, the student teacher Miss White drew, her assistant, was a six-foot-four, cast-in-bronze Sioux football player, Ambrose d'Eagle, huge guy. He played professional football and had been in the service and, boy, he was about as Sioux as anything ever got. I mean, he had the great big handsome nose. He was most certainly proud of what he was. So she really shriveled up at that point and there were no more of those remarks about naked savages and my barbaric tendencies and things like that! You just sometimes look up and say, "Thank you, Lord!"

Well, I think it was Cal Ashenburner who was principal, and he and I were really good friends. He knew school was easy for me, probably too easy. So he found a lot of little things to keep me busy: planning things for students, coming together to discuss what the temper of our particular classes were, what I thought of the teachers, and things like that, which is pretty amazing. I think he must have had something to do with the student teacher in my classroom because he must've known that Miss White hated Indians most thoroughly and, I think, anybody else who was from a different culture, which was a bad thing for a person who was a social studies teacher. He made it possible for me to spend my lunch hours with Ambrose. Ambrose was teaching me Lakota and I knew sign language. He knew a lot of sign from his grandfather, so we had a lot of fun. We had our little internal jokes on Miss White! Little sign-language gestures and things! She was, I think, the first person I ever ran into who was really openly, overtly bigoted.

There were a lot of things that interested me more than going to school, living there on the main highway to and from the capitol at Salem. It was the road the Indians usually took to get through to Portland, or to go down

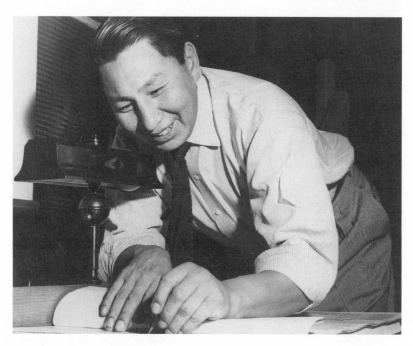

Ambrose d'Eagle, a Sioux who was a student teacher in Don's elementary classroom, served as an important role model for Don and made it possible for him to withstand the intense bigotry exhibited by at least one of his teachers. Here Ambrose d'Eagle carries out his duties as a voting clerk, November 5, 1952. Photo courtesy of the Oregon Historical Society. Photo CN 002389 no. 24P389.

to Chemawa Indian School to see their kids, or to go to Salem to fight with the government. That got me pretty well associated with the Warm Springs and the Yakama people.

I was still intent on learning the answers to all the questions that I was left with from growing up around my grandfather. Got some answers; but you know, you get one answer and you get two more questions. That is what makes it so much fun. You just get into a whole can of worms. You usually end up with more questions than answers, and it was what I really wanted to do. The other kids in our family—Dick, Patty, and Smitty—were all interested and they went to a lot of the dances and feasts. There weren't many powwows then. Plains Indian dancing[8] and all hadn't really taken form, and the big things were the religious feast and the Washini religion, the

Longhouse Indians, some people called them. That was the doctrine of Smohallah. I knew a lot of the old Washini priests, a lot about their religion, which
is really quite beautiful.

By that time, the craft work was a bigger part of our income and Dad
got the job at McClaren School for Boys. I carved a lot of little horses, a lot
of Indian dolls. Boy, they sold really well. Tourists, collectors, and people
like that bought them. Mom already had lots of contacts that bought her
work. She wholesaled a lot of the stuff, miniature saddles. She made literally tens of thousands of those. Gram used to help her. I used to help her
a little. But she turned out thousands of them. Of course, when the war was
on, it wasn't quite tourism, but there was a lot of money around and a lot
of people were going places to get away from the war—fairs and things like
that were very good. The coast was very good at that time in spite of the
fact that gas was rationed. People still seemed to find a way to get over
there. So business was really pretty good.

Mom sold thousands of little saddles to Soaper's Leather Goods and Saddle Shop in Walla Walla, Washington. I remember as a kid going out to get
the mail in the mailbox, and, boy, that was a red-letter day when there was
a letter there from Soaper's because it was usually a check and so Mom
would go to town! I would catch a movie or wander around, pick up some
paint, brushes, and things I needed for my work. I might go down and see
if the old soldier [who knew Grandpa] was hanging out at the photography studio there.

Mom never had much formal training. Her one trip into higher education, I guess you would call it, was going to a business school for a while
when she was a girl in California. Grandpa had a business there, in between
wars and shots at trying to cattle ranch in Wyoming. But, yeah, Mom was
a marvelous teacher. She let me know how I was doing, Indian style, "The
Look!" I tell you, I've never gotten beyond its reach. I learned, though, by
watching Mom and just doing it, but, man, I got scars, scars, scars. She
didn't want any weeping about that stuff either. It was all right to holler a
couple times when you were getting patched up, but that was part of the
job. And of course she always had her medical kit for patching up. If it was
real bad, why, she would run you to town and get you sewed up. A couple stitches took care of the big stuff. But she and Gram, I tell you, were a
great pair.

Don in full Plateau/Plains regalia, in front of the family museum and store at about the age when he dropped out of school and turned to Indian arts and crafts for a living. Photo courtesy of the Lelooska family.

When I was in the ninth grade, I went to Prairie Junior High School outside Salem. I went from a country school to there. I had a great year, I had good grades, elected student body president, all that kind of stuff, and then Dad's business went kerflooey. Mom had bought the property, the house, and everything, through craft work, and let Dad mortgage it to open and run the service station. So that went and we ended up out at Hubbard and decided to open a little shop, a kind of tourist thing. I had been selling my work from the time I was twelve, thirteen years old. So between Mom and I, we figured one way or another we could scratch out a living and buy another little piece of property. I thought about going to high school, but at that time you had to go for about an hour and a half to get to school in Salem because they hadn't finished North Marion High School. I just never seemed to get back to going to school.

THE PENDLETON ROUND-UP

. . . where it isn't all storybook Indians. . . . Oh, it was a great place to learn.

There are many ways to learn and many places to do it. Don was a life-long learner, as clichéd as the term may sound. His willingness to listen, ability to remember, and skill at communicating the different "stories" before him were among his most powerful tools. These allowed him to see the world from many different positions between the poles of "Indian" and "white."

Don's experiences at the Pendleton Round-Up amply illustrate this. Following in the tradition of the Wild West shows, Native Americans looked to the growing numbers of rodeos, fairs, and powwows in the early twentieth century for opportunities to share traditions and present-day experiences. Powwows and Indian-run rodeos have long histories and stand as significant sites of opposition to forced assimilation for Native Americans. Yet even non-Indian rodeos and fairs, in which Indian participants knew that the crowds saw them only as "color," served similar purposes. At the Pendleton Round-Up that Don frequently attended, for example, the organizers of the rodeo used Indians in the pageant to signify the passing of the frontier and at special events to give the rodeo an "authentic" Western atmosphere.[9] The knowledge that they were being used in this fashion did not automatically prevent Indians from finding their own reasons for attending. Don's networks of friends from eastern Oregon tribes introduced him to those reasons. Like his grandfather before him and his own actions later in life, at the Pendleton Round-Up Don saw in such performances the potential for more than just caricatures of what whites thought Indians to be.

I think I really decided I wanted to be an artist pretty early on. The idea of ranching didn't really appeal to me much. I wasn't a devout horseman like my brother Smitty would've been if he had had the opportunity. Mom and

Grandpa would sit and whittle. Grandpa loved to whittle. A lot of people of his era were whittlers. A lot of the whittling really didn't come to anything, it was just kind of a relaxing exercise, I suppose. With him, a lot of it was kind of traditional teaching. He would make a little raccoon or something and while he was doing them, he was telling you all about the raccoon, mythology, some of the funny little stories about raccoon and bears and all these things. So it becomes, if not a Sunday school class in a traditional belief, at least something pretty close to it.

A lot of our income came from Mom's work when I was small—her painting, her carving, her drawing, her saddles and things like that. I thought that might be a very nice way for me to make a living, too. Then, too, that wouldn't interfere with going different places or learning things that I wanted to learn so much because I always had more questions than answers. You have what you love to do. You love doing it so much you would pay to do it if you weren't making a living at it. It is a major blessing. Anyone who can make a good living doing what you so love to do, I don't think there is a nicer thing the gentle Creator could do for you than that.

Well, we had sort of a roadside museum, I guess you would call it, at the place at Hubbard. The collection of things I had traded for or that had been given to me had grown to the point that it was really too big for the house. We didn't have enough room for it. So we had it as sort of a tourist attraction. It didn't amount to much, but it paid the bills. People would come in and I would give them a little guided presentation. Then the schools got to bringing the children and I would talk to them. It just sort of drifted from talking to the schools, to going to the schools, and finally into a full-fledged program—the dances and stories and things. Mostly Plains, Plateau kinds of things at that time. We were close to the Nez Perce, the Cayuse, the Umatilla, and, of course, we've always been close to the Sioux, the Cheyenne, and the Blackfeet. All were my grandfather's old associates. So we got to doing that.

We used to rent a booth down at the Oregon State Fair and sell our work. You would meet an awful lot of people, but most of the Indians came to the little shop. They would bring two or three dead eagles—at that time eagles were varmints—and I would make war bonnets and dance bustles and things. It paid very well. I did a lot of that kind of thing and I had sources for a lot of the things. There weren't the craft supply places around that

Don and Mary in Plains/ Plateau ceremonial dress, in the mid or late 1950s, probably at the Oregon State Fair, where they regularly displayed and sold Indian and Western Americana curios. Photo courtesy of the Lelooska family.

At home in Hubbard, Oregon, the family hosted many visitors, some of whom stayed for days at a time. That tradition of hospitality continued when the family later moved to Kalama and then to Ariel, both in Washington. Here Don, in his mid-twenties, stands, left, with (standing, from right) Dick, Smitty, and Patty Fawn; seated are (second from left) Flora Thompson and (at far right) Mary. Photo courtesy of the Lelooska family.

there are now. But I dealt a lot with Pawnee Bill's Indian Trading Post in Pawnee, Oklahoma—they handled a lot of that stuff for the Oklahoma Indians—I dealt with them and I could trade with them. I could get just about anything I needed. I also did a lot of trading. A lot of my collection began to come together at that time.

Indians would come to the place. Sometimes they would stay overnight, sometimes they were there for two or three days. It was just kind of nice. It was just traditional hospitality that the family offered. It was expected. When we went over to eastern Oregon, why, they always put themselves out. It was just good manners. And Gram, of course, was very, very patient. Boy, there were some *really* Indian old Indians who used to come from Warm Springs—the braids and the moccasins.

One in particular, in the old days a renowned horse thief and horseman, was called Stick Joe—I don't know as he had another name. He was Warm Springs but he had this great big black mustache in addition to his braids, and that forelock hairdo that they wore. He was really a wild-looking character. And Stick was lousy. Most of the time, I mean, you could see them going up his braids sometimes. It was not wasted on Grandma! Every time he had been there very long, man, she just practically fumigated the place, just following him around with the disinfectant in the box! It was kind of funny. He knew an awful lot about horses and turned out he knew a lot about traditional remedies for horse ailments, all that kind of thing.

All of us kids had a pony. As we got bigger, why, the horses got bigger. They were easy to get, too, because I could always trade my work with the pony farm nearby, places like that. So my work became a kind of currency for those expensive little goodies! Sometimes there wasn't money, but there was work. That made a real difference.

Well, after Patty, Dick, and Smitty had learned to dance the Plains, Plateau stuff, we got to going up to the Pendleton Round-Up.* The Pendleton Round-Up Association hired us to go up and help them with the publicity and the public relations. One reason was I was always sober. The other was that I was on pretty good terms with a lot of the old people, because I made a

---

* The Pendleton Round-Up began in 1910 and quickly became a major regional rodeo drawing several thousand Native Americans to its encampment each year. With the exception of two years in World War II, the Round-Up has taken place annually up to the present.

"Our teepee was kind of the refuge for nondrinkers." Dick, Kenny Lambert, Don, and Mary in 1954 at the Pendleton Round-Up. Photo courtesy of the Lee D. Drake Photography Collection, Special Collections, University of Oregon Library.

Indian Chief Clarence Burke, Pendleton Round-Up, September 15, 1960. Don established a friendship with Burke, whose many public appearances as Round-Up Chief made him among the most photographed Indians in the country. At the otherwise raucous Round-Up, Don learned much from quiet conversations with Burke, about everything from quillwork and beadwork to nighttime storytelling in the Indian encampment. Photo courtesy of the Oregon Historical Society. Photo OrHi 102795 no. 855-U.

lot of costume stuff for their grandkids. They would come by the place, we were on the highway there that went to Chemawa Indian School, and at that time there were still a lot of Northwest Indian kids enrolled there. So I met a lot of them.

Old Clarence Burke,[10] the Round-Up Chief, would set up two big teepees for us in the village and we would stay. Here was a village of about 1,800 Indians, tribes from all over the Northwest, lot of fun. On Saturday night, our teepee was kind of the refuge for the nondrinkers. Pendleton goes up on Saturday night in the biggest drunken, Western-type mess you can imagine. So here we are, the little band of sober people, or the people too old anymore to get in on that stuff, all in the teepees telling stories and listening to the shrieks and screams, and the shooting going on downtown—blanks, of course.

You hear lots and lots of folktales then. The encampment used to be a great place because the old people weren't out whooping it up with the young ones. They would usually all get together in somebody's big lodge and swap stories and sing. Oh, it was a great place to learn. It was a real-live seminar because there were the Cayuse, Umatilla, Walla Walla, the Nez Perce, Flathead, Assiniboin, Blackfeet, Crow—lot of people came. They would all get together and they would drink coffee, eat jerky, and play Indian all evening until the wee small hours of the morning.

They would tell lots of stories. I kind of like the Nez Perce story that is a version of the tortoise and the hare. White Buffalo, this big, powerful creature, was a character in some of the folktales. He was a very fast runner and he had outraced all of the animals. Little Turtle comes out of the water and challenges him to race. The bet would be themselves. White Buffalo was insulted, but Little Turtle keeps after him until finally he agrees to the race.

It was agreed that Little Turtle would pop up out of the water a quarter of the way through the race and then halfway, and then again three-fourths and then finally at the stop—just pop up to prove that he was still there and in the race. So he did. He popped up and he would say, "Here I am, just going along." White Buffalo would just run like crazy to get to the next place before Little Turtle. He'd get there, sides heaving, and Little Turtle would pop his head up out of the water and say, "Well, here I am, I'm just going along." On and on they went. Finally, when Buffalo raced down and eventually got to the finish line, why, Little Turtle was sticking up his head at the finish line. He has beat him, saying, "Well, here I am, just going along." So Little Turtle won.

Turtle made a feast for everybody out of White Buffalo and *all* of these turtles come out of the water to the feast. They all look just alike! The moral of it is, if you're going to bet with somebody, you had better look for the unseen parts of the contract![11]

But that is what helped Smitty to make the connection. See, Smitty is the youngest, so he never really was able to get close to a time where he really remembers Grandpa. But he does remember living in a teepee for a couple of weeks every year in a camp where it isn't all storybook Indians. I mean, they're drinking, fighting, getting arrested, going on all night. Thunderstorms come; being in a teepee in a thunderstorm is *spectacular* because when the big flashes come, all the poles go up in black silhouette and the canvas cover of the big teepee is just like a Chinese lantern turned inside out. At Pendleton, usually there was one good thunderstorm when we were there.

Smitty remembers the prize dances and the old people. Dick was a great dancer. He was a champion. The old people say that is when your ancestors can talk to you. Well, they don't mean that literally. What they mean is, there are those moments when you are in touch with some very fundamental, spiritual aspects of your culture.

There were no powwows years and years ago. There were the big ceremonial feasts to honor the various natural crops, the salmon, the roots, the berries, and things. Of course, people did those guardian spirit dances, which have never really been encouraged in public—the Smokehouse, they call it. The powwow stuff is great socially. Helps people keep their identity while living in the city, where the young people are away from their grandparents and elders. But there is so much that is going to get lost if we're not real careful. Then we've got all the people who are giving courses in shamanism and all the phony medicine men, medicine women. It is appalling. I would be frightened to death.

There is a lot of that going on now. I'm frankly amazed. A lot of Indians are *very, very* offended by these New Age shamans, shaman schools, and shaman's diplomas you can get for $500. They have sweat lodges and pipe ceremonies and they have a Sun Dance. There are a few disconnected urban Indian types who take part and then there are the wannabes, the New Age types.[12] Some of it is pretty sorry. There are a few Indians who take it as a compliment to their culture and they also think it is pretty funny that they don't know how to do it correctly. But there are others who are just down-right offended. No, it is sad. It is so confusing to youngsters growing up.

The Pendleton Round-Up is in late September, so Dick, Patty, and Smitty had to get themselves out of school so they could go. We started going when I was still a teenager. The Round-Up was a great entrée beyond the fact that I made good war bonnets, dance bustles, and stuff and was knowl-edgeable. The kids all danced and I went to prize dances and things like that.

I had beaded some outfits. Beaded a pony bead dress for Mom. I felt very self-conscious about doing beadwork. There used to be this very, very *strict* division between what was man's work and what was woman's work. The old art of quillwork is sacred. It is like a guild. The old ladies and the girls go to the sweat lodge and perhaps have a dream. There has to be a spiritual connection. Wouldn't be enough just to be a very, very talented quillworker, you have to have a spiritual connection or it has no value as far as the old traditional Cheyenne are concerned. I enjoyed doing it and it was one way I could get something done just the way I wanted it, but beading was women's work and it bothered me a lot. Then I discovered, lo and behold, one day I popped in on Clarence Burke in his teepee there at the Round-Up. He was sitting there just beading up a storm. I was sur-prised and said, "Jimminy Christmas, Clarence, I didn't know you did that!" "Oh, I don't, *I* don't talk about it," he says! Yeah, it kind of liberated me a little bit.

I started out with that old book, *The Quill and Beadwork of the Western Sioux,*[13] which isn't bad. There weren't a lot of people doing quillwork; but then, showing up at the Round-Up one year, were these people from Poplar, Montana. They were Assiniboin, and Genie Clark was the wife of a guy I knew. The Clarks go way, way back to the fur trader times. She did beau-tiful quillwork. So I sort of hung around and I brought along a carton of Coca-Cola. I watched her quill. She talked and talked and talked! My head is going round and round, like a little recorder: why she was doing it, how they did it in the old times, and how it had changed now. Sometimes they made or traded for quill flatteners. She used her teeth. She would keep the quills moist; you have to keep them moist. She would just pick one out and pull it between her teeth, *dzuit*. She would lay them down on the material then she would stitch them down. They always think it is very funny when a guy wants to know about these traditionally feminine things. She would just get this little grin, and have these little *zingers!*

The women are really the culture bearers. A lot of the men got into raising horses and cattle and sheep. A lot of their traditional crafts of hunting and war and everything disappeared, long, long ago. But the woman's work went on and on and on. They're actually the ones who, in a lot of cases, have kept the spiritual connections alive. Most of the Northern Plains people, why, the ceremonies require the participation of women. The man's role you would think is a superior one, but it is *nothing* without the other. It is just like life comes from the two. The one is impotent within itself, so it requires the two. They have terrific responsibilities. In the Sun Dance and certain aspects of medicine bundles and things, women have an important role. But there was always that little division that in the old days nobody crossed because that put things out of sync and they didn't work and were bad luck.

My dad really made it possible for me to do so much at the Round-Up. I suddenly became a good old boy because they remembered him. They laughed about some of the stuff he used to pull. Long John Parr and my dad liked to go to Athena [Oregon, on the road to Walla Walla] when they were younger. They would get drunk on lemon extract. Well, sometimes you couldn't get the good stuff and there was more alcohol in the lemon extract than in a lot of that bootleg hooch. So they would go and get drunk and ride over there. The old sheriff who could barely get around had an old Model T. Well, they would run up and down the board sidewalks, break them in with their horses, yell and scream and holler like wild Indians, I suppose. He would get in his car and chase them. They would head out of town with him right behind them, screaming, yelling. Just when he was getting pretty close, they would cut off through the sagebrush. Well, if they had really made him mad, he would turn off the road into the sagebrush and, first thing, he would turn the darn thing over or high center on sagebrush or something. When they were long gone, they would sit down, let the horses breathe, and they would just laugh and laugh! Probably fall asleep out there lying in the sand and the sagebrush. Well, Long John Parr was from the line of Chief Joseph, so that started my dad's friendship for him—all of his relatives were part of that Walamushkin band. It opened a lot of doors.

The Round-Up Association wanted some presents for the governor or something like that. Well, I made a lot of Indian dolls in my time. I'm not proud of it, but I did. I made *hundreds* of them. In fact, Pawnee Bill's bought them by the hundreds. They weren't great, but they traded good. I got a lot of nice stuff trading! Well, anyway, I made some and I made one of Chief Joseph. Sometimes you overreach yourself. I mean, you go beyond your skill and you do something that is great, and for a long time you're never able to catch up to that one little moment. That doll was really good. When we went over for the presentation, I was about thirteen years old. People kept saying, "Here is this child-artist who did the doll" and all that baloney. Well, the Nez Perce elders were pretty impressed with the Chief Joseph doll. So we got to talking. I knew sign, from Grandpa, knew Chinook Jargon—that helped. Here I am, a "breed" kid who has absorbed, they figured, a lot of the culture and had good Indian values and nice Indian manners. They all put their heads together and decided that I should be given a name: Lelooskin.

It was years before I realized where the name came from. It was a fine name. I was real pleased at the time. I already had Sioux names, I had Arapaho names, I had a Pawnee name. So this was no big deal, I didn't think. Well, Lelooskin means "whittling," or "shavings off a stick of wood with a knife." It isn't Nez Perce. The word is Flathead. The young fellow who had it was one of a group of young warriors that they called the Red Capotes. They all wore these red blanket coats. Well, they had all been killed. Lelooskin was killed in the Nez Perce War,* and the name had not been taken up in all that time. So "Cutting Off with a Knife" was a good name and it was in the family of two of the old guys. They gave it to me and it got changed into Lelooska, but originally it was Lelooskin. It was a Flathead name that belonged to the Nez Perce, because the Nez Perce and the Flatheads banded

---

* The famous attempted flight to Canada in 1887 of Nez Perce under the leadership of Chief Joseph is misnamed the Nez Perce War. Disagreements over treaty status and land seizures by non-Indians, combined with the retaliatory murders of four white settlers by three young Nez Perce men, prompted a military crackdown on the Nez Perce involved and the attempted escape of some 600 men, women, and children.

together to fend off the terrible Blackfeet when they went into the buffalo country. There're a lot of Flathead connections among the Plateau tribes. That is where it came from.

It does carry a responsibility, when they give you a name of some honored person. A name couldn't be taken up for a long time because you don't take a dead person's name for a couple of generations so you won't bring them back by having the name spoken. I didn't realize the name had that much significance until I got older and I got acquainted with a lot of the old guys on the Plateau. We would talk about the Nez Perce War, which is another one of the things I *really* was interested in. So I got to know some of Joseph's relatives.

The best teacher was Tom Moxmox—Tom Johnson was his whiteman name—and he was husband to Annie Moxmox,* who made the parfleches and the elegant beadwork and all of that. Well, he was Joseph's nephew and he knew everything. His mother was still alive. Now, she was Joseph's sister. They would bring her in the car and here is this little dried-up, bird-like creature in this gorgeous Pendleton blanket. He adored her. Everybody went out there and she would be in the car. She couldn't get around, but everybody would go out there. She would hold court and everybody had to go and see her, and to touch her—kind of a blessing because of what she had survived. Tom used to ride over to her little cabin and see her, I learned from my half-brother Cecil. He would ride over there on his old gray horse to see her about three times a week and make sure she was all right.

He rode like an Indian. You can tell a rider who is an Indian a *long* way off because there is kind of a rhythm between the quirt, which just goes *pat, pat, pat, pat,* and the heels' kick. There is this funny kicking, a little prodding along with the quirt. Just keeps them in rhythm with the movement of the horse. You can tell as far as you can see them. Well, they don't ride that way anymore. Old Tom, that was how he rode and that was how all the old guys rode who could still get on a horse. You could tell them miles off. If you took their quirt away, they couldn't ride! They wouldn't have any rhythm. Tom was great.

He had lots of things. He had the quirt, which is in our museum collection

* Annie Johnson and Thomas Johnson were members of the Cayuse tribe and lived on the Umatilla Reservation. Both were strong keepers of tradition.

Even before Don, as a teenager, earned the name
Lelooskin (later Lelooska) for
carving the Chief Joseph doll,
the young left-handed carver
could be found whittling
instead of playing in his sand-
box. Photo courtesy of the
Lelooska family.

*The broad network of associations that the Lelooska family developed in the 1940s and
1950s included people like Annie Johnson (Cayuse), pictured here in 1961 at the age of
seventy-eight with her great-grandchildren Pauline Sam (left) and Anna Marie Chapman
(right). She also served as one of many ethnographic informants for Don in his quest to
learn more about Indian arts and crafts. Photo courtesy of the Oregon Historical Society.
Photo OrHi 102794 no. 855-U.*

up there at the A-frame. He had Joseph's bonnet. It was weasel skin, with the beaded horns and a spine of eagle feathers down the back, a trailer. He would open up the old metal suitcases, get it all out and talk about it. He would get into how it was made, where it was used, and who it belonged to. Great stuff, but you could tell when it was getting to him because there would be these long, long silences, kind of a reverie. You wouldn't say anything. You wouldn't move. You wouldn't do anything because you felt like you would be intruding in something that you just didn't quite understand, but there was something going on. Then he would take it up where he left off. It happened quite often.

He was a whipman for the dances, which was a very respected position. In the old days, a whipman had the quirt and if the kids weren't dancing, or if they were kicking at one another or goofing off, or not behaving as he thought they should, well, boy, he would whip their legs. He would shape them up. The whipman was a *very* respected warrior.[14] In Tom's case, he was a man of very good character and of excellent pedigree, just universally accepted. Boy, all he had to do was show up and the kids would get real quiet or real scarce. He was pretty impressive to look at. He had a deep crease from his blind eye that ran down to the corner of his mouth, gave him a real ferocious kind of a look. Great old man.

Tom was a wonderful old man. He knew he was going to die. That's another eerie thing that happens. I can't explain it. Most people wouldn't even believe it. They know when they're going to die and sometimes they'll even tell you. Early morning, we all broke camp at the Pendleton Round-Up. It was Sunday and the guy from the mission had been out there gathering up his parishioners who were still comatose from the big toot on Saturday night. I go out there and that ground fog is coming out. Look down the rows of teepees and there are these scattered bodies. It was kind of funny at first, and then you would think, "My God, this is how it looked at the Battle of the Big Hole* when the army jumped them and killed so many of the people in the camp." I remember, that morning I went out and that ground fog was there, kind of cool and strange. It had been hot.

---

* This was one of the most intense battles between the fleeing Nez Perce and the U.S. troops and volunteers pursuing them. The battle on August 9, 1877, at the Big Hole River in Montana left nearly a hundred dead and many wounded on both sides.

I walked over toward Tom's teepee. When I was about halfway there, he came out to meet me. I shook his hand and I thanked him. Always sad to go away. They break camp, everybody goes off for the winter.

I say, "Well, Tom, next year."

And, boy, he looked at me, the saddest look, and just in total finale he said, "No, no more Round-Ups."

I said, "Ah, sure, you'll be here."

"No, no more." Then he kind of smiled a little. "You remember," he said, "you keep me here and our people here," and he pointed at his heart.

I thought, "Well, maybe he is tired or something." He died a few months later and no more Round-Ups. He was totally resigned to the thing. It was sad, but this was the way it was going to be. And he did, he died. A lot of people have gone that way. You tell that to a scientist or an anthropologist or something, they wouldn't believe it: "Oh, that is just superstition, it is just romancing the whole thing." It was not like that. That has happened so often in my life, now I really think they know.

The old cowboys and the old Indians were really something. There were people like Texas Jack Omahandrow: "Killed my first man when I was fourteen years old, boy." What a character, what a charlatan. I loved the old varmint, and he was a varmint, Texas Jack Omahandrow. The original Texas Jack Omahandrow, and he had worked for Buffalo Bill, he had worked for Pawnee Bill, he had worked for the 101 Ranch Show. He was an old Wild West show type, an authentic fake. His persona was probably fake, but he was a good shot. Apparently he had done some people under in defense of his family's rights during the range wars.

Grandpa always enjoyed him. When Jack got going, Grandpa had a way of looking at me, and he would take his hand and make the sign for laughter when Jack wasn't looking. The thing was, "Don't take this too seriously!" He was from that era of the Wild West shows and all. They were the forerunners, of course, of our Western movies, and a lot of the old rodeo cowboys were our first stuntmen.[15]

There were more like him. In Pendleton, this guy came up to me and handed me my wallet. He came out of Happy Canyon there where the gambling and some of the best drinking is done. He handed it to me. "Knew your grandfather, oh yeah, we worked for the Cody show together." I said,

"Really, gee, I, uh. . . ." He had picked my pocket. He was there in Pendleton, and he knew who the kids were, because they took part in the thing. He just said, "A lot of dishonest people here. I know that for a fact, I'm one of them!"

Turns out, old Louie McClare was the crazy man when the Cody show played New York City. The Deadwood Stagecoach, which is now in Cody, Wyoming, in the museum, was filled with press people and they were going to go around Central Park as kind of a publicity stunt. Boy, I'll tell you, Grandpa used to laugh about that. Louie took them around Central Park in that old coach—six-horse team full tilt! Grandpa said, "You could hear them screaming and praying for miles." Well, the press guys kept hollering: "We'll never get there, we'll never get to Denver this way," going on and on! I guess when some of them got out, they couldn't even stand up. They were pretty terrified. That was old Louie.

He was quite an old cur. He married a Warm Springs woman. That was where he finally settled in. If you were going to make a movie and you wanted an old half-breed, just one of those leather-tough old men who stands between two worlds, that would've been him—Louis McClare. Great character. I've always liked characters.

RESPECTING THE SACRED

Little by little, all these things began to accumulate.

Don was uncannily adroit at negotiating different cultural patterns. He folded his experiences with different individuals into his own understanding of the world around him. As he came to adulthood, he became a teacher as well as a student. He continued to learn more stories, but began to tell them as well. The strong cultural patterns instilled in him from his early years gave substance to the malleability of his individual identity and to this, his narrative.

All of those who followed traditional religions had an effect on me. Well, when you talk about being superstitious, Mom's uncle Harley used to say, "Superstition, that is the other guy's religion!" It is extremely personal to me. I have a deep and abiding respect. I have seen some things that I can't credit happening in reality. There is something there that can't be defined in scientific terms or even maybe rational terms, but they *are.* The rain *is.* A thunderstorm *is.* Sometimes you can question the thing to the point that it shuts off. So you *accept,* and you don't pick it to death. Little by little, all these things begin to accumulate.

I *will not* touch certain things, like that Shaman Staff at the Chicago Field Museum. I wouldn't touch that. It was taken, I think, by Emmons from a shaman's grave.[16] It was a strange sculptured piece. Must be about four feet long with a combination of a bird and a man. It was a little weathered, time had acted upon it. I remember the first time I ever saw that thing in person. You know how you can look at an iron stove and you can't see that it is hot, but you can *feel* it? It was almost like putting out your hand to a stove. It isn't heat you feel, but there is something that comes off of that thing. They went to hand it to me up in the little storeroom. Boy, I wouldn't touch that thing for a million dollars. I let the guys from the museum handle it. I didn't want to touch it because it wasn't meant to be touched. I don't think it was meant to ever be in a museum. I think it was sent with the person who possessed it and who possessed the power that animated it. It can work bad.

I remember once, Tommy and Flora Thompson and some other people, including Martha McKeown, went to the Maryhill Museum.* Tommy and Flora were so good to me, and indeed their whole extended family were—great teachers. If I had a set of gurus in my life, they certainly would've filled the bill! They talked so much. But at Maryhill there was a good collection. We went and Flora touched something. She picked it up and didn't realize that it had been taken from a grave, and that night she got very sick. Her hands, her wrists, and her face swelled up and she was very, very ill. That night Tommy was singing and using his power to get this out of her before it killed her. She was pretty good the next day, and after about a week she was okay. I've seen these things happen. You can say this is psychosomatic: she realized, so she panicked and this caused a histaminic reaction or something akin to a bee sting. It was more than that, I think.

Mom is very much in that vein. Anything from graves and things like

---

* McKeown was a local historian of some note. The Maryhill Museum of Art is located near Goldendale, Washington.

that ought to be given back. Well, I'll tell you something I did. A lot of people think I was a superstitious dummy. Nice elderly lady gave a box of things to us that had been in her family for years. In with the things that they gave were arrow points, some stone artifacts, and some trade goods—the kinds of things that had washed out along the rivers or that wind blew out of the sands there. They're not necessarily from graves, although they may have come from graves, but they had been purified by the sunlight and time, so I don't get that funny tingly sensation when I look at it or get close to it. But there was this bone, part of a skull that somebody had picked up, and there were these teeth in it. You can recognize right now where they came from. They came from the Columbia River. They were ulcerated because that blowing sand would get into that pulverized salmon pemmican they used to make so much of there and the teeth were worn. Lewis and Clark mentioned it. Boy, they were *classic* examples, if you had been of a mind to collect them, because you could see what they were talking about.

I was a little horrified . . . because those little bells began going off. Now most people say, "This is superstition. He has just been around this stuff too much." But it was no joke to me. So I had my niece Lee take it up the hill. We wrapped it in red cloth. We put tobacco and things with it and I told her, "Take it up on the hill and put it in a very sheltered place where nobody is going to find it. Go off and leave it. You don't look back; you come straight back." She took it up and put it on the hill. It is still up there as far as I know and I hope it is always there. Somebody had to give it back to the earth. I don't know where it came from, so I couldn't really take it to *the* place, but it seemed a good place to do it, and I tried to do the things that should've been done to return it. It is a small incident. It is showing respect. It assuages what some people would think is a superstitious streak or overdramatizing myself. But I felt very much better after it was done; and Lee was a pure person, so she was the ideal person to do it. She was a virgin, so she was armored by the fact that she had just gone through puberty and the life forces were so strong within her that she was at that dangerous energy time in her life, by old standards. So it was better she did it than I did it. It wasn't so much cowardice on my part but "here is the perfect person to do it in the *right* way." Lee understands those things very, very well. I mean, you don't even have to tell her a lot of these things.

STORYTELLERS

*They always reveal a little of the culture
or a little of the personality of the times before.*

Don loved stories, and often his public presentation of them centered on
the simple fact that Indians have a sense of humor and can laugh. He
consistently tried to deliver this message in his public performances. It
was also his way of making sense of the people he had known and loved
as complex individuals, not stereotypes.

Older Indian people seem to have that kind of kinky thing where they turn
something that is really, really bad into something that in the end comes
up being something really funny. Old Tom Brown was from Warm Springs.
He was a real character, always looked like an unmade bed. I shouldn't say
that about anybody, but his shirttail was always out at least a couple of places,
his belly button would be showing, his jeans about half mast most of the
time, old beat-up boots or moccasins. His hair just grew straight out. He
would have looked like a tumbleweed if Sadie hadn't gotten around to giving him his shearing, as she called it.

He was talking about wildlife on the reservation. He says, "Yeah, used to
have lots of them black bears. Used to be up here on the hills. You know,
one time I saw one of them black bears. My horse and I, we chased him
and roped him. The old bear, he could sure pull. My horse, he was just digging in the whole time. That old bear, he was just *dragging* us along. Pretty
soon that bear turned around and he took his paw, put it on the rope, then
he put the other paw on the rope, and he just started *reeling* us in like he
was fishing. And he reeled us in. Before he got too close, I *jumped* off and
I run. I just left there and I left the horse and everything."

I'm listening, pretty excited, and it was all pretty plausible up to a point,
I suppose. He says, "Yeah, that was pretty exciting. You know, a lot of people
don't believe me when I tell them that, but I always tell them, 'If you see
that bay horse of mine and he has got a brand-new saddle on and it is being
ridden by a black bear, then you'll know it is true!'" They got a lot of those
shaggy-dog things. They're very fond of that.

The raccoon story is common all the way from the mouth of the Columbia River clear through the Shahaptian country—the Nez Perce, the

Don, in Plains/Plateau dress, surrounded by Patty, Smitty, and Dick at a storytelling event during the family's brief stay in Kalama, Washington. By the late 1950s Don had gar-nered acclaim as a storyteller and was increasingly in demand. Photo courtesy of the Lelooska family.

Cayuse, the Umatilla, the Palouse all have a version, and it turns out the Kwakiutl have a very similar version. Mius (Little Raccoon), a mischief-maker, is one of the Animal Kingdom dancers.* I'll tell it the way the old ladies tell it, because I like the way they put things. (Sometimes their English isn't perfect.)

Grandma's got to go and get some material for her baskets. She says to her grandson, Mius, "While I'm gone, you get wood in here. You bring it in. You go down by the river. You drag the wood up, you break it up, and you put it in the woodpile." And she says, "While I'm gone, don't, don't,

---

* The Animal Kingdom Dance is the re-enactment of the ways in which some Kwakiutl families originally gained connection to supernatural powers.

don't, don't (four times, don't, this is the big *don't*) go out there where we buried them acorns."

They used to bury baskets of acorns, and that was where people would go urinate, on top of the ground where these are. It would leach out the tannin from the acorns. That makes the black Chinook olives that some of the early fur traders mentioned so lovingly! Well, anyway, Grandma goes off. It is really funny to see one of those old ladies, some of them big and heavy. You just see this old lady waddling down the trail. Little Raccoon's ears go up. He thinks, "Don't hear Grandma. Can't see Grandma." Goes around behind the lodge. "Oh, there's the place. All those baskets sleeping in the dirt, all full of them good acorns. Well, Grandma won't care." Digs up the dirt. Starts eating those acorns. "Oh, they're really good! They're just right, just right. Little bit salty, taste good." Well, pretty soon he eats all that first basket. Then he goes over, digs up another one. "Oh, they're so good." He just can't quit. He just keeps digging them up and eating them and pretty soon, whole bunch of holes. He has eaten all the acorns. Big belly. He is all swoll up. Well, he falls down, goes to sleep.

Well, next thing he knows, Grandma comes back. She has got a big load on her back, grass and bark and stuff for her baskets. She looks at that Little Raccoon. She knows what has happened. She yells at him. He jumps up. He runs into the house. She chases him. She picks a stick up out of the fire. Old black stick, it is all burned, and she is going to hit him with it. So he runs outside. He hides in the woodpile. The woodpile was pretty skinny and it wouldn't hide him. His tail sticks out over here, nose sticks out over there. Grandma slapped him on his tail, and every time she hits him with that burned stick, it makes a stripe. And she goes around where his nose is sticking out, and she *whacked* him across the nose. That is where he gets that black around his eyes and his nose. Well, he was really punished for that because he was bad.

So it usually stops there, but that is not the whole story. Little Raccoon waits and waits. Every time he looks in the water, he keeps trying to wash the black off his paws and his face and his tail. Can't get it off. So he is going to get *even* with that Grandma. One day Grandma says, "You bring me some fresh water from the spring, good cold water. I'm thirsty." Well, that Little Raccoon goes down and gets that little water basket and he fills it up; then he gets him a whole bunch of those blackberry brambles and wads them all up and puts them in there—all those brambles 'n' stickers. Grandma takes the basket, "glug, glug, glug, glug, glug, glug, glug, glug, glug, smack." Drinks it all down. Those brambles, they catch in her throat, and she chokes, and she chokes, and she chokes. He is just standing there. Poor Grandma falls down on the ground. She rolls around. She knows that she is in real trouble, so she changes herself into Grouse. And that is his grandmother, Grouse. When you ever watch a grouse as it comes out in the road, its head moves back and forth, back and forth. That is because of the sore throat!

That is the *whole* story. Children aren't supposed to get even with the grandmas in tales, but that is the whole story. It is pretty consistent in its detail, only as you get on over into the mountains, the acorns become camas roots or something that is the local food. But basically the story remains the same. Women are good storytellers.

The old ladies, by choice, usually will tell you stories that have this little advisory or "that's how" kinds of things. The heavier stuff, men would do. With the exception of one story I collected. I wasn't a kid anymore when I collected this one.

I went to The Dalles. I used to trade with Curly Smith there. Now, they call him Curly because he didn't have a hair on his head. He had been an Indian trader there for ever and ever. He was a great gambler. One of the few *suyapos* [whites] who ever was any good at stick game and really was the guy you would hand the bones to and expect him to win.* He was very good. And an honest trader, and he never overpriced his stuff much. For that reason, Indians *really* brought everything they had to sell in to him in preference to somebody else because they trusted him. Trust is a very big deal.

I traded Curly out of a salmon-packing pestle. It is up in the case at the A-frame [the Lelooska family museum at Ariel, Washington]. It is the one with the ring top, the phallic top, archaeologists call it. Maybe some of that is not so far from the truth.

---

* *La'hal* and *sla'hal,* the stick (or disc) and bone games, respectively, are among the widespread and classic gambling/guessing games played by Northwest Indians.

I go by Old Gus George, and I've got this thing in my hand. I'm going back to the car. Old Gus is an old Klickitat, real old reprobate, but he knew all the songs. He was a bag of knowledge. I was very fond of all the Georges. I go by, and he says, "Oh, you going looking for Wahguhgkmughk, huh?"

I come to a screeching halt and turn around and make the big mistake, the direct approach. I say, "What do you mean, Wahguhgkmughk?" I shouldn't have done that!

He says, "Ah, I'll tell you someday." If I had been a little more adroit, I would have gotten the story then. He says, "I'll tell you someday."

It was hot and I wanted to put the stuff in the car and go downtown to the saddle shop. They usually had some good moccasins and stuff, and I said, "Okay, next time you can tell me."

He says, "Oh, sure, sure."

Went on to Celilo, stopped off. This old lady was sitting there, one of the George bunch. I say, "I passed by Gus George and I had a salmon-packing pestle." Little grin starts. "Yeah, he said I was going looking for Wahguhgk-mughk." Man, she just nearly collapsed with laughter. I just kind of stood there.

Pretty soon she quits laughing and she quits shaking. She looks at me and she says, "Did he tell you about the Wahguhgkmughk?"

I say, "No, no, I don't think he had time."

She laughed and says, "Oh, he has got nothing but time. I'll tell you, but you never tell anybody that *I* told you, because this is a man's story."

Now, they call it Wah-ka-mah-ta Mound.[17] Apparently, Wahguhgkmughk was an ogress. This ogress could charm men. She would sing and they would see her as a beautiful woman rather than the monster that she was, this twisted, horrible creature. She would lure these men off and they would start to have intercourse with her. Her vagina was all full of these sharp teeth— the toothed vagina is a common theme in mythology. Of course, "crunch, crunch, crunch, crunch, crunch," as the old George woman put it. "Oh, it's all over, they would die, bleed to death, running out of men." This is not really an elegant or poetic telling, "Running out of men."

Coyote comes, Speelyai,[18] and the women are all crying, their faces are all black, all scratched, their hair is cut, and they say, "Oh, all of our men are being killed by this thing that is up there. Coyote, help us, help us." So Coyote sits down and grabs his toes, and he rocks back and forth and consults with his power that lives in his stomach. It is four huckleberries in his stomach. He has to trick them every time in the stories. He has to do something to get the huckleberries to come across with a hint as to how he can accomplish this. He usually threatens them with thunder and lightning and hail because everybody knows that spoils the berries. So he threatened the little huckleberries and they said, "Oh, well, you go and you take a salmon-packing pestle. You go up there and when you think you're going to make love to this, what looks like a beautiful woman but isn't, why, then you take the salmon-packing pestle and you knock out all her toofs!" "Toofs," that was her word, not mine!

He hears this singing and he sees this beautiful woman. So he goes over and pounces on top of her. He is just about to make the fatal mistake and then he remembers what the little huckleberries told him; he takes that salmon-packing pestle that he had hidden under his robe and he breaks off all the teeth. That is the way he got rid of the teeth, and then he starts to walk off and all of a sudden these babies start coming out, one after another and another and another and another and another, whole bunches. He takes them down and he washes them in the river. He brings them back up, gets them all sorted out. He puts some babies over here and puts some over there, some another place, and that was how we got different tribes. Really ugly babies, why, they're the tribe that *that* storyteller doesn't like. Good-looking ones that he washed and gave special care to, why, that is our people!

That was how it went. Anyway, that woman lived in the area where that mound is, where old Wahguhgkmughk the ogress lived. That was where a lot of the tribes came from, in this story. But women usually don't like to talk about things like that with a male. It was really hard to get a lot of details about birthings and abortions and things like that. I've been lucky quite a few times, but it has to be a thing you're never supposed to tell that *they* told you! That particular version is very likely Klickitat. A lot of people called the Georges Klickitat and a number of other things, but they were from that area around Goldendale. *Strong* Washini people. Boy, they really knew a lot. Gus, especially, was a good singer.

Storytellers are great. Delford Lang was a fine storyteller. Now Delford was one of those mixed-bloods who didn't look at all like an Indian but he was Klamath, and he was chairman of the tribal council for a long time.

That is his little red Early-day Shirt in that cradle basket up on the wall in the A-frame. Just not long before he died, he brought that shirt and showed it to me, and we're talking about it and he said, "Yeah, this was made for me and put on me the day I was born." Then as he was leaving, he says, "You know, this shirt is the last thing that I will ever give you." That was literally what he meant. When he died, that shirt was sent to me. And that was what he meant. He treasured it, so I guess he figured that it should be enshrined in the collection, which I did.

Delford knew lots of stories. He knew a lot of the Klamath language. At the time, I had lots of time to spend with Delford. He was married to a Nez Perce woman, Ruby. He knew lots of Coyote stories and a lot of songs, lot of gambling songs. He tells the story about Coyote. I like stories like this because a lot of times they betray some of the customs. In this case, the burning grounds. They cremated the dead. You encounter ghosts and things. There are *countless* stories that go with the burning grounds and having adventures with ghosts.

In this one, Coyote's wife gets sick and she dies. Well, when somebody dies, you have to mourn. For a while you can't have anything to eat. You give away *all* of your property, just down to your naked self. So Coyote does this. He gives away all of his food, he gives away every stitch of clothing, all of his weapons, all of his tools. Everything he gives to the people because they will conduct the funerary rites for his wife. (You see, here are some significant little cultural hints in the stories.) Coyote starts off down the trail—road, I think Delford would say. He is going along, going along, keeps singing to himself:

Hah-na-wah, hah-na-wah, mah-la-gah mo-din-o-lit
Hah-na-wah, hah-na-wah, mah-la-gah mo-din-o-lit

Hurry up, hurry up, sun go down
Hurry up, hurry up, sun go down

Because till sundown he can't have any water, he can't eat any food, can't own anything, nothing. He is just going to wander until the sun goes down. So he goes along; pretty soon, lying in the trail, here is this bow case—

arrows, nice bow, *beautiful* bow. Oh, Coyote looks at it. He *sure* does want that bow and that bow case and those arrows because he can't get food without that. Well, he goes along, passes it up, steps right over it, goes on down the road. He sings, "Hah-na-wah, hah-na-wah, mah-la-gah mo-din-o-lit (Hurry up, hurry up, sun go down)."

Well, he goes a little farther. Hmm, here are these beautiful clothes there, nice shirt, leggings. He stops. He is just about to pick it up and then he remembers that he can't have anything. He is going to get in big trouble if he breaks the rules. So he steps over the clothes and he goes on down the trail, singing, "Hah-na-wah, hah-na-wah, mah-la-gah mo-din-o-lit (Hurry up, hurry up, sun go down)."

He goes through a whole series of these things. Everything you could possibly want, including a beautiful woman, is sitting in the trail and *he* goes right on by. The last one before his disaster is the woman. So he passes her up. He just steps over. She is lying there in the trail looking most appealing and, "No, no," he just steps over her: "Hah-na-wah, hah-na-wah, mah-la-gah mo-din-o-lit."

Well, *now* he is way down the trail. His skin is getting all itchy and hurting from the sun and he has got nothing in his stomach. Sounds like rocks are rolling around inside. Comes to a wild plum tree. The wild plum tree is *full* of dead-ripe, big, juicy, wild plums—the sort Coyote likes more than *anything.* So he looks at that plum tree. He looks at the sun. The sun is still *way up:* "Hah-na-wah, hah-na-wah, mah-la-gah mo-din-o-lit (Hurry up, hurry up, sun go down)."

"Oh, maybe one." Looks around. "Nobody is going to see." Eats one of those. "Oh, that is so good." Takes care of his thirst, takes care of his hunger, spits out the pit, *splut.* Takes another one, eats that. Another one, eats that. Spitting out the pits. "Ah," he eats about *all* those big dead-ripe plums in that little tree. "Ah," then he lays down, "ahhh!"

Pretty soon he doesn't feel so good. Belly begins to hurt. It is making noises, not like rocks rolling around, sounds like something boiling in a kettle. Oh! He jumps up and he runs down off the trail where there is a little pothole, a dry wash made by a creek. He gets in the middle of that pothole and he is looking around because he has got to do something about what is about to happen. Oh, he just starts going. Just going lots. And it just keeps

going and keeps going and keeps going. Pretty soon, old Coyote is floating around in a pool of his own . . ."shit" is what Delford said, and Coyote
keeps singing: "Hah-na-wah, hah-na-wah, mah-la-gah mo-din-o-lit!" I love
stories! They always reveal a little of the culture or a little of the personality
of times before. Delford Lang, yeah, Delford was full of them.

5 / "A Kind of Hunger"

search for identity—cultural and political—was arguably one of
the key features of Native American struggles in the twentieth century and continues to be so in the twenty-first. Yet identity is a
tricky, elusive matter. What choices individuals and groups have and how
differences are given meaning make identity formation particularly political. This was certainly the case for Don. Aside from his family upbringing and his appearance, over which he had little choice, there were few
"official" items to which he could point to claim a specific tribal, much
less Indian, status. Yet he never doubted he was Indian.

In many respects, Don's life was very much like that of the Métis or
"mixed-blood" people whom Native American author, literary critic, and
academic Gerald Vizenor speaks of as "Earthdivers": those beings who
dove to the depths of the seas and retrieved the lumps of clay from which
they shaped new worlds. For him, these peoples are "compassionate tricksters" and "uncertain creator[s]."[1] Vizenor's visions stand in stark contrast to the much dated but frustratingly persistent social science tradition
that seeks to salvage "authentic" Indians before they "vanish." Proponents
of this tradition argue that modernity inevitably erases "premodern" cultures or, by implication, that intermarriage with non-Indians or even members of other tribes makes each successive generation "less Indian" than
that before it.

Other schools of thought explain this supposed demise as the triumph of civilization over savagery. In the past generation, this vision has been inverted. It now shows a not-so-pleasant Western imperialist juggernaut that inevitably destroyed Native cultures. For all of its recognition of the inequities of power and the role of diseases, this newer vision is a romantic victimization in which Indians play no real role.

Following on the heels of this victimization narrative is an even more recent argument, that the cultures of Native Americans (indeed, "minorities" in general) persist. "Ethnics" offer up resistance to assimilation and refuse to change. Some may find merit in this heroic model, but it still falls into an easy either/or fallacy. The scholar Arnold Krupat argues that those who analyze societies as being either purely "modern/progressive" or "traditional" engage in an ineffectual "ethnocriticism."[2]

Even recent attention to identity formation among American Indians such as that proposed by Vizenor does have its critics. An emphasis on "mixed blood" literature and histories, they argue, is unconnected to the politics—cultural and especially economic—of being "tribal" and denies the reality of material oppression and the fierce resistance to it.

Don's experiences, however, suggest that scholars need to not only think beyond the older dichotomies—civilized or savage, modern or premodern—but also take care in drawing stark lines between "mixed blood," non–federally recognized Indians on the one hand and "full blood," "tribal," federally recognized Indians on the other.[3] It is true that the promise of and positioning for federal moneys reinforce, even dictate, a need to make those lines clear,[4] but in the process, it is too easy to lose track of those important, even critical links between reservation and off-reservation lives. It is time to take up the question of how they interact, how they can be mutually beneficial. It is important to allow Indian peoples the opportunity to be complicated, to be full of the very human contradictions that make up who we are as individuals and groups.

Still, politics make a difference. The 1960s and 1970s marked another sea change in federal Indian policy, one that dovetailed nicely with the decades-old drive by Indian peoples for self-determination. Much as in the 1930s, the federal government turned its attention and resources back to reservations. In education, it promoted Head Start programs on reservations, encouraged and supported conferences regarding K–12 and college and university programs and curricula. In economic realms, it gave much attention to finding ways to bolster reservation economies, usually trying to focus on resource management and industrial development. It also took up arts and crafts programs with renewed vigor, and though it tended to see such efforts as only marginally remunerative, federal officials argued that support of cultural efforts raised self-esteem and gave Indians a place for their talents in a modern world. Paternalistic as those constructions may have been, they nonetheless helped swing the balance toward greater self-determination.

Those same decades also marked a time of increased militancy, not only on the reservations but also by urban Indians enmeshed in a powerful sense of pan-Indianism. The American Indian Movement, its predecessors, and its progeny helped to articulate political positions for "Indians" that included tribes as well as individuals. They also pointed out and strengthened critical connections between Indians on reservations and those in urban centers.[5]

For Don, this was a critical period as well, when he made the transition from a person involved in "Western" art and Plains and Plateau cultural production to a renowned Northwest Coast artist. The role of the federal government was indispensable in making that leap, not only in its monetary support but also in helping Don make links to tribes such as the Makah in Washington and the Kwakiutl in British Columbia. It brought Don into contact with James Sewid of the Kwakiutl, arguably the single most important acquaintance Don would ever make. With Sewid, Don made a connection comparable to his earlier experiences among the peoples of the Plains and Plateau. The result was a wonderfully complex tableau on which Don painted his life as something much more than just a disconnected "trickster" and something slightly short of direct tribal politicking.

TRANSITION

Just little by little, it began to swallow me up.

It was always one of those nagging questions: just how *did* Don Smith, a Cherokee raised in such an obvious overlapping of Plains, Plateau, and white cultures, come to do Northwest Coast art? I had to ask. Having heard so much about how Don learned to ask questions, it seemed odd and out of place for me to ask directly. When I finally did ask, it took many hours of taped interviews spanning decades of Don's life to begin to reach an answer.

Northwest Coast art had always been there, in the back of my mind, and it always just kind of tugged at me. Every time I got close to pieces in a museum collection, I had a feeling of déjà vu. It was almost uncomfortable sometimes. I kept on doing the Western, Plains, and Plateau things we were doing and improving that and all, but Northwest Coast art never really let go—and then I began to experiment with the carving.

I think when I *really* began to get intrigued with it was when I was making some Northwest Coast puppets: a Haida, Tlingit maybe, but northern Northwest Coast chief. I would burn them if I could get my hands on them today. That was when I began to really open up something that seemed to need my attention. In researching those and the masks, I don't exactly know how to express it, but something kind of took hold. All these siren songs of things I would like to know or have an explanation for: who, what, where, and are they like the people I know? I wasn't satisfied with some of the books and their description of them as being lazy, fish-eating, untrustworthy critters.* There had to be more to people that could have developed that art. Behind the art, there must have been a *powerful* belief system. Just little by little, it began to swallow me up.

Then I ran into Norman Feder, who at that time was the editor of *Indian Hobbyist* magazine.[6] He was an art collector, Indian culture addict, anthropologist. He and his bunch were very interested in getting some replicas of Northwest Coast materials, for some of their demonstrations. So I made them some masks, frontlets, rattles, and things like that. And of course the more I did, the farther down the slope I slid, as it were! Hubbard was where it started. It just sort of grabbed hold and it has never, never let go. It just seems to grow stronger with the passage of time.

I just read everything I could find, and then I discovered the Rasmussen

* The presence of so much visible art led several generations of scholars to speculate that the sheer abundance of nature allowed these nonagricultural people to become producers of art. Most current students of the peoples and art of the Northwest Coast and American Indians generally espouse much more complicated theories.

By 1960 Don was immersed in the production of Northwest Coast artwork. He grew increasingly adept at the art form, as suggested by the variety of pieces around him at the family's museum and shop in Kalama, Washington. Meanwhile, he maintained a connection to the Plateau/Plains people with whom he had associated for so long. This broad mix of cultures influenced him throughout his life. Photo courtesy of the Lelooska family.

Collection. At that time [in the mid-1950s], Tom Colt was the curator of the Portland Art Museum. I met him through Mrs. Halverson, the director of art for the Portland Public Schools. She got interested in me through the superintendent of schools in Salem, who was the one who ran all those tests on me. Mrs. Halverson, that poor mistaken lady, thought I was some kind of a genius or something! I wish she was around to see what I finally turned into. She knew I was already fascinated with Northwest Coast and, in fact, anything Indian. She got wind that the collection had been shipped in and they were going to open it. She talked to Tom (one friend introduces you to another friend) and I was invited up to see the things as they came out, which was a delight. It was like I suppose some kid would feel if he went to the Academy Awards or the Grammy Awards. It was like seeing celebrities. Wonderful, ancient pieces. That was a great thrill.

They had just received the Rasmussen Collection in the mid-fifties. I think it had been stored in Seattle during World War II for safety. Tom was responsible for bringing it to the Portland Art Museum. What is the old religious term? Epiphany? When they opened the crates and those things came out, I mean, these weren't pictures, these weren't descriptions, my God, here they were! Boy, that was it. Again, there was this—I had it since the whole Northwest Coast experience began—this déjà vu: "I know what that is" or "I've been here before." Sometimes explanations would be there long before I finally discovered a source to confirm the notion. If I were to believe in reincarnation, as a lot of the Kwakiutl do, I would think maybe that somewhere along the line I had been one of them because it was a wonderful voyage of discovery, but it was kind of a rediscovery, a feeling! Boy, to finally see and touch those things. And none of them really had that frightening feeling. They seemed friendly, warm things that had something to tell and teach.

Those Kwakiutl pieces in the Rasmussen Collection had the most meaning for me. I mean, that wasn't just art, wasn't just *"Indian"* stuff. There is a wonderful theatricality there. I think I'm a ham at heart and that appealed to me, the concept of making the unseen world of the supernatural real and tangible for the uninitiated, to use the mask as a portal to the spiritual world. Wow, it will *never* let go of me. As old as I am now, with so much of this, I always have this list of things I would just love to make and experiment with or bring back. I got to know Tom fairly well, through my interest, and he came to the place a number of times. He kind of took an interest in me.

ARIEL

Sink or swim doing the better things.

From that moment of awareness, Don plunged into the challenges of carving Northwest Coast–style poles and masks. Serendipity and timing combined with his skill and ambition, taking Don on paths he could scarcely have imagined.

When we moved from Hubbard to Kalama [Washington, about 1959], Dad leased the service station from the guy we leased the building from. He built the building for the shop and the little museum sort of as a drawing card for the Columbia Inn Restaurant there. We had been there about two years, maybe three, and we thought about moving to the Oregon Coast. William Weinberg had been a customer and when he heard that we were thinking about moving, why, then, he came up with this proposition. He wanted some totem poles carved for the inn and he said, "Well, we've got the lot over there and we'll lease you the building at one percent of the cost per month." It was a good deal, especially for those times. It seemed like an easy way out. There was room for everybody in the top of the building there. Everybody had their room and there was a big kitchen and family room. Then the museum and the shop were all under that one building, which seems *terribly* small now. It seemed immense at the time.

Kalama is where I carved those big, long, single-piece poles. Someday maybe an earthquake will claim them and then I won't have to look at them anymore. At that time, they were fine for what they were—tourist poles. But certainly not the quality I came to admire. I'm never satisfied. I had done carvings for the Zombie Zulu and the Mayan Jungle, a couple of Eddie Polaski's nightclubs. Well, just before we moved to Kalama, coming up on the 1959 Oregon Centennial, Eddie wanted a big totem pole carved for the Hillvilla Restaurant in Portland. I said, "All right. I'll carve you one as big as you can get a log for." Well, he got one that was about four or five feet across the butt and fifty feet long. Sharpened up the tools and, oh boy, I mean, jimminy Christmas, this was something you could get your *teeth* into, this thing. So I spent about six weeks whacking that out and driving back and forth to the thing.

Apparently that was one of the things that had inspired Weinberg. He wanted some totem poles for the inn. He was thinking then of building a motel complex, but his aspirations kind of ran afoul with the Internal Revenue Service—which is not to denigrate him; I mean, a lot of nice people get clobbered by the IRS, but there we were. Weinberg got himself into a real tax mess with the federal government. Mom took things in hand and

Don laying out the pattern for a large pole commissioned in 1962 by International Paper. By this point Don was well on his way as a Northwest Coast artist and was making important artistic and cultural breakthroughs. Note the initial design sketch on paper, and the grid lines on the pole itself. Photo courtesy of the Lelooska family.

she bought this place at Ariel [Washington] and we just moved very quickly here. Boy, this place was a mess, but it was the best thing that ever happened to us. We've been here for thirty-two years. It probably was the best move we ever made. And it also was the time to make the break from the commercial, souvenir kind of things, tourist-trap stuff, to something serious. By that time, I knew the difference between the two and I wanted to do the better. This afforded the opportunity, so Mom and I decided we would sink or swim doing the better things.

We built a coasthouse for our own amusement, more or less, about the time we moved up here. You see, we spent the first summer in Ariel in a teepee. We had the TV in the teepee, right out here. It was a very rainy summer, not unlike the one we just went through. So the teepee is mildewing and all. The teachers who had been to that little old place we had down there on the highway at Kalama were clamoring to come and all, and so there had to be a way that we could do the school thing. I enjoyed doing it and I thought it served a purpose. So I get to thinking. Well, the thing is, we have a teepee in a place it doesn't belong. The people who lived here, the Chinooks, had things solved rather nicely.[7] They had the plank houses and they had their summer houses—the mat lodges—that they could take out to different places, or else they could just pack the boards off the house and go someplace and make a temporary camp.

I got the idea it would be nice to build a Northwest Coast house. The easiest type to build is the Kwakiutl house. We had to figure out how big it could be made, and of course it had to be done on practically no funds at that time. So the Columbus Day Storm of '62 blew down some cedar trees that belonged to our friend Ralph Bozarth's dad. He donated the logs, and Ralph zipped around and found a little mill that would saw them—and all of a sudden the pipe dream was rather rapidly turning into a real proposition. With Ralph's help and, again, the friends—my God, I don't know what we would do without our friends—they all pitched in. Ralph is such a quick study, a genius, really. He grasped, very quickly, all the concepts of the construction and ways it could be done, and done better and stronger without compromising the appearance of the thing.

We put it up and then OMSI [Oregon Museum of Science and Industry][8] got interested and began bringing a few people up. It was kind of a meager program. Of course, that was before Jimmy Sewid entered the picture. Before that, I always felt I was kind of walking on somebody else's lawn a little bit. We were very careful about what we did. But that was the way it started—a bunch of blown-down cedars and a lot of friends!

It was a very *pivotal* year, actually, '62. A lot of things blew in besides the storm! Building the house really changed a direction. I had been very much involved with the northern Plains and the Plateau, and it was an interest, the Northwest Coast. I was *fascinated* by the art and just voraciously reading and studying and talking to as many people as I could find who knew something. That was, I think, the turning point. The building of the house was one of those things that pleased something or somebody when we did it, because things began to fall into place pretty good after that! I think it was meant to be. Sometimes you go along and you don't know why you do something and then after you look back at it for a while, it looks like, well, gee, you couldn't have done anything else! Eventually we outgrew it, and then we built the second one, same way, mostly friends.

When we put up the second coasthouse, we had a feast, a salmon bake, and had lots of people down. We had some of the Plains and Plateau people and we had some of the Makah again. They had come down for the last major do we had in the little house, too. Jimmy Sewid and some people came down from up in Canada. It was a lot of fun. We weren't really sure it was going to go as well as it did; it was just amazing.

NEAH BAY

You'll not see, when I hide the bones.

The story of federal involvement in Indian peoples' lives during the twentieth century is problematic at best. Federal patronage of Indian arts favored men's work over women's. In the Pacific Northwest, for example, Indian women had powerful and lively traditions of producing baskets for personal and ceremonial use as well as for the tourist trade.[9] Yet in the 1960s when the Indian Arts and Crafts Board consultant looked for artists in the region, he focused on Don and his carvings for demonstrations around the region, not women weavers.[10] This flowed from the line of thought among art critics and Indian art promoters that utilitarian items, especially if newly produced, were crafts but not art.[11]

The Indian Arts and Crafts Board demonstration projects in which Don participated did not generate, as the federal officials had hoped, a sudden rush to carve Northwest Coast–style masks and poles for the market. Yet government actions did bring results, difficult though they may be to measure. Don's association with the Indian Arts and Crafts Board gave him increased exposure and confirmed for him the validity of his desire to know Northwest Coast cultures as he did those of the Plains and Plateau peoples. It gave him vital connections to people he might otherwise not have met, and it helped him define his "Indian-ness" in new ways.

After we had been in Ariel about a year, one of the things that happened was the Indian Arts and Crafts Board sent a guy out. That was when we got into the Kennedy era and all that money for arts and stuff. I was sort of the one person around that he could use as an example to keep his job, I guess, because there wasn't a whole lot happening. Some of the first publicity of any quality came through the Indian Arts and Crafts Board. Bob Hart of the Indian Arts and Crafts Board was very interested in what we were doing. So it just sort of went from there.

I went out to Neah Bay for the government.* The Indian Arts and Crafts Board wanted me to go out there and demonstrate carving to the Makah people. Now there was a supreme arrogance, for a carver who didn't feel he was hardly fledged to go up there! I could've done a trip to Yakima, but Neah Bay was the place that seemed to me to be the most mutually profitable. I mean, the Makah could see the tools, find out how to make them, and experiment and all. I passed on some of the tools. Besides, the Yakama and the Umatilla hadn't suffered the *acute* destruction of their arts and crafts that the Makah had. Theirs was a case where practically everything visible had been bought up or carried off or was hidden.[12] The Indian Arts and Crafts Board paid my expenses and bought the pieces I made in the demonstrations.

So we went up and we set up the demonstration in their general store in town. The Makah gave us space in there to set up a chopping block, the tools, and the cedar, and then I just sat down and went to work. See, what happened was, it was like it was winter and you're feeding the birds! You throw out some seeds. And pretty soon, here comes one bird, two bird, three bird, four bird. Pretty soon a whole bunch, and the birds kept getting older and older and older. Pretty soon we had some who practically had to be *carried* in.

They came and they watched. About two days, nobody said anything. They watched, and the Arts and Crafts Board guy got chairs so they could sit around. Hear them talking in Makah, the old people. The younger ones didn't seem to speak it much. So I just kept whittling away and sharpening the knives. Letting them look at anything they wanted to look at. Very, very quiet. Didn't know which way the wind was blowing. About the third day, old guy comes in. He was just about as wide as he was tall. He wasn't fat,

---

* On the northern tip of the Olympic Peninsula, Neah Bay has long been a relatively isolated place, not easily accessible to outsiders even after the state highway reached it in the 1930s.

he was just like a block of rock or a big gnarled stump. His name was Luggi. Boy, was he a real picture, just this massive old man. He watched me awhile and hummed to himself; a lot of old Indians hum old songs. Pretty soon I turned my head around and looked at him, kind of smiled.

He says, "Kloshe mamook." That is Chinook Jargon, means "good work." And he said, "Mahsie," which means "thank you." "Nowitka," he says, "nika waum tumtum kopa mika." "Yes, my heart's warm toward you."

I was too stunned at that point and I said, "Thank you."

And he says, "No, I should thank you. I want our young people to see this."

So we talked. Well, we didn't actually talk, I mostly listened because he was talking about how their masks had been in disfavor with the missionaries, and the government really put pressure on them for sneaking off to potlatches and things like that. And my brain was going ninety miles an hour and I was trying to run my mental tape recorder and remember all the little rules and tricks that would help me remember everything he said.

Later on another old fellow came in and said, "You know Luggi?"

I said, "Well, I just met him, but seems like a great man. He knows lots."

And he says, "You bet he knows a lot. He's the last, he and his brother are the last ones who went out whaling, the old way."[13] So bingo!

Next day he came in early; just about the time we got in there, why, there he was. Again, you've got this problem about asking direct questions. So try to think how to go about this, all the time trying to keep my fingers and not mess up my work. So I said, "Yeah, Makah were great whalers. Would take a very, very brave man to go out and take whales."

He says, "Like to think so!"

I said, "Ah?" Kind of a nasal "ah." Not quite as "yes," but kind of a little question.

"I was a boy," he says, "my brother and I went out. We were whalers." Bingo! Then you can just let it flow along. He would talk about it, going out and harpooning the whale, the sounds that it makes and the way the blood smells when it comes out of the blowhole. And it is lanced to death; then towing it in, and the songs and the rituals and the taboos, and whew. . . . Great old man. Sebastian. He was Luggi's brother. He was a little younger than Luggi, maybe a year or two. Mom got to meet a lot of the old Makah. They're all gone, all gone. That was a great living history experience for me.

Then we went over to the church. Patterson, the missionary, said, "Well, you can use the basement."

I said, "Use the basement?"

He said, "Yeah, you're going over to make some patterns for button blankets for the ladies."

I said, "Oh?" First I had heard of that.

He said, "Yeah, they saw your blanket. Did you cut the pattern for your mom and she sewed it?"

"Yeah," I said.

"Yeah, they'd like you to make some patterns."

I went over there. They had all this tagboard and *everything* you needed. They gave me a *real* nice supper, what they call buckskin bread and fresh salmon. They had baked all kinds of good stuff. Then we went to work, started in right after supper. We went down there and we're drawing up blankets and everybody, it seemed, was talking about their family crests. Thunderbird was one of the big important things, that being connected with the whaling and the lightning serpent and all that. So I would draw the patterns on the tagboard and some of the younger gals, why, they were cutting them out on the piece of plywood. The old ladies were watching and talking alternately in English and Makah. I don't know how many we made. They're still using them, Patterson told me, those cutouts! They wanted their blankets back. There were probably people more skilled than I around there somewhere, but they weren't going to be the first one to stick their head out and do it. And so anybody that wanted one, we just sort of took turns. They seemed to know whose turn should be first. I think it was the ranking maybe that made it work that way. But it was four o'clock in the morning before I got around to thinking about looking at a watch or something, and they're all still there. The whole time they were singing songs, whaling songs, and telling stories and all sorts of things just *pouring* into my ears. You just almost feel like you're just going to overload and smoke'll come out of your head! And just on and on and on.

Finally they were singing gambling songs and kind of chuckling. Here we are in the church basement and we're singing these gambling songs! They sang one, and I sang along on that one because I knew it. I had picked it up from the Yakama who had been over around the Puget Sound area working in the hop yards.

The ladies of the Makah Club in the mid-1960s, when Don went to Neah Bay with Indian Arts and Crafts Board consultant Edward Malin. Photo courtesy of the Lelooska family.

They said, "Where did you learn that song?"

And I said, "A Yakama Indian. He worked in the hop yards over here and he liked that song. He learned it here."

They said, "Oh, that's not surprising. People used to come from many, many tribes and work in the hops and we'd *all* kind of trade our songs because we'd all gamble in the evening."

So that was kind of interesting; here was this cultural transfer. The song goes like this:

Ha lalah yahwa, ha lalah, ya lalah, yahwa lalah,
ha lalah yahwa, ha lalah yahwa lalah, ha, lalah yahwa.
Halo mika nanitsh siah, yukwa nika sla'hal,
nika halo tseepe youtl.
Ha lalah, ya lalah, ya lalah, yahwa lalah, ya lalah yahwa,
lalah, ya lalah yawha, ha lalah yahwa,
lalah, ha lalah yahwa.[14]

Words are in Chinook Jargon. Which should instantly tell you that this is a bi-tribal product. "Halo mika nanitsh." "Halo" means "no." "No, you, see." So the words are ordered like you were speaking traditional Indian. "Yukwa nika sla'hal." That means, "When I hide the bones." It is sla'hal game. "You won't see, when I do it, so you're going to be totally in the dark." "You'll not see, you'll not see, when I hide the bones." It is really funny the way these songs get around, in the old days.

They really identified with one of the figures I carved when I was there. They told me about Cha'chik, which I don't think has made it into *any* of the books.[15] Well, Cha'chik was a whaler and a warrior, and he was huge, just immensely powerful. Sounded something like a sumo wrestler. They valued huge, heavy men. Most of their whalers were. They loved to wrestle, that is a Nootka thing.* The way I looked might have helped a little bit on that score, at least with the old people. Like Samoans, they appreciated lots of beef!

Ship came in, probably an American whaling ship; it sounds like some of their activities. They lured Cha'chik on board and they got him drunk; when he woke up, he was chained down in the hold and they were shanghaiing him. He is this great big powerful guy. He is a good seaman and they would just take him along. Well, he sobered up before the tide was right for them to sail out, and they weighed anchor; he yanked the stanchions out of the ship, went up on deck, and laid waste to the crew. Then he jumped overboard and, still with the chains and stuff all fastened to him, made it to shore! The ship sailed away, probably glad they were rid of him.

The Makah saw me carving this guy killing a sea lion. It was a northern strong-man type,† so they dubbed that Cha'chik. He could drag two sea lions, they said, on the beach. They would tow them in behind the canoes and they would let the tide bring them up and he would just get them and drag them by the lines—all kinds of these wonderful feats of strength. That carving belonged to the Indian Arts and Crafts Board. I did several pieces up there that went to the Arts and Crafts Board.

The sea lions are *really* big—that was the first time I ever got close to

* The Makah and Nootka (Nuu-chah-nulth) are closely related in cultural practices and language.

† Stone Body or Stone Boy had supernatural powers after his mother bathed him in the blood of a mythical serpent. Stories about him abound in coastal British Columbia.

The Cha'chik figure that Don carved for the Indian Arts and Crafts Board demonstration at Neah Bay struck a chord with many Makah, who identified with the superhuman feats of the sealing and whaling culture hero. Photo courtesy of Edward Malin.

one. Oh, man, they are so big when you get up on them. They didn't have a whole lot of fear. Nobody was shooting at them or anything like that; you could get really close. But boy, when they finally did move it was amazing, something that big, how quick they could come down off those rocks and plunge into the surf and be gone.

The Makah really had it in for the Bureau of Indian Affairs at that period; the government had threatened the Makah. The Makah have salvage rights on different stretches of beach and anything that washes in there, no matter what it is, belongs to the family that owned the salvage rights. Well, the old people still believe they have those rights and I believe they do, too. The navy didn't believe that. The navy families were going down there and picking up Japanese fishing floats and neat stuff that floats in and getting some of the olivella shells that the Makah make necklaces out of for sale in the souvenir shops. Well, this was an infringement of Makah rights. The Makah were not really hospitable to outsiders on their beaches. So they told the navy people to get the blazes off the beach, what was there was theirs.

The navy families went back and complained to the commandant. Commandant complained to the guy on up the ladder. So some official sends this letter to the tribal council: "This will not be the way you're going to behave toward the navy; you are guests and you should be glad to have them there for economic reasons. Besides, you should consider the fact that termination is being considered for many tribes even larger than the Makah tribe."

That was all it took. I mean, they're really proud people. That had them in a very, very bad mood, so much so that on our second visit, when we came out of the little restaurant that was down almost on the dock, there're about six great big Makah kids about eighteen, nineteen years old, maybe twenty. And a lot of Makah have this *massive* build, I mean, big, strong kids. They looked sort of like a young Luggi. The government guy was out there, nervous kind of a guy.

One of the kids says, "You're the government man."

And he says, "Yes, I'm an official of the BIA."

"Oh, idiot, idiot, idiot, idiot," I said to myself, "your Arts and Crafts Board would have been bad enough, but idiot, you, BIA!"

Then one kid says, "I think we ought to wash the BIA guy." They were going to take him down and throw him off the end of the dock.

So I said, "You know, I'm just sort of a guest up here. I just came up here to sit around and whittle and get to know the Makah people. You want to throw him in the drink, okay, but I can't get home without him! Unless you guys want to feed me all winter, don't drown him!" So they thought that was funny. They laughed. Then I thought things might be a little better.

They say, "Well, okay. We won't throw him in there *tonight!*"

I said, "Well, thank you kindly. It's really hard to wring out a bureaucrat." They thought that was funny. He didn't know which side I was on and, really, I had one side and that was me! Never occurred to me to worry. I was light enough complected to be mistaken for something else easy enough! I never had any problems.

I was up there three times. Every time it got better, but they were in a bad mood toward the BIA. The Arts and Crafts Board guy said the absolute wrong thing, and he had that official gray government car. When we got back to the motel, I said, "You know, they're going to see that car parked there. They're going to know just which one of these units we're sleeping in tonight." Boy, that scared him to death. Once they laughed, I figured there wasn't any big problem. If you can't get them to laugh, why, then otherwise, I think they might well have done it. He just was a little scared of them and that was a mistake. They know!

I think the spookiest thing that ever happened had to do with an old man, just an elegant old man—as opposed to a lot of the Makah, he was kind of tall and rather slender in build—who came and watched a lot. Name was Johnson. Trying to think of his Makah name. . . . Can still see his face. . . . Talked a lot about the whalers. His relatives had been whalers, father had been a whaler, his uncles. Talked a lot. The whaling equipment; I was very interested in how they did some of that. He knew how a lot of it was made, too. Then I mentioned the sacred aspect of doing this and he said, "You know, there aren't people alive who would ask that question. That is the strongest part of your whaling equipment, it's the soul, the *tahmahnawis* that is put into it when it's made."

So anyway, the Arts and Crafts Board guy and I were back in the motel. I had forgotten all about the kids on the dock. Comes a knock on the motel room door. Fortunately, that time I had a room of my own. Next door is the government man. Knock on the door. Open the door, some of these big Makah kids again.

They said, "Old Man wants to see you."

I said, "Oh?"

Said, "Yeah, he said you were to come along with us."

"Oh?" I said, "Well, all right." Because the old man had been very, very friendly and all, I said, "I'll have to tell the government guy that I'm going. He might wake up and wonder what happened to me."

They said, "No, don't tell the government man *anything*."

I thought, "Oh boy." So there I am; I wasn't scared, but I was wondering what the *hell* was going on. So went down and got in the pickup. Only about three of us could get in the cab of the pickup. The others got in back. We go down this one little narrow road, the brush is going clear up on either side. If you've been to Neah Bay, you know how some of those little roads run out there. Pretty soon it opens out into a little farm, big barn. Here comes the old fellow out and a bunch of lanterns. He has got them all lit, and the boys take the lanterns. He says, "Come on." Got over and went into the barn. Had a big loft in it. Went up these creaky steps—and I wasn't sure those steps were going to hold me, but I wasn't going to chicken out at this point. Got up there. The kids and all but one of the lanterns went up beforehand. So when I got up there, all I could see was lanterns. Pretty soon they moved away and then kind of out of the dark, you know, out of the gloom comes this shape. And it was just like seeing a ghost. It just went right down through me like somebody had poured ice water over the top of your head and down your back, and a big whaling canoe, forty feet if it was an inch, big old wolf's-head canoe.

You could see the shafts of the lances and the harpoon shaft and everything sticking out of the boat, and the mice and rats had just about eaten up the floats. The cedar rope was still there, it was still in pretty good shape. The paddles—whole darn thing is there, sitting up on blocks in the loft of that huge barn. I mean, any museum in the world would have given their eyeteeth for the darn thing. And it was a *gorgeous* canoe. Boy, I spent hours just poring over it, seeing how thick the gunwales were, how they had sewed in the thwarts and the seats. . . . And the old man was talking all the time and telling about it.

He said, "I put it up here because I was afraid that the white people would just come and take it. They've done that with things."

I said, "Yes, I know."

He says, "Yes, well, this one they won't get. I wanted you to see this because you understand."

And I say, "Well, yes, but I understand the better because of what you, Luggi, and Sebastian have told me." And he grinned real big and talked and talked and talked. Morning's starting to get there. It is about four-thirty, five o'clock. The sky is getting streaky. And I said, "Well, better go feed the government man." They all laughed.

He said, "Now, did you want to see it again?"

"Just hold up the lanterns," I said, "I want to see it one more time, the way I first saw it." And I looked at it.

He said, "I feel like there were ghosts sitting all around us all evening and I think they're happy; somebody understands." So went on down. They hauled me back in the pickup. I got back in my room and no sooner in the room and getting ready to lie down and nap a little bit and *bang, bang, bang* on the door. There is the government guy.

He said, "Were there some Indians out here?"

I said, "Yeah, there were some Indians out here."

"Oh, what'd they want?"

I said, "Oh, I think they just wanted to visit," because I wasn't about to tell him about what I had seen because I would never see anything again if I mentioned it.

I heard the barn burned the day after the old guy died. I think some of those boys sent that canoe with him. He didn't want the white people to have that canoe. Any museum in the world would have loved to get their hands on that, the whole thing was there.

They're neat people. I like the Makah. They gloried in their bloodthirsty past and all the fights they had with the Klallam.* An old lady said once at a big dinner, "We fought with *everybody!*" They had come over, apparently, from Vancouver Island and they drove out the Klallam and pushed back the Quileute† and everybody else. I think they were headed down the coast at the time of European discovery and change.

Culturally, the thing that did it for the Makah was when they first started to discover that village site at Ozette.[16] That stuff began to wash out. I went down there with some of them—Judge Parker was one of them, some of the Greens went down there, some of the old Makah ladies, the Makah Club, they called themselves. They were the custodians of all the songs, most of the oral histories. The stuff was just washing out. Makah were saying, "Yeah, it's really neat stuff, canoe paddles and all kinds of things. When it gets dry it just all falls apart." . . . Lo and behold, some of it begins to find its way down into the scientific community, and they come and that was when they "discovered" what was there. The Makah would not allow one thimbleful to be taken away. So they got the museum.[17] It has been a marvelous thing for the Makah people and their pride, especially the younger ones, who hear all this stuff from the old people, and unless you've been schooled to listen to old people, why, it is just so much hot air to the youngsters. But boy, here is stuff from their ancestors and it is important, and people come from all over the world to see it. It is so great. They're really working hard to revive the culture.

The last major do we had in the first coasthouse was when the Makah came down from Neah Bay, which surprised everybody who knows the Makah. We just had a great evening. They wanted to come down, and some of the old people thought it might be a good idea if they revived some of their dances and things, and maybe got into the idea of trying to educate

---

* The Klallam, part of the Central Coast Salish, live to the east along the Strait of Juan de Fuca.

† The Quileute live south of the Makah along the Pacific Coast side of the Olympic Peninsula.

the non-Indians in what really was their culture rather than letting the anthropologists interpret their culture; that they should develop a voice of their own. They came down and so did the Pattersons, the missionaries who were very, very supportive of Makah art and traditions.

It was a wonderful evening. We did the program and then, when we were pretty well through the program, why, they sang a lot of songs—the complimentary songs, the thank-you songs, and, of course, we saw to it that everybody was fed. We had presents for all the major players in what they call the Makah Club, which are the old nobility. I had learned enough about their culture to know the niceties, so we tried to get in all of those. They ended up singing and dancing and just everybody having a great time swapping stories. Went on until the wee small hours of the morning! Once they get rolling, why, they really know how to party! It was just really a terrific experience for me. I have a card here somewhere from the Pattersons, the missionaries. They were here and were thanking me and telling me that there had been a profound effect. That makes me feel good because you never see it at the time. You don't know what is going on. I do know the old people were *terribly* good to me. That canoe episode and a lot of things like that told me that apparently there was no resentment.

I can remember on one of the visits there, I stopped to make a picnic lunch and look across the Strait of Juan de Fuca at Vancouver Island. I looked across and I wondered, "Gee, will I ever get over there? After all these years, reading Boas and Drucker* and all of the material, I wonder if I'll ever get over there." It seemed a *long* way across the Strait. But I finally made it!

MORE GOVERNMENT WORK

The old people knew quality.

The Indian Arts and Crafts Board also sent me to Boise, Idaho, as a working Indian artist supposedly earning a living. It was just to make a little talk. I didn't demonstrate carving or anything like that. I went as an interested, supposedly knowledgeable party! I knew people that the Indians there knew,

---

* Franz Boas and Philip Drucker are two key early figures in the anthropological research on Northwest Coast peoples. Boas was active from the 1890s to the 1930s. Drucker began his career in the 1930s and was still publishing in the 1960s.

so that helped quite a bit. Some of the ones who were there were Piegan, and my grandpa knew lots of Piegan. I had some Blood friends in Alberta. See, the Blackfeet are made of Siksika—the true Blackfeet—and then there are the Piegan and the Blood. It is a confederacy, and their language and customs all are bound together. That three-fork design you see on a lot of shirt stripes, that represents their people. The three are one in a way.

It was just great. Especially the older guys. Just sit down and talk about crafts and old materials, where you can get this and where you can get that. I was pretty well grounded in that because for years I had been doing that. They were interested in finding materials: the conch shells, that flat bone wampum, weasel skins, feathers, all kinds of craft supplies. Well, for years I had traded with Pawnee Bill's Indian Trading Post. Pawnee Bill was Gordon Lilly, Colonel Gordon Lilly some people called him. He was an old friend of my grandfather's from the Wild West Show days. So things link together. It was a very small world indeed when you think about it. But I could give them sources of supplies that they didn't know about. I think that may have helped. At least it gave them resources for things they couldn't get any-more because the Indian trade had dwindled to nothing practically.

They hadn't *really* started this rebirth of crafts, so it was really tough to get stuff, the bone-hair pipes for the breastplates and things like that. It was a kind of a hunger, I think, with the old people because the grandkids are coming of age. The older women couldn't get *good* beads, they hated the crummy beads they were getting. Czechoslovakia, Bohemia, was the great supplier of good seed beads along with Venice, but the Commies took care of that. There were great quantities of beads in the country, and I gave them the names of places like the Eliot Green Bead Company, which had been around since the fur-trade days, almost.

So it was just a matter of getting these things. The old people knew qual-ity. They knew what their work ought to look like. They had the basic raw materials, still. They still had people who were tanning skins. There were people who still were going and getting the mineral paints like we talked about with the parfleches and stuff like that [see chapter 4, "Learning from People"]. But a lot of the other things that the traders had once supplied in abundance were hard to get, and they just really didn't know where to get them. We talked about that and marketing, galleries, dealing with gallery people, and just a whole lot of things.

There were some younger people who wanted to paint and were thinking about sculpture. Some wanted to make outfits. It was just kind of dumped out in a free-for-all. I made my living doing this kind of thing. That was what they wanted to do. I took the approach "Well, this worked for me and you want to try it, why, I'll tell you what I did." You tell them where to get things and places where there might be markets. Emphasize the importance, I felt, of keeping the identity rather than taking the popular powwow stuff, which is kind of a homogenized thing culturally. "Why don't you go and get the old people and listen to them?" Give them a chance to talk and to open up their ears because the time is very, very short to get these things. And they can't get it out of books, so they have got to go to the original source, which was the old people. And approach the old people in the good old way. If your family possesses one, or you have a close friend who does, then take the pipe and make the formal appeal to an old person for instruction in sacred ways and things like that. That shows your respect and then you can go from there. I just went from my own experiences.

Teenagers most of the time are pretty inarticulate, except among themselves. When they begin to talk and then begin to ask questions, it was very hard for a lot of them to admit ignorance on these things. They began to ask questions. I think, "We are making some headway." I was learning a lot, I know that! And it was hard. You can't go in there and say, "Okay, here I am. I'm this, or I'm that. I'm going to teach you guys." You have to go in and say, "Oh, I'm learning, too, and this has worked for me. I'm making a living doing it. I feel lucky to do so. I'm very grateful to our old people who were good to me." A light-skinned breed is not always welcome among old people and, so, I just tried to take what had happened to me and show them that something could be done. There was so much to all of that. It was hard to cover, but you could kind of at least tell them where some of the sharp edges are and how to get started. And as long as their old benevolent enemy the BIA's got some bucks, why not?

CHOOSING THE ART

"Well, a Cherokee certainly could not do anything of quality."

By the mid-1960s, Don found himself in a difficult position. How was he, a Cherokee, to be taken seriously as a Northwest Coast carver? He had done his best to achieve a technical expertise on a par with Northwest Indian carvers of his generation, but his own self-imposed restrictions, and people who refused to recognize that he had any legitimate reason for pursuing Northwest Coast art, blocked his path. As indirectly as I could, I asked him about this conundrum.

A certain anthropologist who was the director of a well-known museum in the Southwest decided he was an enemy of ours early on by reason of the fact we were Cherokees doing Kwakiutl art. He was such an obnoxious little varmint. This guy was supposed to be an authority. My gosh, he writes *books.* When Jerry Levy, who was a professor of psychology at Portland State University, a customer, and a friend, asked him about me, he said, "Well, a Cherokee *certainly* could not do anything of quality. It's a waste of time."

Jerry had bought a lot of my work. So Jerry took my pieces in to this guy and put them down in front of him. Jerry asked, "What do you think of these? I have a chance to buy them."

The guy says, "Oh, my gosh, gee, yeah, rattle, nice masks, this is *excellent* quality. These must be 1885, 1890," and he was going on and on. "You could tell, this is the old paint." Jerry saw me use acrylic paint. He knew that and he just drags this poor guy way out on the limb.

Then Jerry says, "Well, if I told you that these pieces that you've just been admiring were carved by that Cherokee, would you be at all surprised?" They were never real friends after that, as Jerry puts it! But there was always some of that disbelief to overcome that a Cherokee could do this. Some of these types feel that this is *genetic.* It is not. I know Bill Holm, who is an excellent carver and a wonderful dancer and very, very good in the language.* It is much less genetic than it is intellectual.

This idea that if you become an artist and you happen to be of Indian ancestry, why, you just have to stick with *your little tribe.* You can't ever look over here for inspiration or over here. You're boxed in. I don't think that is entirely fair. We have some Native American artists such as Fritz Scholder

---

* Holm is perhaps the best-known non-Indian scholar and carver of Northwest Coast art in the second half of the twentieth century. He has been a vital part of the renaissance in Northwest Coast art since the 1960s.

who kind of picked and chose.* He was mixed-blood, but his paintings were very, very powerful—Plains Indians in a very modern style. I just think it boxes a lot of people in, stunts their intellectual growth. I really don't think that you can interpret your *own* culture unless you've been exposed to other Indian cultures. I think the more you know about other cultures, the better able *you* are to kind of back off a little bit and look at your own culture, the mores of your people. I think it is much better. Otherwise you get like a little snail in your shell and you're dragging it along behind you. Anytime anything comes up, you just shrink back into the shell rather than going out to find out what is going on in the world.

I think my whole life has been *very* enriched because of my grandfather. I didn't have a lot of tribal prejudices. Lots of tribes detest one another: the Crow and the Sioux; some of the Cherokee don't like the Comanche. Well, my mother doesn't like Comanche, either, come to think about it. Those are old feuds and old times, but they cannot accept that any other tribe has anything of any value other than their own particular group. I think they kind of shortchange themselves a little bit.

My argument to the ones who say "Well, Cherokee shouldn't be doing Northwest Coast art" is: "Well, good grief, the whites do not fetter themselves with the idea that theirs is the only culture in the world. Why else would we send people off to Venice and to France and all the places where great art can be found in the world?" It enriches you and it makes you better when you do finally find your particular niche. I think I've done pretty much the same thing that the white people are doing all the time, only I didn't go to Venice, I went to the Northwest Coast because this was the richest, deepest art tradition in North America and a culture that has been very, very little exposed to the general public—or had been at the time I started. It is the *one* place in North America where you had artists working as commissioned artists with patrons, great chiefs, who came to them and commissioned them to produce works for display on the great occasions that they wanted to mark their life climaxes.

Here is this great wealth of tradition. One of the great traditions of

* Born in 1937 and a California Luiseño, Scholder is known for the breadth of his artistic styles and subjects.

humankind in the arts can be found on the Northwest Coast. The art authorities all over the world agree on *that* now, that it can stand with the works of the Egyptians or any other great culture. So I just chose that particular school of art, you might say. When you really get interested, there is no aspect of the art that is not touched by the culture, the language, the religion. Even things down to birthing babies and recipes. So many of these things are tied to rank and privilege and then back into the mythology. The wellspring of the art is the mythology. So it was a matter of becoming pretty thoroughly Kwakiutl between the ears. Learning to think the way they thought, their values and all. It still goes on, it is such a rich culture. You could mine it for a thousand years. Now the old people are disappearing so quickly that it is going to hamper a lot of the oncoming generation.

6 / Openings to New Worlds

W ell into the late nineteenth century, European and American exploration, the fur trade, and early mining, fishing, and lumbering brought waves of change and devastation to the aboriginal inhabitants of the Northwest Coast—but they were not overwhelmed and the destruction was not wholesale. The Indian peoples did more than just survive depopulation and cultural change: they participated in it by choosing among limited options, creatively responding to their circumstances. The result was a stunning renaissance in the ceremonial regalia and monumental statuary that has come to be known as Northwest Coast art. The art itself flourished as people struggled to claim or maintain rank and status, which stabilized the social order disrupted by depopulation and the new sources of wealth that trade with the newcomers promised.[1] Because performance of songs and dances was intimately connected to religion, and because the regalia was integral to those performances, the production of art was also part of a spiritual revival in the face of the rapidly changing world.

The bulwark that these cultural productions provided was not static and, like the people who created it, it changed. An elaboration of existing themes emerged with the introduction of new materials, from a new and relatively easy access to iron and other metals (some had been available in limited quantities before regular European and American contact) to new sources of pigments for paints to traded blankets, buttons, and beads. A growing demand among the new arrivals for Indian "curios" expanded the preexisting trade in artwork, and the producers of these goods did not hesitate to shape the work to the demands of their customers. The small argillite renditions of poles, houses, and pipes with figures (some of which ridiculed Europeans and Americans) are the most striking. Ceremonial regalia, too, found its way into the trade nexus. Sometimes it was offered for sale willingly, sometimes under varying degrees of duress and coercion. These peoples were not bowled over by the arrival of Europeans and Americans.

In the second half of the nineteenth century, though, the arrival of missionaries and the regional emergence of European American political systems that demanded extreme cultural change of Native peoples slowed the open artistic renaissance among the Indians of the Northwest Coast.[2] In 1884, Canada's missionaries and politicians conspired to amend the 1880 Indian Act to outlaw potlatches and other ceremonies on the grounds that they distracted Native peoples from the business of assimilation and, in the case of potlatches, drove them into poverty as they flagrantly "gave away" their material possessions. Less explicit, but no less damaging U.S. policies affected the Native peoples of the Northwest Coast Culture Area.*

Until 1921 revisions of Canada's Indian Act put teeth into the prohibitions, the Indians of the Northwest Coast sometimes modified practices to avoid persecution and at other times openly defied the Canadian laws and U.S. policies. In 1921, at the Doug Cranmer and Emma (née Bell) Cranmer marriage contract potlatch on Village Island among the Kwakiutl, Canadian officials seized hundreds of ritual objects and jailed a number of men and women for months at a time. Although the people won their release from prison, most of the objects went to Ottawa, though some filtered out into the hands of private collectors and museums.[3]

That repression drove the ceremonies deeper underground or into even less obvious forms such as church potluck dinners. Still, memory and func-

---

* Anthropologists and other social scientists define a culture area as a human ecosystem in which lifeways, demographics, and environment are roughly similar though tribal or band affiliation, language, and religion may vary significantly. This allows for broader generalizations, but also obscures important differences. The concept remains useful if its limitations are recognized.

tion persisted. By the 1940s, enforcement became sporadic once again, and then in 1951 the Canadian government reversed the ban. Although the First Peoples of British Columbia quickly restarted the open celebration of their rituals, more than a decade passed before direct calls for the repatriation of materials began. In 1963, James Sewid traveled to Ottawa to demand the return of items taken from various Kwakiutl families in the early 1920s. Progress was slow but finally, in 1973, Canadian officials agreed to return the "Potlatch Collection." They insisted it not go back to individual families but, instead, be put in a museum. Both sides reached a compromise. The families at Cape Mudge on Quadra Island and at Alert Bay near Campbell River on Vancouver Island, respectively, opened the Kwagiulth Museum and Cultural Centre (1979) and the U'mista Culture Centre (1980), at which Kwakiutl families store and display their property but are able to take them out for ceremonies.[4]

Don Smith arrived on the scene just as James Sewid embarked on this upswing of cultural politics. Jimmy saw in Don a skilled carver anxious to find some way to gain legitimacy and an opportunity to expand the very public political statement he and other Kwakiutl were making in British Columbia across national borders. This gave Jimmy a chance to establish what amounted to a Kwakiutl colonial outpost in the United States. No doubt, the serendipitous access to another carver afforded Jimmy new opportunities to fulfill social obligations required of a person of his rank and status. Still, the adoption, naming, and granting of rights and privileges to Don and his family did bring new obligations for the Sewids as well as the Lelooskas. Yet the two families embraced these new relations far beyond what any mercenary objectives or political aspirations required. They developed a deep friendship and respect for each other. Indeed, after the deaths of Jimmy Sewid and Don Smith, Sewid's daughters Dora Sewid-Cook and Daisy Sewid-Smith formally transferred the rights and privileges Don had held to Don's youngest brother, Tsungani Fearon "Smitty" Smith.* At that time, they once again declared that the Lelooska family was part of their extended clan, ignoring political boundaries and bloodlines.

As federal relationships with Native tribes and bands grew in impor-

* Tsungani is a Cherokee name.

tance during the twentieth century, scholars, politicians, activists, and tribal leaders have highlighted the differences between "reservation" and "urban" or nonreservation Indians. Likewise, with growing numbers of Native Americans living in cities and off reservation during the period, issues of racism rose to the fore in urban areas. As strategic and necessary as the separation may have been for political reasons, drawing distinctions between reservation and nonreservation Indians too sharply obscures important continuities and connections, as the Sewid-Lelooska alliance demonstrates. No matter where they were located, Native Americans sought dignity and self-worth through many channels. Don was no exception, but he was fortunate in the tremendous payoff. In the connection he made with Jimmy Sewid, all that Don had done in his life came together in what can only be understood as the transformative moment for him as an individual and as an artist.

CHIEF JAMES SEWID

Jimmy made it all right.

When I made the masks for Jimmy's family, that was when I felt, as the Hindus say, that I had paid my teacher's reward or price. To bring those masks back to the people made me feel good. I'll always be kind of proud of that. It started with X̱wix̱wis*, which was a stunning compliment from Jimmy Sewid.[5] That came to happen from the Kennedy era when the Bureau of Indian Affairs received funding for the Indian Arts and Crafts Board and they were sending out people to try to renew the arts of various Native groups in the United States. They sent out Ed Malin, and he had run into Jimmy years ago when he was an anthropology student. I went up to Alert Bay with him, and it was a fact-finding trip to see what was going on in Canada. Malin needed to find out what the Canadian government was doing in reviving the arts and crafts there to see if something could be done down here.[6]

So, went up and that was when I met Jimmy Sewid. For some reason Jimmy and I just totally hit it off. I mean, he talked and talked and he was

---

* Also spelled Kwikwis. The X̱wix̱wis mask is a transformation mask with the eagle of the undersea represented on its outermost mask and a sea hawk on the inner mask with a sun enhanced by a concertina-like attachment to represent the sun's rays.

busy—they were trying to get their coasthouse done and all. But he just spent so much time and invited us up to the house. He was talking about how he grew up and his grandfather, and I told him about my grandfather. The way Jimmy had grown up and the way I grew up—we're so similar in so many respects. It was just like I was talking to a brother, a close kin of some kind. Just like a feeling of going home or déjà vu, the whole thing.

They had just finished the big house at Alert Bay. Jimmy had been responsible for the building of that along with Old Me-Cha—Herbert Martin, Jimmy's uncle and Mungo's youngest brother. Three brothers: Mungo* was the middle; Spruce was the eldest; and then Herbert, or Me-Cha as we call him, was the youngest. Last Hamatsa initiated in the old way, a living library. He and Smitty just hit it off. Smitty looked after him many times and kept him from falling in with his bad companions so he would be in good shape to dance. Interesting fellow, spoke English with a strong Kwakiutl accent. Plus he stuttered, which made it a real experience to understand him, but Smitty never seemed to have any problems.

We went up there; the house had just been finished and, my God, there is this house seventy feet long, twenty-four feet to the ridge, fifty feet wide, whew![7] And Jimmy Sewid, everything that a chief should be, hospitable, dignified, just like meeting a relative. Shook hands with them and then, surprised the heck out of me, he hugged me just like a big old bear! He had seen a lot of pictures of my work that Ed Malin had taken up there when he had been on a trip a little before, and they gave us every courtesy and attention. We got to see that first potlatch, I think it was Chief Knox's initiation of his son as a Hamatsa.[8] So this was Boas's social organization and secret societies, the great work on the subject done in 1897, and here it was alive and kicking.[9] A lot of writers said this was all entirely moribund and the whole culture has decayed away. Not so. All they needed was the law off their back and some encouragement, and they were all ready to go again.

Well, came back, just couldn't even sleep, thinking about it. My mind is just whirling, the images and thoughts and ideas—and questions, questions, questions. Not too long after that, we got a call and Jimmy wanted to come

* Mungo Martin (1881–1962) was a key figure linking nineteenth-century Northwest Coast artists to those of the twentieth century.

down, visit. Jimminy Christmas, I mean, if the President had called, I wouldn't have been any more astounded or pleased. Jimmy said he wanted to come down, that he wanted to talk to me, he needed to talk to me. He had never been out of Canada to that point.

We had an opening mask we used for our little school things, that Bella Coola* Eagle opening mask. Again, I felt that was a reach when I did that one. That was a copy of an old mask, which is good for a student to do, but you really haven't achieved your stature until you're able to work within the discipline of the art—the thing that makes it what it is—and create new works *within* the art traditions without having these little bastardizations creep in on you. Technically, I think that mask was a reach for me at the time.

So when he came to visit us, Jimmy saw Smitty use it. He was very impressed with that and Smitty. That was when he commissioned the mask for the Redeeming Feast, their big potlatch, to acknowledge his fortieth anniversary, which was a signal honor.[10] Actually, they usually had the Redeeming Feast about seven years after the marriage, but the Potlatch Laws originally stood between Jimmy and that ceremony. With the law out of the way, then, Jimmy wanted to do this. It was an honor for me to have Jimmy commission the mask. Although I was delighted, it also scared the poochies out of me because I didn't know whether I was going to pull this off or not!

Now, in some cases it was obligatory that you commission an outsider. With the Kwakiutl, it is kind of shaded over. Good carvers have grown more and more hard to get. I know when Jimmy was initiated Hamatsa, his [paternal] grandfather, Aul Sewid, went to Willie Seaweed, who is another one of Jimmy's uncles. In fact, he was the one Jimmy was to be apprenticed to as a carver at one point in his life. So they were already at that time going to members. But, of course, he belonged to another tribe on one side. It is more strict among the Haida and the Tlingit. A Raven never carves for a Raven. You have to go to one of the Eagles or Wolves, as they call them in the southern Tlingit country.[11] So you always reach outside the clan. It's

* Bella Coola, or Nuxalk, are closely related to the Kwakiutl in cultural practices and live just to the north of them near Burke Channel.

just like any funeral arrangements. The traditional funerals were all arranged by the opposites and that was obligatory.

Turned out the reason he came down was he wanted to commission me in the old, formal way to make a mask of X̱wix̱wis for the Redeeming Feast. So I said, "Yes, I'd be delighted to do it." I didn't feel worthy to do it, so I told him, "Please forgive whatever I do, because it will have been my best for you." I just felt totally inadequate to have such an honor, to be picked. They've got carvers all over the place up there.

So I made the mask. Took it up in secret. Utilitarian things were always around to be seen, but masks were usually hidden. The Kwakiutl put them in those big caves. The place is full of caves, those old village sites. There were some islands that had caves in them. A lot of ceremonial regalia as well as bodies were placed out there and hidden. Every so often they turn up something at the University of British Columbia—a moldering old box with a bunch of stuff in it. But they kept them pretty secret. When you take a mask up there, you go very quietly. Nobody sees it until they lock the door and pull the shades! The family gets to see it first. So it is all a big surprise when they use it. This is good theatrics, and they certainly are the most theatrical of any of America's Native people.

So we snuck X̱wix̱wis into the house. They were preparing a costume, a suit of coveralls coated with glue that had eagle down stomped into it; very effective suit to go with it. Showed them how it worked. I put it on Smitty because we had one we used in the school program here at Ariel, and I had him show Jimmy how that one worked and thought something similar to that would be just exactly what they wanted. They were pleased with the mask.

The potlatch came on and here was all the family and it was just great. There was just no describing it, really. I mean, if you take your best fantasy about something and then have somebody make it about five times better than that and all, why, I just couldn't believe it. Came time for the dances; they usually have the Hamatsa first, then they have the Tła'sala Dances in the later part of the evening.[12] In the old days they were two separate dance complexes, but now they're usually done together.

Well, Smitty had been kind of sitting there beside me, and he disappeared. I didn't know where he went and I thought, "Oh, gee whiz, where the heck did he go? Maybe he went to the rest room or something. He's going to miss seeing the mask." They're all sitting there grinning and then, you know, you have this feeling something is going on, but you're not sure what. They have their Tła'sala Dance, that is the dance with the big ermine headdress and the frontlet, and they tease the dancer. The dancer goes out and then you hear this noise, a whistle. It is outside the door of the house, then they open it up and they clown around like they do with the Tła'sala. They're holding up the blankets as the thing is coming into the house, and I can see the yellow top of the beak up above the blankets. I said to myself, "There's X̱wix̱wis. Smitty's missed the whole thing." And they bring him into the house and I looked at the feet and then I knew: "That's Smitty!" Smitty has these kind of distinctive, teddy-bear feet. And lo and behold, my little brother is out there. This house is full of 750 very Kwakiutl Kwakiutls, all the old chiefs, everybody. This is the mask and now it is my brother who is involved. I keep thinking about what happened in the old days. When things failed you're expected to commit suicide or they killed you by witchcraft! I keep saying: "Well now, look, this is a whole other era!"

He comes in and he makes this nice turn and then he pauses and he makes a turn. You're supposed to go sunwise around the fire. And I think, "*Oh my God,* he's going to go the wrong way." And no, he turned around. Old Herbert Martin's helping him. Apparently somebody had pushed the mask down and he couldn't see out of it. Old Herbert kind of got him started around and he got his bearings from the light of the fire. Went around, popped it open. Bingo, worked great. Turned around, closed it, *bang.* Worked fine. Back behind the screen very quickly, little Herbert and all the gang. Smitty had been blind as a bat through most of it. *"Sheew!"*

So then Jimmy got up and he threw the blanket over his shoulder that I had given him when he came down. (When you go visit somebody, why, they usually give you gifts, so I gave him a Pendleton striped blanket.) Anyway, threw it over his shoulder and started this speech and it was in Kwákw'ala. My Kwákw'ala at that time was pretty skinny. But then I heard him mention my name, and then he mentioned Ariel, Washington, X̱wix̱wis, the words for carver, and on and on. The family are all smiling and grinning and going on. He made a long speech about what we're doing down here and how important it was that people should know about Kwakiutl culture so that never again would the government undertake to forbid them their potlatches, break up their potlatches, and seize their regalia and treasures from them. That it was important that people should know, and we were the ones who were going to tell the story; that was when the adoptions began, at that point.

It was just one of the great moments of my life, really. No way could I have anticipated it. And then when it was all over, you wanted to ask somebody: "Did that really happen? Gee, did that really happen?" X̱wix̱wis was like the Chief Joseph doll in spades!

In the nineteenth century, the Kwakiutl were dropping from some 10,000 down to probably 1,000, maybe 900. This left a great many ceremonial positions unfilled, and it was kind of like knocking cogs out of a wheel in the potlatch process. So they were having to adopt people into these positions from other families and from other groups, just to keep the seats filled.[13] Several old Kwakiutl have told me that. Adoption was a legitimate way of doing this, but you don't do it like you do with politicians, where you stick a little feather hat on their head and give them a ridiculous name and get your picture in the paper. Jimmy's potlatch—he expended probably $10,000 on Patty and my names.* You know there was a *lot* of *desire* there to accomplish this. When he announced the names, I didn't even know it was coming. I still can't believe that it ever happened, but it was *very* expensive to make it right in the old way, and boy, Jimmy was generous with that. He had the bucks to do it, but still, I mean, good grief, how many people would do that?

It felt like I was coming home. Everybody was so great. They knew this *awful* hunger that I had, to *know*. That the books were inadequate and in some cases inaccurate. They did everything they possibly could to help. Of course, when you become part of a lineage and you become a member of the family in the old way, they distribute great amounts of property and money to make this good—why, then immediately, their enemies become your enemies. So that was when we got some of our most devoted enemies. Which, in a way, kind of made me proud, too, because a man is as

* Protocol demands that gifts be distributed for such activities at a level commensurate with the rank intended. Giving valuable gifts or large sums of money indicates the intention to bestow a high rank. Don and Patty were adopted first because they were older; other Lelooska family members were adopted later.

much judged by his enemies as by his friends! It was a fabulous experience! There is just no way of ever describing it.

Up to that point, I had been experimenting and making Northwest Coast pieces for maybe ten years or so. Always I knew with the things that these were hereditary privileges and there was a place beyond which I felt I had no right to go. For instance, we never would've developed a program using the actual dances, the actual songs, the myths, and all of it keyed on one great inheritance of a lineage. All you could do would be just very minor vignettes or demonstrations of pieces. There wasn't that real feeling of participating or knowing that it was correct in every way possible. Well, Jimmy fixed that without ever having discussed it or anything. Jimmy made it all right. He instinctively knew why I was reticent about some things. He thought he would take care of that and they would have a carver in the family and it would take care of the whole thing—my problems, their problems—which is what families are for. It just opened up so *many* things and really just was a great validation of the direction I wanted to go, but was very hesitant to go there because that was a privilege, something that belonged to the people and that they had prized *so* much.

A lot of anthropologists would say, "Well, it doesn't make any difference now, the culture is totally gone." I could not believe that. It might have gone underground, but I always knew there was a lot more there than a lot of people credited. I know a guy down at one university had a big argument with a friend of mine, saying, "There's nothing going on up there. The culture is totally dead." The guy is supposed to be an authority. So by that time, Jerry Levy and his wife, who is a Hopi, had been up to a potlatch, so they knew doggone well that when you spend tens of thousands of dollars, you're not kidding. I mean, this isn't tourist stuff. This is a very powerful family force of pride, honor, and tradition there. Boy, I'll tell you, it was a great, great moment, and it just went on and on and on, got better and better and better.

POTLATCH POLITICS

Everything gets paid for.

When he was talking to me, Don knew the tape recorder was running. He knew he was speaking to me, the family friend–become-historian, and he was also addressing a much wider audience. He tried through his narrative and stories to explain his understanding of the depths of privileges Jimmy Sewid had granted him.

Everything gets paid for in the old society. I really saw it with the big potlatch because Jimmy was very, very generous. He had all of these traditional potlatch debts, which were repaid without ever having being asked when the big potlatch came. I mean, he was up to his ears in eulachon grease, dried eulachon, smoked moose meat, dried halibut, and just all sorts of good stuff—herring eggs and the seaweed like they use in making the soups and stuff. He was just traditional.[14] Foods and things just poured in, and that was showing respect and it was also repayment. A lot of gifts at potlatches are not outright gifts. They're repayments.

It all had to be done *just* so and everybody had to get *just* what they were supposed to get. They kept their debts very straight in the old days. They used notched sticks or strings with knots tied in them to remember their debts. They taught young men early on to learn to remember all of their debts and all of their obligations. As soon as writing came in, why, then the chief always had his scribe at his side. He had these old ledgers and in them he had who had given what at what potlatch and when. They had all the names in order of rank. There was an awful lot of protocol and if you goofed, then that cost you even more because you had to give away property to wipe away the memory of this faux pas. It gets very, very complicated. A lot of this now has fallen off.

Part of what potlatching does, if your family has a little faux pas that they want forgotten, you give a feast and you give presents. If the guests accept the presents, it is kind of unspoken that they know why this is being done and their mouths are closed. If not, they're disgracing themselves. That was very common. I remember one of my early trips up there, I was sitting where the ferry docks. There was a bench there where usually some of the old guys were hanging out. It had a nice view out across the straits. This young fellow came and sat down. Well, he wasn't all that young, he was probably thirty-five or forty. He had come in, I guess, couple of days before. I hadn't seen him around Alert Bay.

I look over and I say, "Hi," and smile.

He looked back. He didn't say anything.

I said something about something that was going on and I looked over.

He looks at me right square in the eye and he says, pointing to his face, "You see this?" Boy, he had a big long scar there. Hadn't been sewed up apparently. Really a big weal of a scar.

I say, "Yes."

He says, "That cost my family a *lot* of money."

I said, "I know what you mean. No one should say anything about that. I don't see it."

"Well," he says, "you must been around here long time! Cost a *lot* of money!"

Jimmy was just a boy when they broke up the big [1921 Cranmer-Bell] potlatch. They had them all locked up in the schoolhouse and Jimmy was looking in through the window, kind of standing on his tiptoes. A mounted police sergeant or constable kicked Jimmy, ran him away. Jimmy was just trying to see what had happened to his relatives. He was a really worried little boy. Then at Jimmy's funeral, the Mounties in their red coats standing there in that heat *sweating* in those *red wool* tunics and directing traffic. Here was the Premier, Vice-Premier, all the bigwigs of British Columbia turned out, and the celebrities. I just thought to myself, "Jimmy, you've come a long way. I wish you could see this." And then I thought, "Well, I think he does."

Jimmy used to talk about when he was a little boy. Kids will play and get into fights and things. Well, his family would never permit him to fight back. If a kid insulted him or something, why, he couldn't fight back because if he hit the kid, then his parents could come to them, like suing is now, and demand indemnity because he was from a noble family. So he was to just turn around and walk away. It must have been very difficult because I know from my own experience there are people you just cannot walk away from in this life. But the nobility were expected not to do things like that.

There were an awful lot of things placed on noble children; responsibilities that they had to uphold. Must've been really, really tough. The higher your rank, if you were the eldest heir to the position that your father held, why, that really put you in a hard place. They wanted to raise Jimmy traditionally and they weren't going to let him go off to the white man's school because they beat the kids in school, and his family wasn't about to have the future chief of the lineage struck by a white schoolteacher. So Jimmy ran away and lived with his grandmother Lucy and got his three years of education in defiance of his uncles.[15]

See, Jimmy's father was killed just about the day he was born. A tree fell on him and crushed him. His uncles kind of took over Jimmy's upbringing. The three uncles kind of got together around Jimmy because they feared Aul Sewid, Jimmy's grandfather. He was a strong chief, and in his younger days had really been a terror as far as exercising chiefly privileges and things like that. They were afraid that he would brush Jimmy aside and usurp all of Jimmy's positions, names, and rights and take them unto himself.

They took Jimmy down into the street in Alert Bay. They called all of the people; they took the biggest copper* they had between the three chiefs and laid it down on the ground, and then they took Jimmy and laid him, the little baby, down on top of the copper. Then they took the Gikumps— the little Tsonoquah mask, the little glossy black and red one with the human hair, the chief's mask and only a few chiefs can own or use that—and they put it over the baby's face, then they all stood up in line and together they said, "This child, we will protect him until he can protect himself." That was a flat-out warning that if Aul Sewid moved, the three of them would use all of their wealth and prestige to maintain the rights of the baby. So that was how Jimmy managed to keep his rights in the face of a changing society and a very, very powerful grandfather. I would've loved to have seen that. That must have been a really dramatic moment. Tells you a lot about Aul Sewid, because it took three big chiefs to stand up to him. Jimmy, too, had lots of enemies he made politically when he was elected chief councilor and did a lot of things that made a lot of people jealous—and, of course, there are always your traditional rivals.

MORE LESSONS

It depends on how you're raised.

Having stepped through the door Jimmy Sewid opened for him, Don did not stop his relentless quest for greater understanding of the many peoples

---

* Coppers, shieldlike copper plates sometimes several feet high and with a T-shaped ridge dividing them into three sections, represent wealth and status.

of the Northwest Coast. As in his childhood, Don continued to ask astute questions, listen, and learn.

The first trip I took up there was in the mid- to late 1960s. I went up with Ed Malin, the government guy who had known Jimmy when he was a student. Just after the war, he had been up there and met Jimmy, been to Alert Bay and some of the other places, and purchased some stuff that he later resold to the Denver Art Museum. A lot of the pieces he collected were in there.[16] He was working for the Indian Arts and Crafts Board, and the Makah trips had been successful and all. So when he heard about the completion of their big house up there, he got the government's permission to go and to take me along.

Every time we would go up there, we would take the little ferry that started near the Seymour Narrows—used to be Ripple Rock there. It was a menace to navigation; they blew it out years ago. They called it the Death Hole because sitting on it were the Lekwiltok tribe. They were renowned for their piratical activities, and if you didn't pay a toll, boy, you could expect to be attacked. They were in a perfect spot to really squeeze the people who were passing back and forth, and there was ever-increasing traffic because a lot of the tribes were trying to get down to Vancouver and Victoria to work in the mills and things like that.[17] Just north of there is the little place they would take off from and it was six hours, *clunka, clunka, clunka, clunka, clunka,* on this ferry. There was asphalt that they had blown in with a kind of plaster mixed with it that would fall down from the overhead into your soup when you're eating or it would fall in your hair! A lot of the seats had been taken from old British planes, old military transport kind of seats.

Sitting on that ferry was kind of like sitting in a church hall or something. You have a lot of people there and you're stuck for six hours. There was no TV or anything on the *Island Princess.* And the poor little thing would go along and you would hear it go *boom, boom, boom* when they would run into the drift logs in the Inside Passage. You could just hear them banging down the side, *boom, boom, boom.* The cook was a one-eyed Chinese who looked like something out of some pirate movie. He could cook. Man, could he cook. He would feed everybody in the little cafeteria down there. Never forgot an order. Sounded like somebody out of a Charlie Chan movie. It was his accent. *Almost* seemed put on, it was so perfectly out of a movie or something! But boy, could he cook. And he wasn't terribly courteous to anybody who was not courteous to him. He was a real genuine character.

But then, after about everybody had been fed and all, they just kind of sit down in these little groups and the old people would get to talking. They would pass a certain point and then they would start in:

> Oh, yeah, my great-grandfather told me he came by there going fishing and he saw the stern of this big canoe sticking up out of the brush. He looked a little more and he could see two or three big canoes had been hauled up. It took a lot of people to haul up a big fifty-foot northern canoe. So, boy, he headed right quick back because it was the Haida* and he'd discovered them and they had beached, hauled up to rest and get out of sight and travel when fog would be in or it would be dark.

Things like that. You look out the windows of the ferry and you can almost see the canoes sheltered in the brush there waiting to go down and beat up on some of the Salish.

We were up on the Skeena River some years ago. It was 1967, the year they had the Arts of the Raven.[18] It was the Canadian centennial. We went on up from the potlatch at Alert Bay to Prince Rupert and then we drove inland through all the Tsimshian villages. That was a wonderful trip. It was spring—late May, early June—and the ice was coming down the river and the river was getting close to the flood stage. There were these big trees with roots and stuff coming down. Well, around the bend in the Skeena comes this big shape, absolutely perfect image of a big canoe with a bunch of people in it. It comes around the curve of the river and it was so perfect: the paddles and the people who were in it. The shape of those big northern canoes is just so striking in itself. I saw that thing. It got closer and closer and then, all of a sudden, it changes and it was this big log that was coming down and the roots are sticking up and all. It created this image of the canoe. That is what the non-Indian interpretation is; this is an optical illu-

---

* The Haida conducted occasional raids into Kwakiutl, Nu-chah-nulth, and Coast Salish territories for the capture of slaves and plunder.

sion. If you're a Tsimshian, why then, you realize that it was a canoe full of ghosts because the smallpox came there and swept lot of those villages into oblivion in just a few weeks.*

So I could look at it in two different ways. I saw a canoeload of ghosts from the time of the epidemics, which is what the people would've interpreted. The other one was that it was an optical illusion, but it was certainly a *striking* one. How much the illusion was influenced by the fact that those big canoes were common on that river and, in fact, we were standing on what was an old village site at that time, I don't know. The big white pieces of ice were coming down in the current. That was a striking one. Things like that happen and it depends on how you're raised. I can kind of go back and forth between the two. I'm more comfortable in the traditional interpretations, even sometimes if their portents are unpleasant, than I am with just the cold, unvarnished, supposed facts. . . . It is so easy to pooh-pooh things.

On those ferry rides, listening to the old people, it was just that feeling not unlike being in a big house or something and everybody was there. They're talking and laughing and remembering. The old people were traveling and seeing the various places along the way. Old Beaver Cove was one that seemed to spark the memories of the old people, and they would talk about when the Hudson's Bay Company ship *The Beaver,* the first steamer on the coast, would come in there. They would point out there, they would say, "They would anchor right there." They talked about Aemilius Simpson, who was a cousin of *the* Simpson, the Lord of the company, how he always wore white gloves.[19] They would sing their song. They had a song they made for him to coax him out, because then he was obligated to give them molasses and ship's bread or something as a little present. Sometimes he took charge of the trading, because they had confidence in him. So they would either come up in their canoes beside the thing or sometimes they would warp *The Beaver* right up against the rocks—it is very deep there—and put a gangplank across or they would just throw the sea otter skins, beaver pelts, and stuff over. Port Simpson [near Prince Rupert], I guess, they finally named after him.

* Smallpox was the greatest killer of Native Americans in the region, sweeping through in periodic epidemics that killed as much as 30 to 40 percent of the population at any given time.

I was sitting there next to one old guy, one old Kwakiutl chief, turned out to be one of Jimmy's uncles. With a lot of people I'm meeting, eventually you bring up Jimmy Sewid, why, they would say, "Oh yes, his father and my father were brothers," or some such thing. And you begin to see these elaborate things come together. Made it very real. But this one old guy was telling me about a Kwakiutl chief who was so taken with *The Beaver* that he took one of his big canoes and he had these wooden things built on either side, looked like paddle wheels. He decked it over with canvas and boards, put a bridge on it, fixed the thing so it would smoke, and concealed the paddlers so it was a kind of an imitation of this big white man's ship!

Again, I got to know another of Jimmy's uncles pretty well on trips up there on the ferry; we're talking about the big houses, told him about our little one. He said, "Well, in our house we had two big house posts, slaves holding up coppers and the other end were wolves, head down and coppers in their teeth—Tsawataineuk [also spelled Tswatainuk] tribe. Someday, when you build another house, I give you permission to put those in your house." That was how we got the ones picked for the second house. Well, clearly we needed a bigger one. And by that time things were beginning to fall into place. Things just sort of clicked along.

On the ferry was where you had a lot of people sometimes from fairly *remote* villages, bored for six hours and their memories are all coming out. It was just a matter of kind of priming the pump and sitting back and listening. Yeah, met a lot of interesting people. Sometimes there would be people there from the west coast of Vancouver Island who were coming up because they had relatives or were just interested in what the Kwakiutl were doing. There might be some Nootkas there from different places, and then there was the year the Métis came up for the conference.

That was really interesting. They had a big meeting up there. There had been a schism between the the Métis and the tribes. The Métis resented that they didn't get any land and the full-bloods got the land, the reserves, and the Métis were just totally left out. They sort of blamed their cousins for that, along with the government. There had been a schism between the two for a long time, so they were thinking of trying to heal the breach and talk about everybody uniting. That they were all really relatives and should be friends and they had *common* interests in the resources and all. It was sort of the put-the-cork-back-in-the-jug-and-get-down-to-business meeting.

They were, to say the very least, a very, very *colorful* group! It was interesting to see them in their sashes and hear the way they talk and the *warmth* of them. Just a wonderful joie de vivre—they just loved life—singing, and they had the fiddles along and all!

The cork did not quite get put back in the bottle, but they're getting along much better now. A lot of the Métis are associated with the very minor terrorisms that have taken place.[20] That appealed to some of the younger, angrier Métis people. Jimmy felt that violence and demonstrations and things were, really, in the long run, very, very counterproductive. He was against that.

We happened to be going up; I went to sit in on a lot of the sessions of the conference and got to talking to a lot of the old guys and learning a lot. One old guy sitting there was talking about the French, the Indians, and I say, "Yes, yes, we have a Frenchman back in our family, too."

He says, "You have French blood and Indian blood?"

I say, "Yes."

"You are Métis. Oh, my friend! I salute you." You know, kiss you on both cheeks. You're standing there looking like an idiot! I certainly admire them and like them.

NAMES

A metaphor kind of thing.

I was curious about how Don saw himself, and thought that asking him about the names, aside from Lelooska, that he had acquired over the years might provide some insights. Determining the meaning of names is a tricky business. Names do have power over people but, given the contemporary popular fascination with mysticism and ubiquitous stereotypes about Native Americans, the unilateral adoption and display of "Indian" names by some trivializes the whole affair. What names mean thus offers only a partial explanation, which must be viewed alongside how the names were acquired, understood, and employed. In Don's case, these fell into three categories.

The first were those names given with the purposes of connecting to specific cultural traditions within the family. Many families employ this strategy and simultaneously honor the past while hoping to impart the favorable implications of the name on the individual for the future. For Don the leading force in this naming was, not surprisingly, his grandfather Enoch Hinkle.

In the second category were those names various individuals conferred on Don. Such names not only honored him, but also placed him in the familiar cultural patterns of the individuals bestowing the names. These were the equivalent of mnemonic shorthands that conjured up not only an image of Don, but also the context in which people knew him. In some instances, namings of this sort are exactly the type that too many people publicly display as their claim to an "Indian" identity or an affiliation with a romantic and mystical "Indian-ness" common among those who uncritically engage New Age philosophies. In spite of his penchant for public performances, Don was uncomfortable with such unilateral appropriations, and he did not flaunt these names in public to make himself appear more authentic.

Formal, public bestowal of names within tribal contexts constituted the third category. These names were of a vastly different order from those acquired through informal means. In these formal, public contexts, the granting of names by ranking individuals had important political as well as cultural meanings. When Jimmy Sewid gave Don and his family names, Sewid recognized Don's achievements and at the same time made certain that important names remained within his clan, for their possession potentially provides a means to assert political and cultural pressure. Don's friendship with Jimmy, cemented as it was by mutual obligations, meant that Don did not try to exercise the power of the names other than to support Jimmy by simply keeping them within the family. For Don, however, the names offered him a way to be "of" the Kwakiutl. They gave him and his family cultural connections that Don understood intellectually and emotionally. In a sense, they provided the same kinds of links to a family past as the name his grandfather had bestowed upon him.

The moniker Lelooska was akin to the Kwakiutl names. As Don recounts in chapter 4, "Learning from People," that name came to him in a public ceremony and gave him the ability to define himself in new ways (see "The Round-Up"). It fit who he was and who he became. Pride, force of habit, and the appropriateness of the name meaning "he who cuts shavings off a stick of wood with a knife" led to its lifelong use.

For the most part, Don had always been quiet about the many other names he had acquired over the years. I asked him about names, hoping to get them down on tape and then paper. Aside from the personal insights, I believed they might provide evidence of his many associations over the years. He openly spoke about some and successfully avoided discussing others.

I've had lots of names from different people. Someday, when I'm through this, I should write them down because I would like to keep them in the family. The-Man-with-the-Belt is my Warm Springs name, from that big concho belt I used to wear all the time up there. My baby name, *Yana,* was from my grandfather. It means "the bear," and of course to the Cherokees, Bears are the wisest and oldest of the animal people. In the beginning, bears are big with most all tribes. When I was born, I was the first. . . . I gave it to my nephew Jay. I have a special responsibility to him because the maternal uncle, among my grandfather's people, is really more obligated to shape the character and the future, if he can, for the nephew than the father. But Yana means "the bear." Now, whether or not the first birth certificate I think Grandpa had seen, with the footprint on it, had something to do with that or not, I don't know. I've always thought he thought it must have looked like a bear track. He thought that was the most ridiculous thing in the world, that piece of paper to prove you were born. My God, the fact that you were standing there should indicate that you *had* been!

Among the Kwakiutl, two are the most important. Gekun,* which comes from the Ma'amtagila, means "Chief of Chiefs." It is really a ridiculously grandiose name. My potlatch name is A Bembis Gyikima'i, which means "Mother of Chiefs." Now this is a strange concept. Here is a man whose name is Mother of Chiefs. Kwakiutl are very fond of this kind of metaphor concept of naming and songs and things. So what it means is that this chief, through his wealth and his power, is like a mother to the other chiefs. They're like little children and they come to him and he feeds them. That is, he has wealth, which he pours out in potlatching. So they're like little children in his hands. That came from Jimmy's uncle Nagedzi, "Great Mountain." He was big, like some big old gnarled stump. He came from Kingcome Inlet,

---

* Gekun, also spelled "Gyik'in," was James Sewid's grandfather.

from the Tsawataineuk tribe, and he was the song maker, the oldest man in the Kwakiutl nation at the time he died. Had that wonderful singing voice.

Another important person to me has been another of Jimmy's uncles, Jim King—Kwagi'la or Tłakwagi'la, "Coppermaker," a name from the Seamonster's house. Yeah, we've been working on the Seamonster Dance and researching it for years. I found out all the copper names come from the house of 'Kumugwi, the Lord of the Undersea World, and one of the names is 'Kumugwi, Coppermaker. "Precious-As-Copper," Tlakwastililumga, is Patty's name. That is from one of the wives of 'Kumugwi. Smitty's name, Qa7axtal'es, means "Inviting into the House Early in the Morning," the young noble who is so anxious to share the wealth that he is out there in the morning getting people to come into his house, greeting them. It is a big name. Dick's name is Kwenxwadzi, "Big Thunder." Susan, his wife, has the name Kwenxwelugwa or "Little Thunder."

Smitty's daughter Mariah has one of the very, very powerful names, Ts'eikami, the ancestor's wife's name—"Supernatural-Power-Woman."* They gave that first out of respect to my grandmother Lady Elizabeth Hinkle, who they just loved. When she passed on, they decided that Mariah should have it, because in a way, the older people really felt that Grandma and Mariah are the same. You see, she passed, then Mariah came. Well, the night of the baby shower for Mariah there was this little saw-whet owl outside the place. When they told me about that, I kind of worried because owls sometimes have to do with ghosts hanging around in hopes of getting a soul or getting a body and coming back. Sometimes, they also say, I learned later, the owl is a relative who so loved the family that it didn't want to leave and it is just waiting for a free ride back into the human race by being reborn. So we talked about that.

Old Granny Ack-koo†—boy, you want to get into something *deep,* why, she was the one to talk to; she was the one who taught Jimmy's daughters, Daisy and Dora, and she was the reason that they are who they are. Anyway, we talked about it. "No, nothing to worry about," she said, "nothing to worry about. It's as much good as bad, so let's just see." Well, Mariah came into the world. Her eyes were that blue—Grandma had those eyes:

---

* Supernatural-Power-Woman is also known as Ts'igilhilaqu.

† Agnes Alfred, James Sewid's mother-in-law.

sometimes they were like glacier ice and sometimes they were like wildflowers. I love those eyes. Grandma had a way of putting her hand on her hip when she was about to exert herself, which was *very* often. The Sewid family knew Grandma, and respected and loved her. That was why they gave Mariah that name in the first place.

So we were up there at Cape Mudge, I forget what the big occasion was, and we were talking and just kind of dancing informally; Patty was going to do the Thunder Dance. She was going around showing them how the Thunder Dance went and Mariah wanted to dance, so she was out there. She is going along behind, and Patty is not moving ahead fast enough, so Mariah tried to bite her! She was about two, three years old. They thought that was funny. It just cracked the whole place up. Then Mariah turned around and she was peeved. She thought she was being laughed at or something. She put her hand on her hip, and she looked *right* at us. I was sitting by Granny Ack-koo. Granny turns around to look at me and she points with her finger, and I knew what she meant—Grandma was the owl and she is back! Granny Ack-koo just stuck her finger and pointed. "Just you wait" is what she told me—hand on the hip, the eyes—"we'll see!"

We put on a "play" potlatch, too. Well, it was fun. We had mostly Indians, but we had non-Indians participating in that, too. We were all trying to outdo ourselves. They gave me a name, and translated into English, I suppose it would've meant "Wobbly Ankles!" You know, this is the guy who is always worrying about everything that is about to happen. I am a worrybudget: "Oh boy, now what's going to happen? My God! My God!" Wobbly Ankles! It is kind of like "Knock it off, chill out!" But those are fun names. It stuck with old Willie Seaweed, Kwaxitola ("Smoky-Top"), Jimmy's uncle. He was a much beloved person and, I think, their greatest artist of this century.[21]

Names are very, very, very important. Mom has the same name that Julia, Smitty's wife, does, but they're from two different lineages. Mom's name is Tl'alilhilugwa. Julia's is Tl'axtl'elidzemga. They mean the same thing, "A Whale Is Rising." A whale is kind of a metaphor for a noble lady and a noble lady is also a sort of a metaphor for a whale. The nickname for the whales, the noble ladies, comes from the days when they were hunted by some of the Kwakiutl tribes. Among the Nootka and some of those tribes around the end of Vancouver Island, when they went out whaling, the wife of the harpooner or the whaler chief had to lie very quietly in bed, wouldn't move all day. She was to think calm, calm thoughts. That was so when he harpooned the whale, it would be docile. There *are* stories about women who didn't like their husbands very much; a wife like this would lie there, wait and wait and wait until she thought that her husband was harpooning the whale, because she was supposed to be able to sense this. Then she would jump up and flap her arms and kick her feet in the air, throw herself on the floor and do all kinds of things. Sometimes he got his canoe busted or he was drowned or killed! There are stories like that.

But there are few of the Kwakiutl who did take whales. Of course, the whale they preferred was the gray whale, which is a very docile whale. The finback was a fighter and the humpback was also a fighter. The gray whales were pretty easily taken. But there was this connection between wealth and whales because of the whale oil and all of the things that came from the whale; the prestige and the honor and all that are bound up in it. So a lot of noble women's names are "Whale-is-rising" or "This-is-the-whale-coming-up-it's-going-to-spout-and-reveal-itself-and-give-itself-to-the-whaler," because you can't kill them unless they're willing, and then there are a whole lot of things you do to apologize and welcome the whale. The Nootka and the Kwakiutl are bound together by language in that they're both Wakashan-speaking, and they're also bound together by marriages: Flora Alfred, Jimmy's wife, is from Maquinna lineage over on the Westcoast.[22] So there is lots of whale stuff that goes on, but it has to do with the female nobility very, very often. It is this nickname, a metaphor kind of thing.

Well, in the old days when you received an ancestor's name, you *are* that ancestor alive again. This is very, very true of chiefs' names and the great names of families. Jay's name is that of the Strong Man, as some people call him. Now, Stone Body was sired by a man with Tsonoquah. Stone Body's father said to his wife, "Well, Tsonoquah came to me in a dream—I thought it was a dream but, really, I was under a spell." A half-supernatural baby is the result. Stone Body's father says to his wife, "Not to worry." He chanced at that time to catch a Sisiutl, a Lightning Serpent, in his fish trap.[23] He bathed this half-supernatural baby in the blood of the Sisiutl and it made his body hard like stone. Sound familiar? It is this parallel in mythology you find all over the world. And there was one place, a spot on the chest, where the baby had thrown up a little bit so there was some dirt there from that and the blood didn't soak in there. In the final chapter of the epic, Stone Body is killed by a wound in that spot. Before that, though, he traveled all around the world and took princesses and wealth from all the tribes. Brought them back and gave them to his brothers—the three lineages that were founded by the three sons of Kulus.* So he brought it back and he just gave the wealth to his brothers. Well, they gave my nephew Jay that name because he is a big, strong guy and always seems a little formidable when you first look at him. They thought that was the name he should have. It, too, is another very honorable, powerful name from the lineage.

Then usually people have their Winter Dance names that are only used during the Tseka [Winter Dance]. If you use their name at the wrong time of the year, you could get yourself in trouble. They have *endless* nicknames that you find out, like Jimmy's uncle, old Herbert Martin, who was the youngest of the three brothers, the last one initiated in the old Hamatsa way; they went and stole the corpse, the mummified body, out of the grave box and they used that in Herbert's initiation as Hamatsa. They call him Me-cha. It sort of means "bashful," the way it has been translated to me. According to Jimmy's other uncles, this was a good nickname for him because he was the opposite, he was a *lover.* I mean, he liked ladies *a lot.* He had a lot of girlfriends. When he was eighty years old, I mean, he still liked ladies. He had this thing he would do with pretty ladies he liked. He would kiss their hand *very* elegantly. So here you have this scruffy, old, *rugged* guy all scarred up from fights and fishing and everything, and he would elegantly kiss her hand. He did that to our friend Doris Gruber.[24] Doris had this kind of funny, surprised look. Here was this guy who looked like he was just off the fishing boat. He elegantly takes her fingertips and kisses her hand quite elegantly. She gets this look on her face and somebody behind me said, kind of half under their breath, "Watch out, Doris, he's not kissing your hand, he's tasting you! He's Hamatsa, you know! He's just tasting!" He had many names, too.

Herbert spent most of the latter part of his life with Jimmy. They were very close. He stuttered a little bit and he spoke English only with quite a Kwak'wala brogue, I guess you would call it. He and Smitty really hit it off.

---

* Kulus is the younger brother of Thunderbird (see Holm, *Smoky-Top*, 43) and another of Don's crests.

They were great buddies. Smitty kind of looked after him and would keep his friends from luring him off down to the Harbor Inn so he would be in good shape for the dances. He was one of the ones who was imprisoned when they broke up the potlatch, and he taped all of his memoirs of that for Daisy, which was the material she used intact in *Prosecution or Persecution*.[25] There are lots of nicknames; they're fond of those.

7 / Producing Art

In the 1970s and through the 1980s, Don excelled in his artistic work, his confidence buoyed by his relationship with Jimmy Sewid. Just how important that connection was and how central a cultural understanding was to him as an artist comes through in his recounting of how he went about carving. For Don, possessing the technical skills to carve and knowing the practical and secular uses and histories of each ladle, rattle, mask, or pole was not enough. He sought knowledge of how the art functioned within the culture from which it originated, how the material and spiritual uses of the items were connected. He also understood that this was not just a simple dichotomy of "traditional" and "new," but a continuum of change within tradition.

Don's experiences with Jimmy Sewid, his making of masks for the Kwakiutl ceremonies and his participation in them, and the enhancement of the programs at Ariel, Washington, made him a part of Kwakiutl efforts to recast public understanding of their past as well as the present. Yet Don's efforts expanded beyond just the programs, and he began to think very carefully about the growing demands for repatriation of artifacts. This fit well not only with the Kwakiutl but also with a host of tribes that pursued the return of artifacts housed in museums worldwide. Although repatriation did not carry the same economic weight as land claims and other treaty concerns, Don's participation in that issue, indirect though it may have been, indicates how nonreservation Indians can still be connected to tribal politics. This came to be so much a part of Don that, although he continued to identify as "Indian" in that broad, pan-Indian sense and never lost a sense of "being Cherokee," he moved more and more toward "being Kwakiutl."

CARVING

The payoff is really in the doing.

There is something magical and mysterious about the ways in which Don brought his carvings to life. Powerful blows from his elbow adze sent chips flying and revealed the rough form hidden in the blocks of cedar or alder. Precise and meticulous cuts with a dazzling array of razor-sharp hand-made knives—some straight, some crooked—gave the pieces their individual aspect and expression. Hours of sanding, followed by a coat or two of linseed oil mixed with turpentine, and then paints, completed the piece. I never tired of watching this process, and I had seen it many, many times since my debut as what the Lelooska family jokingly referred to as a "professional sander" for Smitty, Don's youngest brother. I felt self-conscious, then, asking about the technical aspects of carving. I asked anyway, thinking of some future audience who might be interested, despite the fact that I had no clear end product in mind for the interviews other than a transcript of them. I should have guessed what Don would do with such an occasion. As he responded to my query, the technical very quickly moved into the cultural and political.

I really enjoy wood. I love getting a big piece of cedar, just chopping away, and making the chips fly. You can really work yourself into a sweat. Totem poles and things like that are just a heck of a lot of fun. Good exercise. Get out all your aggressions.

You need good, clear, fine-grained cedar, the best. You can use less high-quality wood, but the best is such a pleasure. It just makes the carving a joy. I've often wished I could find somebody who can make me a shaving lotion that smells like wet cedar. You first cut into it—that kind of spicy-sweet smell is plicatic acid. It can be poisonous as hell.[1] Working on big things like a totem pole and canoes, especially, you got your head down

"Don Lelooska" in the late 1960s or early 1970s, carving a large cedar frog bowl at a show held at the Heard Museum in Phoenix, Arizona. Beginning in the mid-1960s, Don and his family traveled to museums, galleries, and art shows across the country. They displayed their work, staged programs, and gave lectures. This combination gave audiences much more than just artwork. Photo courtesy of the Heard Museum.

inside; you'll see flies come in and light on the wood because it is moist. That fly'll go "goota, goota, goota, goota, goot" and he'll stop. First thing you know, *blook.* Deader than a doornail! You wonder, "Is this *really* where I should be?" Then I say to myself, "They say always that carvers live to great ages."

You have to see the design for a piece in the wood, and a drawing helps you to clarify this. You *have* to do that. Without a vision, pencil lines aren't enough. You can do your details with pencil lines, but you had better darn well know what you're going to do when you go to work with an elbow adze, because they're really destructive. Now, I personally think—and I got a hunch Bill Holm[2] might agree with me—that the old-time carvers had a lot more ability to envision something on the surface and then lay it on by eye just using a few templates to keep their balance.[3] I think they had more of that ability. Of course, they had charred sticks and things like that they could have used, or just scratched impressions on the wood. But I just have a hunch that they were very, very good at *envisioning* these things—perhaps better than we are today. I'm used to laying it out on a piece of paper and it is all clear.

I experimented making tools, but it took a long time to get it just right. Stupidest thing I ever said to an elder was to Old Man Tsimshian. He worked teaching carpentry for a long time down at Chemawa Indian School. We were talking once about tool making and the formula for tempering, which I found among many, many different old carvers who knew the trick. Anyway, we're talking about the apprentice, who had been born to the right to be a carver. First thing he was taught by his master was to make his tools. Dummy, dummy, dummy, I said, "Well, what if he couldn't make his own tools?" Old guy gives me "The Look," you know, this old Indian "Look!" He says in that deadpan voice of his, looking at me like I'm the most stupid creature in creation, "Well, then, he wouldn't need them."

He knew about tempering, the link from elbow to wrist for elbow adzes, and making a real short blade projection for the D-shaped adzes. He knew a lot about Native tools. He was a good woodworker, but he had gone on and become a carpenter because there wasn't a lot of work for ceremonial carvers at that time. He told me the tempering formula for metal. You heat your metal to the color of the sun when you look at it through your closed eyelids. That is when you quench it in urine, eulachon oil, or seawater—it just depends on whose formula you're thinking about.

I really think *everybody* who is going to carve seriously has to make their own adze; you can't really buy your adzes. The adzes have a ratio and I've never been quite able to make a formula out of it, but I think it has to do with the length of your strike. A part of it comes from your elbow and the other part comes from the wrist. But there is something there. So everybody has to make their own elbow adzes because they become just a projection of your *vision*, what you're seeing. You just . . . you don't think about it anymore. It is a reflex action. Crooked knives, things like that—why, you can give somebody a crooked knife and he can use it just fine. The adze is something *intensely* personal. Yeah, tools are very, very personal to carvers. It took quite a while to get the tools right.

Then there are certain plants and things that you use on your hands. This isn't indispensable, but this is indispensable information from the standpoint that they were doing these things to make their hands supple, yet tough—boiling devil's club and then washing your hands in that.[4] That was also the purgative used by shamans when they're cleaning themselves out before they seek a vision or instruction from the powers. Alder is good, too. If your hands are real sore and you're getting blisters, you boil a concoction of alder bark and then you wash your hands in that; it helps.

After you carve a piece, you've got to let it dry. This is the *great* difference between European carving and Northwest Coast carving. Northwest Coast carvers worked in the moist wood because in this damp climate, you couldn't season wood; it'll rot first. Even cedar that'll last eighty years, supposedly, will be in sad, sad shape if you try to just let it dry. So *they* worked in the moist wood, probably from the days when they had work-hardened copper or jadeite blades or crude iron blades. It made it easier to handle the material. Then when you season the wet piece carefully into its dry state, you have a harder structure than if you had carved it from a seasoned block. People who work for timber and paper product companies *really* know wood, its characteristics and everything. They say this is true; that the carved object will harden and then give you a stronger structure than working from a seasoned piece. It is the idea that there are no stresses that occur while being swollen inside and shrinking outside. I think there are stresses, but it removes so *much* of the stress factor—that might be part of it or it just might get harder. Cedar can get real hard when it dries.

After a piece is carved, it is usually sanded. In the old days, they used shark skin. They also had little shaped pieces of sandstone that they would use. Sometimes they worked it so smooth with the hand tools that you really have to look at old, old pieces, get them into the right light and turn them to see whether they were sanded or just that neatly finished with the knives. [The mixture of] linseed oil and turpentine seals the wood and keeps your paint from bleeding. That, too, tends to harden the wood.

Now, in the old days, they didn't do that much. But nowadays our pieces are going into places that have electric heat and air conditioning, so they're subject to a lot of stresses, and people want them to last. They might have used the old masks for a few years and destroyed them deliberately. The masks for the Animal Kingdom Dance[5] were destroyed after they had been used a couple of years. They would burn them. Whenever it was to come back again, why, it had to be made all over again. That is a Bella Coola trait, which makes me think that the dance complex—Atlakam Dances,[6] they're called—had their origin in Bella Coola. In view of the Bella Coola connection of Jimmy Sewid's family, I think this may be where it came from.

Another thing about it that makes me think so is the term Nawalagwats'i, which is the name the old chiefs gave the A-frame museum at Ariel [Washington]. That is a Bella Coola word for "Receptacle of Magic." That is what the cave on Gilford Island is called and has been within any stretch of memory of anybody I know. The Bella Coola word gives some hints. We'll never be able to nail it down, but I just have a very strong hunch that this Animal Kingdom Dance came into Aul Sewid's hands that time when he went up to ask "Why?" They gave him the girl and he left her because she was so young but he did take the goods! That would have been masks and privileges and things like that.*

As for the colors of the paints, you've got a pretty limited palette when you think about it. You've got a *wide* range of blues and greens but the blacks, the reds, that ocher yellow are pretty standard. You can think about white background, which is sort of contemporary Kwakiutl, or since just before the turn of the [twentieth] century, where you white everything in and then paint over it.[7] Or you can have some natural wood, some white, and the colors.

Now, if it is a mask you're going to be using in performances, seeing as the wood darkens and firelight tends to burn out [obscure] the colors, you're better off with the white background because Kwakiutl masks are a lot like theatrical makeup. They're bigger than life. They were painted that way because your reds die out in the firelight quite a bit and if you've got that reddish-brown background of the cedar, you're going to lose a *lot* of your painted detail. So there are decisions to be made, whether you want to go

---

* Aul Sewid brought to the lineage rights and privileges to many dances, names, and crests, through a number of marriages before his final marriage to Lucy Sewid, James Sewid's paternal grandmother.

an older way or a newer way. That can be dictated by whether or not you took the older sculptural approach as opposed to something a little more modern.

A lot of changes were taking place for the Kwakiutl, and immense changes came just *wholesale* after the British peace was established.[8] You could go back and forth in safety to the north. The tribes were getting together down in hop yards and in places around Victoria, Vancouver, and Nanaimo. There were exchanges of ideas and technology at times like that. They had a good means of communication with the Chinook Jargon. You can get along well with that, and a lot of them are quite fluent in it. I think probably that is when the art began to really take on a lot of the things that we are seeing in later carvers like Willie Seaweed, Mungo Martin, and Charlie James, who was Mungo's stepfather and his teacher.

You have to have several pieces going at the same time because they're done in stages. You carve them. You season them. You sand them. You oil them and then you've got several days there. So in between the times that these various steps in the process are going on, why, you're working on another piece. Now, I recently carved the loon bowl and after I had carved it and set it to dry, I decided I had enough time that I did the loon opening mask, which went out of here this morning to its new owner. You have several things going, but the die is cast once the sculpture is completed. You're committed, and you're feeling good now. You think, "This is going to work." And I have a little time to think about some of the "ticky" little details. I usually'll go about three pieces and keep them going—form one process—and this is good for your muscles, too, and you don't get as tendentious if you shift gears. If you were to sand eight or ten pieces, well, you just get fed up with it. You get kind of dull toward the whole operation. So I like to have several pieces going in stages. That way, while one thing is drying, I can come along and do another.

It is hard setting a price for a piece after getting so wrapped up in doing it. That is the price you pay. You can't ever love your own work. I learned that a long time ago. If you're going to be an artist, your joy comes from the creation and doing your utmost best and in those wonderful little stretches you get. That is it. I get so much enjoyment out of it, it is like getting paid twice. Then the other part is the grim business of making a living. But you can't let it influence you: "I'm going to make this for some white guy who's going to hang it in his office." Nah, you can't do that. It has got to be each piece, I feel, made to the quality that I would want if it went into our program, if I was taking it up north to Jimmy's family, or doing it for some of the old people. I may build some technical things in for the comfort of the dancer in those types of masks that go up there. Everything else, you have a standard and you just don't deviate.

I've never been really sorry to see a piece go because I have already had out of it all I wanted. I have looked at it. I have critiqued it. I have already become dissatisfied and it is time to move on. So unless it's a piece we're going to use in the program that I'm going to have to *live with,* it is all over! You have one technical standard that you try to meet every time. The payoff, really, is in the doing. Pricing gets real hard because you look at it one time and you think, "Oh boy, this piece is going good." Finally, then, the dissatisfaction sets in and you say, "Well, I'd do this differently next time and I'd do that differently and I *wish* I hadn't done that" or "That wasn't such a good choice." By the time you get through talking to yourself about it, your price is going down, *chuka, chuka, chuka, chuka, chuka, chuka, chuka.* That is where you need an objective opinion from someone else, like Patty and Smitty. We kind of jury our work back and forth. Because when you've gone through the struggle, the discontent sets in. As far as your growth is concerned, you've gotten everything out of the piece. You're really not qualified to price it anymore.

I carve year-round, without any real seasonal changes. Some of the carvers did nothing else but carve. A few of them, that was all they did. Then there're other guys who were fishermen, and then in the off-season they carved. It was on, off, on, off. A lot of the artists, the younger ones today, are fishing and then they're working at their art and they just kind of shift gears. It is hard to get fishing out of your blood when you've been a commercial fisherman—the excitement, the weather, and the boats and all that.

In the family, we do a lot getting ready for the shows all over the place. That is when you have to accumulate the pieces. You see, what we do is a little different from a lot of the artists. They pay their own expenses and everything. Somehow, we fell in the habit of: if the gallery wants us, well, they pay the expenses. We bring the stuff and then what we add is the good public relations because we can do the lectures, sometimes even full programs, which help to promote the project, plus it gives us the satisfaction of having done an educational outreach. See, one hand kind of washes the other. The more knowledgeable audience you have, the better your sales are. One creates the other. That is why I think we've got, really, a pretty good system with the programs and all because we're generating new, enthusiastic people who are interested. We're educating the public.

I think we're performing somewhat of a service in that none of us could make a living doing the programs. Takes about a third of our time. But *doing* it is what makes you a good carver. A lot of the young guys who are working at it—I'm not criticizing them—don't have the opportunity to work inside the masks. Having *used* them and seeing them *work* and all, you kind of know the business inside out. A lot of them are just making them. They go to the galleries and they're sold. They're not viable in the old way because an old carver will pick it up and say, "Boy, I'm glad I don't have to wear that!"

Financially, the educational programs at Ariel kind of *cost* me because my most productive thing is the carving. But we've never really been terribly mercenary, I don't think, any of us. I think one of the reasons Jimmy Sewid and the old uncles were so interested in our little educational thing we were doing down here and really *asked* to participate, you might say, was the fact that still in their memory was the terrible breakup of those big potlatches and their relatives sent to prison.

INSPIRATION AND OBLIGATION

The more you learn, the more ignorant you feel. . . . When you get to the top of the hill, you look across and there is a higher one still.

In the process of our exchange about how to carve, I asked Don what old carvings had inspired him, what styles he liked to use when carving. His uneasiness about museums came through in the discussion. I also brought up the topic of when he thought he had mastered the art form, and which carving he thought of as his masterpiece. Somewhat amused, he spoke to me about his perspectives on learning and the obligations it wrought.

I'm still just a student. I haven't made any "masterpiece" yet. You know, everybody suddenly becomes a master carver when he gets his first gallery show or something. I think it is rather harder than that. I think if you let yourself become one, then you cease to grow. No, I like to think, especially right now at this point in my life, that the best is yet to be. You just have to keep striving and never be satisfied, never, ever. Always be self-critical. It is just like the learning process: the more you learn, the more ignorant you feel. You can never let yourself feel that you have a total grasp or the total truth about anything. I think you just have to keep reaching and pulling yourself along. You may climb up to another hill, but when you get to the top of the hill, you look across and there is a higher one still. So I like to think maybe the best one is yet to be. There are some that are kind of little signposts or landmarks along the way, but gee, I would hate to think that I had finally made the best one that I was ever going to make and there would be nothing left!

There really are no simple approaches, I think, to explaining any society. The deeper you get, the more you realize the depth. Even cultures that seem on the surface so basic, so simple—like the aboriginal people of Australia: their material culture is practically nil and yet their mythology is one of the most complex and elaborate, I think, of just about any people on the planet. Their system of ethics is pretty fascinating stuff. That is why I am so fascinated with Northwest Coast art.

For example, as a single piece, probably the great Tsonoquah feast dish in the Rasmussen Collection at the Portland Art Museum first fascinated me the most because I knew there had to be more to that than what the books had to say. I didn't know everything about it at that time, even who it had belonged to, until I really got acquainted with Jimmy Sewid. It was kind of peculiar. The Tsonoquah is very important, it always fascinated me. That is my principle crest, given to me with my name by Jimmy. It came from his Ma'amtagila ancestor.

The whole thing has had a kind of mystical quality. I know that sounds corny and everybody romances everything Indian nowadays to the point that it is ridiculous, but there is a mystical side to it I don't understand. It looks like it was sort of meant to happen. Then I found out later on that Tsonoquah had been from Jimmy's family, and then they gave me the songs and the privilege of owning one. They call it the Mother Dish.

The Hamatsa used to ride the neck of the Tsonoquah into the house. When it was carried in and it was full, it must have weighed a tremendous amount. They would come in and go around the house, sunwise, like dancers do. Then they would turn, then turn back a little, then they would turn the other way. Whichever way the feet pointed when it was set down on the ground, the feet were pointed to the chief, who was expected to give a big feast. This was all arranged, of course, long beforehand. But he would pretend, "Oh my goodness, I am unprepared, totally. Well, I have a few things that I brought and I will give up these." Then, of course, his minions would give out this immense amount of food out of the bowl.

You never put ordinary food in those big crest dishes. Has to be expensive, noble food. Seal meat is considered noble. In fact, certain chiefs are entitled to receive certain portions of a seal. Long clover roots are noble food. Certain kinds of berries are considered to be noble food, but you never put anything like dried clams or dried salmon or anything. It is just mundane, everyday food. Jimmy's uncles liked to put fruit—melons and apples and oranges—in there. They would send a boat down or bring it in by canoes sometimes. Send clear down to Victoria to get crates of oranges and they would fill it with that because they didn't have that every day. So this was really a noble, noble feast.

They used to bring it into the house with poles underneath, a lot of strong young guys carrying it. Two bowls represent the breasts, two are kneecaps, and one they call the bellybutton, but it is really the vulva of the Tsonoquah, the giantess. Those bowls were given to certain men of rank and position. Chiefs of a certain rank receive that portion of the Tsonoquah. Then the belly was full of food and the head was full. Sometimes they would take off the mask and expose the food dish to the public, and sometimes they just let them reach through the holes and get the food out that way, reaching in the eye sockets of the Tsonoquah. I want to make one for us someday, but I don't know where we would put it. It would be nice to have and it would be fun to do that. Of course, with Jimmy gone, it wouldn't be as much fun. But that one impresses me.

That long Hux̱whukw mask[9] in the Rasmussen *always* impressed me, too. Now I know who made it. I know why it was made. I know how it was lost and I think I know how I can send it home. There are six pieces that were seized. That *missionary* that helped to inspire the breaking up of the potlatch and the seizing of the stuff sold a lot of that out of hand. It wasn't all crated up and shipped off to museums like it was supposed to be. He sold a lot of it to Walter C. Walters in Wrangell, Alaska. It was there that Rasmussen bought it.[10] So there is a clear paper trail of how it got from there to where it is. Federal law says that a lot of that *has* to go back. If it comes to that, boy, I will be right in there with my family saying, "Give it back." I've got pretty good documentation with photographs and I know who carved those pieces now. There is nothing in their books that has to do with that. I don't like to be vindictive, but if that big bowl and those Hamatsa masks had to go back, I would feel so good.

Most museum collections kind of give me mixed feelings. When I saw Julie Wades-in-Water's* dress and saddle up in storage at the Denver Museum of Natural History, it gave me the oddest feeling. As a kid, I had seen that stuff in their big teepee when they had it set up for their summer encampment in Montana; all of their wealth was displayed. It just brings a torrent of memories and smells. It just all comes back so quick. It almost makes you sort of out of it for a minute. But in this place it was just an artifact. When I was a little kid it was alive, it had a life of its own in that big painted lodge, with the painted dew cloth around it inside and the buffalo robes and everything. It was a gorgeous teepee. I mean, it was a classic. But the thing, I think, that really got me was this emptiness of the object taken out of context and away from the people and that funny little chuckling, half-chuckle half-giggle that she had. Just everything came back and in that instant it did come alive.

But then it seemed, here is this thing, they're glad to have it. It is good it is here. It'll be preserved. And she might be proud to have it shown to people so they would know the Blackfeet better, because they were very interested in people knowing the real Blackfeet as human beings, not as "wild Indians." And I feel that way about a lot of pieces that find their way into museums. Sometimes, when I'm around a lot of people who deal in old Indian artifacts and things—things that were sacred objects, and baby cradles that had been used and just *lovingly* crafted for the child by their aunties—with the dealers it is just money, the great old war shirts and the painted buffalo robes and some of the warrior society stuff. You see it at some of these shows and auctions, especially. And you know the feeling it

---

* The extended Wades-in-Water family has been prominent among the Blackfeet in Montana.

*Jimmy Sewid walks up from the beach at Cape Mudge during the 1979 opening cere-
monies of the Kwagiulth Museum and Cultural Centre. The Lelooska family chartered a
bus for family and friends to attend the ceremonies and potlatch. Don and Smitty produced a number of masks that the Sewids wore in these and other ceremonies. Broad,
open public displays of cultural vitality remain socially and politically important for the
Kwakiutl. Photo by the author.*

gives me? Have you ever seen that great painting of the Roman soldiers and
they're gaming over the robe of Christ beneath the cross? That pops into
my head every time I'm around all those things like that! They crucified a
race and here they are now, you might say "below the cross," and they're
casting lots. It is a money thing, I suppose, unless you had the peculiar growing up that I had, which was entirely supported by my mother, who was
never quite civilized enough for Grandma's taste. It gives you a different
way of looking at these things, really.

Now, other museums are different. When that little museum was first
finished in 1979 at Cape Mudge, we went up to participate. I gave a set of
Moon masks to Jimmy's family, and they were going to keep Jimmy's masks
there in the museum. So after the performance was over and before they

opened the museum to the public, I scooted over to take the masks over because they asked me to. They had let in a lot of the older people, especially older women in the group. I suppose because men died younger or were killed fishing and all, you really have a preponderance of older ladies at a gathering like that. They're going around and they're viewing the pieces. It was the first time they had had a chance to see them since they were children, when the things were seized and their relatives imprisoned, the whole bitter, bitter thing. Just to listen to them and look at them. And the weeping, the wailing, and recognizing these pieces almost as though it was their dead relatives, the ancestors standing there. It just goes right through you. It is just like an icy shaft going from the crown of your head right to your feet.

You realize how much this stuff still means to those people. I have a hard time sometimes reconciling. . . . We need museums, of course, and these things on display have done a great deal for building respect for the Indian. But I always think about the cost. How were these things obtained? Were they simply taken? Was somebody gotten drunk? Was it somebody who was fired up with missionary zeal? A new-minted Christian is a powerful instrument in getting rid of all that heathen stuff! A lot of it went out of Alaska in just that way. So I get mixed feelings going through museum collections, I suppose because I can't separate it from the humanity, the love that people had for these things, how they prize them, and how they were supposed to go down through generations. So, growing up like I did, you look at things a little differently, you feel a little differently about them.

As for "styles" or "traditions," Bella Coola and Kwakiutl are my two great loves. Now, fortunately, I find out they've been in bed together a long time, even the days when they hated one another. Aul Sewid already had all these privileges and things from the girl they gave him who was too young so he left her.[11] It is an epic. That is one of the great, great stories around.

. . . Haida—they're the "enemy." But I do love Haida monumental sculpture. You see, I'm polyglot enough that I can see in each culture some things that I think they are the absolute masters of. Tsimshians, the Nishga, and the people on the Skeena, the Gitksan, were excellent at what I call the miniature carving: the beautiful raven rattles, the gorgeous frontlets, the small jewel-like things. I think that was one of their best things. The great monuments in cedar, I think, was probably the Haidas' great forte. They were getting lots of their nice ceremonial carving done by the Coast Tsimshians, incidentally.

But when I think of ceremonial art and drama, theatricality, there are no people on the Northwest Coast, nowhere in North America—and, indeed in some ways, I think there is no tribal society in the world—that equal the Kwakiutl in their conception of theatricality and bringing the unseen world of the supernatural into this world for a moment. The mask, all over the world, is a portal to the supernatural. Even Jimmy Sewid said, "You know, once the mask goes on, you are no longer just you." You become part of that which is the mask, the myth, the traditions, and in this case your ancestors. This is the little door that you go through, your time machine. As a dancer and performer, if you can get yourself into this mode of thinking, well, it is no wonder why some of those old guys still chill your blood when they do the Hamatsa Dance.

There are wonderful things to be found, but I think overall the Kwakiutl culture is so complex. They were *tinkering* constantly with their potlatch system. This just didn't stay static. From the time the first trade goods came in, they were tinkering with their system. If it didn't work they threw it out, tried something else. There was this . . . structure, and what they have been trying to do is bolster the structure, enhance it, and keep it strong and growing. They worked at this and they were pretty adroit, really. They took innovations for a long time. I think the Kwakiutl were very good at taking new ideas, new materials, and adapting them to their culture in a way that enhanced rather than caused a breakdown in the culture. It would've been very interesting to have seen how they might have developed, what kind of a society they would have become, had not sickness and missionization and government interfered.

Now, when you carve in Haida style, you have to think Haida. You have to approach it from the standpoint of what they admired. They were the classic people. They were much more hidebound in their art than the Kwakiutl.[12] The Kwakiutl—well, one authority has called it prodigal theatricality. I prefer to think of them as baroque in their approach to art. Haidas are classic. The Tsimshian are in between. They're fairly eclectic in their approach. Their totem poles are usually tall and slim because that is the kind of timber you have on the upper Nass and Skeena Rivers, but they're very repetitious—

little human forms up, up, up, up. With the Haida, you have these great supernatural beings and they just sort of come out of the wood. It is a nice way of illustrating mythology and that is what I enjoy doing. Because what must always remain the central wellspring of Northwest Coast art is the mythology.

With the exception of totem poles, my work is Kwakiutl and Bella Coola. I do the totem poles in the Haida style because structurally they're very feasible to put in a home where you've got electric heat and air conditioning and all these things. A Kwakiutl pole is very hard to hollow out, whereas a Haida totem is really a deep bas-relief wrapped around the cylinder. If you ever take a close look at one, you'll know what I mean. A Kwakiutl pole is a group of sculptures, one on top of the other. You can't hollow them out and carve them in relief like you can on a Haida pole. So you get cracking and all of kinds of problems. Look at really large Kwakiutl poles and you see lots of cracks. White people don't like that, but the Kwakiutl understand this.

Of course, you just raise them up as monuments and eventually they went back into the earth and that was that. I like to do the Kwakiutl poles. I would like to finish ours someday out there in the open shed next to the house. "The cobbler's children go barefoot," as they say. I've got to finish it and raise it, which will be expensive and a lot of fun. Patty, no doubt, will make a great financial coup out of the whole thing. There is a lot of P. T. Barnum in that girl.

EXPERIMENTS AND CULTURAL CONTEXT

It has to rest on privilege and history.

Hoping that I had begun to learn from Don about asking indirect questions, I pushed out one of those "checker pieces" of ignorance, as Don phrased it, to find out about the other types of Northwest Coast artwork Don had done. He took the "bait" well enough but, in his usual fashion, directed the conversation to where he wanted it to end: privilege and history.

I've experimented with lots of things along the way. Bob Hart of the Indian Arts and Crafts Board kind of instigated a lot of it way back when. He got Ed Malin to get me to experiment with the stuff in the 1960s, because they were looking at a lot of these different materials that might be used in craft work. Horn is really interesting. I did some in bighorn sheep and I did some mountain goat spoons. Mountain goat horn is terrific stuff to work. It is just a pleasure, just like carving smooth black plastic. It takes a nice polish. I made some bighorn ladles and a bowl. I think I've got a bowl still kicking around somewhere here.

First thing I learned about it was that it needs to be soaked before you use it. Some of those dried-out old bighorns I have I soaked for about a month before I worked on them. By that time they had acquired a marvelous *odeur* that would cling to you for days after you had worked with it a lot! Then you would boil it and the moisture in it would make it about as supple as an old rubber tire. You could carve it very easily at that point, smooth it up, and work it. Then you would put it in a wooden mold and let it dry. You have to keep them in the mold quite a while and let them *really* dry out or they'll warp on you—I discovered that.

It was kind of a rediscovery process. Anyplace where there were the available horns, why, at least certain people had the skills to work them. I talked to some of the old people over at Warm Springs, Mitchell and Julia Simtustis, a sister of the old guy who was chief over there. I talked to the elders and I kind of picked the ones who had old Wasco bowls and spoons. So without asking that direct question, which is considered ill mannered by a lot of the old people, you could get into the thing. You would say to yourself—you wouldn't be speaking directly or asking a question, but you would begin to say to yourself, "Gee, I wonder how they did that?" Then they would volunteer, "It used to be a hot springs. They used to toss the horn in."

They had a lot of those bighorn sheep up along the cliffs on the Columbia River Gorge at one time. They would put the horn in a hot springs until it got soft and then they would work it. Of course, the art style was very different, but the technique of handling it wasn't. I thought about that, and then I knew I had to reconstitute the moisture in the horn again because some of them were really old. I soaked them until I could bend them in my hands. It was just a piecing together of little bits and scraps, like the mention of the hot springs. Julia could remember seeing him—I guess it was her grandfather or somebody—kind of chop them out with a little hatchet to rough them out, then take a knife and "stretch it out," as she put it, and let it dry. Then lots of scraping. It all began to fit together. When I begin to experiment with the material, what it would and would not do taught me about as much and confirmed a lot of what the old people had said.

The carving is a very, very shallow relief, but the curve gives you an illusion of depth. It is just like Haida totem poles. They're a relief wrapped around a cylinder. On a bowl, you usually do the belly of the bowl with the design. When the bowl was all smooth and just nearly finished, why, then you would sit down and rough out the sculptured part, which was usually the end of the handle. Raven head or something like that, you would rough that out. But for the shallow design, the two-dimensional art, you would just let the contour of the bowl tell you what should be there. You would do an abstract design. If you were going to do a crane, where the long handle of a spoon would be the neck, you would rough the head in. Then, when the time came, why, then you would just design the wings and the belly details in the crane. The whole thing would be like a crane when it was finished. It is different from a mask. You could see the design in the wood. It is just a matter of getting rid of the wood you don't want. With horn, you get the basic shape, and then the abstract design would pretty well suggest itself as you went along. And, of course, when it was all done, why, you could really see what the possibilities were.

I've experimented with argillite,* too. Did some amulets and some little figures. I didn't have any real big pieces. They all went to the Indian Arts and Crafts Board. A lot of those early pieces were done for them. It is good stuff, argillite. Not soft, but nicely workable, sands nicely, works nicely with a chisel, smooth cuts. When you get it smoothed up nicely, then you split a lead pencil open. You could either pulverize the graphite in there or scrape it. You rub that into the argillite and that is what gives it that sheen. It is kind of a gun-metal color. The extensive use of argillite came along with the end of the sea otter trade, and they needed something to trade with the ships for what they needed or wanted from them at the time. So they got into the curio business. That was where we got these miniature totem poles and things. Some argillite pieces were part of the old tradition. I think they were probably amulets and things like that, but not many of them. Of

---

* Hardened mudstone common to the area, this relatively soft stone served as a woodworking blade until replaced by metals.

course, the great, great, great carver Charlie Edenshaw* used argillite and so did his uncle Albert Edward Edenshaw.

Working shells goes way back into prehistoric times. Lots of it comes out of archaeological sites. Of course, the best shell came with the fur trade. The native abalone shell is kind of pallid compared to the stuff that comes from Monterey, California. The Spanish brought the first of the really fine green shells. Boy, the Indians loved those. Word reached the fur traders somehow. They would stop off down there and load up. It is used a lot for inlays. You can work it pretty easily and with simple tools. I made some sets of tools out of old files and things, which were the basic old tools. They've had iron, I think, longer than a lot of people have considered because drift iron would come in. In fact, the Haida have folktales about these trees that would float in that had this wonderful stuff.

I experimented with silver, gold, copper, shell, ivory, antler, bone, and painting on hide, like they used to for the old armor and things like that. Pigments, making old paint. I made some adzes with jadeite blades. You can't really whale away, you sort of bruise it off. I guess I did a lot of different things; my horn and shell carving was what got Patty and Lee started. I got them started and then they got so good, I quit!

Now, the copper making was a whole thing in itself. That was kept very quiet for a while! People had coppers seized and things, but they still had the right to the name of the copper. I learned to do that. That compound bend of the T is the trick. You make a hardwood mold. You get the hardest stuff you can find, yew wood or piece of good old oak or something, and you cut that T in there. Then you anneal the copper by heating it and then plunking it into water. That hardens steel, but it softens copper. You have to heat it several times to get that T-shaped bend.

Coppers really are kind of shrouded in mystery. Once, when all Jimmy's uncles, who were all big chiefs in their own right who had potlatched, and other visiting chiefs were all together, I just sort of brought around the idea of the copper. You make a statement, you say, "Of course nobody knows how these start out." Bingo! Well, they start out because there are certain men who are ḵwagi'la, or tłaḵwagi'la, "copper maker." They have the right

---

* Charles Edenshaw (1839–1924) was a Haida wood and argillite carver and a silversmith. He was also an informant for early anthropologists Franz Boas and John Swanton.

to do that. It is like *practically* everything, it is a hereditary privilege or you have to be granted the patent to do this. They would make the copper and then the copper was presented to what they call the council of chiefs, a circle of chiefs bound into a potlatch circle, and they would bid on the copper. The one who won the bidding got the copper, and the privilege of naming it and having it engraved with a crest that comes from his family. No uninitiated person gets to see the blank copper before it is named.

The bidding starts out at what it costs to acquire the copper and have it decorated. Then they begin to build their reputation. The old guys agreed that was the process. Of course, some of the coppers, over time, became enormously valuable, especially those that had been fought over or disputed or had figured in great important marriages and things like that. In the potlatch period, as warfare became less popular because the queen's gunboats could drop in on you at any time, the copper got to be something that would be "broken." You begin to go into this period of what almost amounted to bloodless warfare.[13] A lot of things that would've been taken care of by revenge raid or something in old times were settled by breaking a copper. That would force the other guy to break one of equal or, better yet, greater value or to tie them to his houseposts at some public event. Sometimes they were thrown into the ocean, towed out to sea and cut loose, sinking into deep water. Aul Sewid broke a copper against each one of the chiefs who refused to participate in an attack on the Bella Coola. When they chickened out, he just bent the copper across his knee, sent the pieces out in the canoe, and they threw them in deep water. There is a staff that has a swan at the top and Jimmy gave me the privilege. It has each one of those coppers on the staff.

They're very interesting. Sometimes they would get hacked up and practically just the T would be all that was left—and the T is two-thirds of the value of the copper. You can buy a copper T. In fact, Max̱'inuxdzi ("Big Killer Whale") was Mungo Martin's copper.[14] It was founded on an old T and put together in the machine shop there in Alert Bay. He finally gave it as a memorial to his son who had drowned.[15] He was going to break it against Tom Omid, but wiser heads prevailed. I think it was probably Wilson Duff[16] who said, "Well, wouldn't it be better to put it in the museum and it will be a memorial to your son and people will learn about the Kwakiutl from it?"[17] So it is there at the Royal British Columbia Museum in Victoria. Everybody knows the history of that copper, but others were so old that a lot of it was lost.

I've made about five or six of them—very quietly. Jimmy had most of his, but there were people who would want one restored. They needed one more or less as a prop for their initiation and all. It was mostly re-creating coppers that were seized in the twenties when they broke up that really big potlatch. A lot of them hid their coppers in the attic or under the houses up there, but some were lost and they needed them replaced. It has to rest on something or it is just an interesting piece of tin.

There was this one Kwakiutl family head who wanted to have Jimmy's family ask me if I would make him a copper. He needed a copper because he wanted to give a potlatch, but he didn't have rights to one. Well, it was like asking somebody to counterfeit a two-million-dollar stock certificate or treasury bearer bond. That isn't the way it is done. A copper can be made, but the copper only has wealth and legitimacy when it is offered to a council of chiefs. I guess he thought, "Oh, you got to have one of those if you're going to have a potlatch. You have got to have a copper. Okay, I'll go see if I can get somebody to make me one." He didn't *understand.* Of course, there probably aren't ten people around who could *really* tell you all of these nuances and niceties. Jimmy Sewid's daughters Dora and Daisy can. Of course, the girls were lucky. When they grew up, Granny Ack-koo was there, and so were Jimmy's old uncles and their father. They were really exposed and these things were *drilled* into them, because that was what noble children had to learn. It was like sending them to a good Eastern college to prepare them for life at a certain stratum in society. So there is a lot to learn, and the books are inaccurate on *many* parts of this.[18]

It has to rest on privilege and history. Of course, they were kind of tinkering with their traditions, which is something they were very good at and they did a lot, especially as the fur trade developed. There is still a lot to know about coppers, and I don't think we'll probably ever know. The old guys who knew these things are gone. The Bella Coola used them and we don't know that much about the old, ancient origins.

8 / Learning from Experience

By the 1970s, Don had moved from being an apprentice of art, culture, and history to a journeyman, even a master, and this set the era apart from the earlier years of his life. Rather than just Don seeking people out, increasingly they sought him. Don embraced these new responsibilities, making deep and lasting relationships. Capturing them all is impossible, but the few stories Don told of those years give a glimpse into where those associations took him. They also reveal his willingness to experiment on many levels. That, in turn, only contributed to the growing body of stories that now make up the legend of Lelooska, for those who knew the Lelooska family have at least one wild story to tell. Through it all, Don's humility and humor shines.

REVISITING THE SACRED

Holy people are holy people.

Don had great respect for people who dedicated their entire being to worthwhile causes. His association with several religious men illustrates how highly he regarded them. It also demonstrates the growing power of pan-Indianism on reservations and in urban centers that is such a hallmark of the second half of the twentieth century. As usual, Don's art carried him into these relations.

I once carved a Kwakiutl Madonna and a Haida Christ for the St. Augustine's Indian Center[1] [established by Father Powell] in Chicago. Father Powell[2] wanted a Northwest Coast piece, so I drew on an old Haida carving for the face and the body of Christ, which is quite stilted and in the old traditional style. Yet I wanted that particular appearance and bound the hair up as a shaman, a person of great power. His hair was carved tied up like that.

The Madonna is a better piece. I decided I could carve her as a noble woman. This is the firstborn son of a chieftain and she is holding him in the wooden cradle. She is offering him to his people for the first time. He will be a chief, so here she stands; this is the mother. The father, of course, is in the background. In a way, he is the heir. I carved it that way because this is a big ceremonial moment when this child gift is about to be offered to the people, the clan. I thought that would be fun to try to carve. This would be Mary and this would be Christ. Offering him to the world that he had come to live in, suffer in, die in, and make better. That was my approach.

How did I meet Father Powell? I guess it was through the Indian Arts and Crafts Board that he heard about me. He wrote to me. He started sending me the center's newspaper. He was kind of in my life before I knew him. He was sending me these things and we got better acquainted, and then I did some work for him, some pieces he wanted.

Father Powell is a man of God. If there really are any running around, why, he has got my vote. He wrote the two volumes *Sweet Medicine,* on the Cheyenne religion.[3] *Sweet Medicine* is really something that you should read if you're interested in northern Plains because these are the people of Lame Deer that Father Powell worked with for so many years. So far as I know, Father Powell is the only non-Cheyenne by blood who can be present when the Medicine Arrows are renewed or when Is'siwon is revealed.* He holds the great name Stone Forehead. Great names are part of your soul, and sometimes you don't ever even tell people what your real name is because among Indians everybody has lots and lots of names. But he holds that name, which is a symbol of the respect that the Cheyenne elders had for him.

---

* Is'siwon, the sacred Buffalo Hat, is a symbol not only of the buffalo as a rich source of food, but also of the renewing power of females—animal and human alike—and of the necessary harmony between humans and animals.

I have a letter from him that I got long ago, and I'm trying to write to him. I haven't written him in a long time. I'm really ashamed to contact him, but of course this goes back to the time we had that schism in the family with Patty over the Yamhill Market.* Families have ways of getting these schisms and breaking apart, then pulling back together. I know I did everything that I felt I should have done. I must not have done something right or it never would have happened. This, for me, was a terrible feeling of failure, because I had really failed my grandfather, I hadn't kept them together. It bothered me for a long time. There was that sense that I had somehow failed in what Grandpa and all of them left me to do, that I let that happen. Now the whole thing is healed and we're stronger for it, but it was in that time that I really ceased to write back to Father Powell. He has always been there. But if anybody will understand when I finally can frame the words, it will be Father Powell.†

Then I got involved in carving the Four Evangelists at Lewis and Clark College outside the library and chapel, which was scary. Paul Thiry, an architect who collected Northwest Coast art, had me carve them for the chapel. Then he cast them in cement. He kept the wooden original, but finally Lewis and Clark College has them all, cement casts as well as wooden originals. That scared the rats out of me, because here I've been raised with respect for the powers, the Divine Intelligence. I've never been able to find a suitable term for my concept of God—Divine Intelligence, Creator—none are adequate, in my opinion. I got to the job of carving the Evangelists: the Angel, the Eagle, the Bull, and the Lion from the "Book of Revelations." That scared me to death. I knew they had to go on top of these pillars or columns. So I took a whack at it. That was still the beginning time; I had turned the corner from the commercial to the better stuff. So I tried to design them and carve them. I knew two people who were really scholars in the area.

So when I got them pretty well done, I wanted Father Halloway to come and see them. He was a Franciscan priest. Wonderful guy. He had been a

---

* See chapter 3, "Family across the Generations."
† Father Powell and the family did reconnect and he officiated at Mariah's wedding, Don's funeral, and Mary's funeral.

priest in the prison at San Quentin, California, for years and an army chaplain, just a terrific guy. He always covered up his collar and he would come up with a scarf or something because he thought it made people uncomfortable. He wasn't one of those hard-sell, look-at-me priests. This is a man whose life was dedicated, and he had pretty well done everything that could be expected of a man in that position. A wonderful, wonderful, wonderful man. Mom was very fond of him. We're not Catholics, but to me these are holy people. Holy people are holy people, despite the labels and any of the other trappings you put on them.

I wanted Father Halloway to come and look at it. So he did and so did Father Schoenberg, who was a Jesuit.[4] He was the one who put the museum together for Gonzaga, which unfortunately has now closed.* He was *constantly* promoting this museum and he was a *great* salesman and fundraiser. It was kind of funny, because one day both of them were here at the same time. Father Schoenberg was just full of his zeal to get the museum going over there and just talking a mile a minute. He bounced down the stairs, out of the building to get in his car. Father Halloway sighed and he looked after him with a funny little smile on his face. He says, "Hah"—he has a slight Irish accent, which is great, I would have cast him as the kindly priest in a movie if I could have. He says, "Hah, the Jesuits, they were ever wild men!"

I wanted them both to see the Four Evangelists and give me their opinions, and I knew in honesty they would. They were good judges. You sit there—and I know what a person feels like in a courtroom when the jury's filing in to decide whether you're going to get the gas chamber or something! Well, they liked it. I was delighted and somewhat surprised. I felt good and I was very, very grateful!

In retrospect, the Four Evangelists are not great, I realize. I look at them now and I wince a little bit. I do that with all my work. There are very few pieces that I can look back on and say, "Oh, my goodness." But there *are* those few where you have overstepped yourself and that is your first step into the next little trip up the mountain. There are so many things I would do differently if I were to take the job on again. But it was fun. I was sure glad that they thought it worked.

* It reopened in 2002.

MYTHOLOGY AND HOLLYWOOD AT SKYWALKER RANCH

. . . kind of dry and academic.

Don loved to study, in the strictly academic sense, nearly any aspect of history and world cultures. The influence of Lady Elizabeth and Enoch Hinkle remained at work in him. As he had with public schooling, Don always learned much in formal academic settings, but those were never as rewarding to him as the deeply personal associations he so regularly established.

In the early 1980s, the people down there at Cal State–Long Beach were responsible for putting together this meeting. I had gone out there and given a talk. The lady who was with their Native American program was from one of those tribes of the Six Nations, I guess we call them Iroquois nowadays, but they prefer to be called by their own name, Ho-dé-no-sau-nee. They asked me to go to Skywalker Ranch [in Marin County, north of San Francisco] and I could at that time. I went down there for a few days. It was an experience, I mean, it was nice for my résumé! It was no big deal thing, but it was interesting. It wasn't the experience that Neah Bay was, or even the Boise trip, but it was very interesting. I guess everybody likes to meet celebrities. Joseph Campbell was a very, very ill man. It was after *Star Wars* had been out; George Lucas had gotten tremendously rich and built Skywalker Ranch. Bill Moyers was there, too. Campbell was willing all of his library to go to Skywalker Ranch, which I think may eventually become a center for religion and mythology, I would hope. It certainly was an ideal situation. I had a lot of respect for Campbell because he, I think for the first time, opened people's minds to mythology, and dignified mythology in the minds of a lot of your WASPs who have a mentality that can't accept that other people have a bible, have their own impression of creation and of the Divine Intelligence!

The family had been going down to San Juan Capistrano, California, for several years, and always when we would go down, there would be some kind of educational outreach. Which was, speaking in the crass way, good promotion for the gallery. It also made me feel like this was something more than just cashing in. It was a matter of paying my dues—like the Hindus, where you pay the teacher. That is what I feel some of these things are, because it is what the old people wanted me to do. They really never would've taken the time with me. Somebody had to do it. A lot of them were a little disappointed in their grandkids, or young people in general, and so it probably contributed to their desire to *put* their knowledge someplace or just be listened to.

It was about two, two and a half days, I guess. They just got around a big table and sat there. They would go at it for about four, five, six hours. Of course, you would stop and have cold drinks and talk and move around. Then they would throw out an idea and then they would run the idea around through the group and kind of see what turned up. It was very interesting to get to know those opinions on the concept of creation and the concept of what really is evil and what is good, and how various societies went about making these things work. I would say it was fun from that standpoint. But it was kind of dry and kind of academic. There wasn't that deep personal thing that you get when you're dealing with the old [Indian] people. They come and they stay with you, or you stay with them, or you sit around like at the Pendleton Round-Up for hours at a time in a big teepee with a bunch of the old people and just *listen* to the oral histories bubbling back and forth or swapping songs and things like that. It didn't have that wonderful *humanity* to it. This was kind of dry. Not that I have anything against academics, but it isn't the traditional Indian way of doing, so it was a little sterile. It was really fascinating. I think I learned a lot.

The others there, the people from the Southwest, have such good manners. They really seem quite sophisticated. You never know when you're impressing old Indians anyway. They handled that so well. They could put on that poker-face routine. I always admired that. You could see it in their eyes a little bit. They're not going to have anybody think that they're some dumb hick just off the rez. They had the shields up the first day. Then everybody got acquainted and we knew what to expect of one another. Of course, the best talks are the ones you had with individuals outside the sessions when there wasn't anything going on.

For example, I really never thought a whole lot about the breadth and depth of Navajo religion or how vitally alive and how powerful Navajo healing, medicine, and ritual is in spite of all the efforts of the army, the missionaries, and the poverty and everything else. It is still very, very powerful. People you wouldn't expect, who have gone to college and have Ph.D.s, have fallen home and gone back to these things. So that was interesting. It is hard to pick one thing out of the bunch, but the Southwest isn't my area, though I know many of those people. I think it was very interesting to be exposed to some of the Southwestern people, their philosophy, and really how well these old people dedicated themselves to tradition and how *smoothly* they adapt to their environment.

THE NOT-SO-SACRED

It would be nice to have a buffalo around.

Don was always full of surprises and, much like Mr. Toad in *Wind in the Willows,* loved to embark on new adventures, only some of which were artistic. In fact, that exuberance frequently manifested itself in his quest for the latest "toys." In my years around the family, the acquisition of something splendid—a rare musket, a special historic medallion, an item of Native-produced clothing, a new big-screen TV, or the latest video release of a movie—was an occasion for celebration. At times, these erupted into hilarious events such as "the great food fight," which rivaled any Hollywood could have produced. Others created controversy within the family. All marked the passage of time and each came with or made its own story that was woven into the fabric of the Lelooska family. Few were more dramatic, humorous, but ultimately unfortunate than "the time Don bought the buffalo." To give people a sense of such a moment, I asked him to recount the tale. In hindsight, I cannot help but wonder what hidden messages there may have been in the finale of the story.

We went over to Moiese, Montana, which is the National Bison Refuge on the Flathead Reservation. I expressed the idea that it would be really nice to have a buffalo around, get a young one and let it grow up, and study the changes at various ages and things because I was doing some Western carving at that time. Buffalo anatomy is pretty interesting. And, of course, I was raised on buffalo stories from Dad because he was there as a boy when they brought the herd into Yellowstone. Patty thought it would be nice to have a buffalo, too. So poor Michael [Cook, Patty's husband] knocked together a fence next door and he took off to Moiese and they bid on a long yearling. That is about a half-, almost sometimes two-thirds-grown buffalo. They got a little bull and they put him in a horse trailer. He was a wild buffalo. He had been raised on the range there. He wasn't a feedlot buffalo.

They brought him home, and I was looking at this pole fence and remembering Dad's story about the telephone-pole corral that the herd destroyed in Yellowstone. They brought them in these big railcars and they put them in this big corral that was made out of telephone poles. This woman showed up with this little fox terrier. He jumped down and tore into the corral, and Dad said they gave one big communal snort, demolished the corral, and away they went. They traveled fifty miles before the last of them got rounded up!

So I was thinking of that. I looked down at the fence; the ground sloped and there was about three and a half feet between the bottom of the fence and the ground there. I said, "Well, if he goes out, he'll go out right there," and I pointed down to the corner. Well, lo and behold, when they let him out of the horse trailer, Pat's dachshund repeated the Yellowstone episode by running out and barking at the buffalo. That was all he needed, one snort. He did a lap of the corral and skidded into the corner on his side and slid right out under the fence. Down the road he went past the tavern and through the park. God knows where after that for a while, but he was out. He was pretty good-sized.

Michael was going to get him back. It was a point of honor with Michael. He hunted him and hunted him. We're getting these reports from everywhere as far as Battleground, Washington,* and places like that, that they had seen this buffalo. And I guess he went by the Ariel tavern just down the road there about a quarter mile. They used to have that bench out in front; some of the good old boys and some of the loggers who had gotten off work were there. The buffalo goes charging down the road there past the place. I can just see them, turning their heads! "Did you see what I saw?" "I don't know, what did *you* see?" I think that was about the way it went!

It was going on; we were getting these reports and things. Finally, they got a good report after almost a week that he was up the Lewis River Road here a couple of miles away. Somebody saw him go up that steep bank. Well, by that time, Michael had armed himself with a dart gun. He knew

---

* This is approximately twenty air miles from Ariel and across two major rivers.

Don in 1985, outfitted for a fur-trade workshop sponsored by Lewis and Clark College and coordinated by Professor Stephen Dow Beckham. Beckham led frequent excursions to Ariel, as did Professor Darwin Goodie of Central Washington University. Don, an avid student of written and oral history, was a treasure trove of knowledge and insights for the many college students and schoolteachers who attended such workshops on Indian and fur-trade history. Photo courtesy of Anna and Harlow Friday.

the weight of the buffalo because when they had him in the chutes, they weighed him and gave him shots and stuff. So Harlow [Friday] was either here or Patty called him or something. Anyway, he got in on the act. When I get a report back from Michael, they've stunned the buffalo and they're trying to get him down. Mom and I jump in the car and go up there and park on the shoulder. I look up the bank. This big tussle is going on in the brush. I would see brush flying up and then I would see Harlow fly up in the air and then I would see Michael fly up in the air. They're trying to wrestle him down.

Finally they got him down and the tranquilizer really started to take effect. They got a piece of plywood. They rolled him over on the plywood and slid him down on the plywood out in the middle of the road. Of course, cars are going by. Then he started to come around. By this time the tranquilizer is starting to wear off because Michael didn't want to give him enough to kill him. Somebody had to hold the buffalo down. Well, that was my job. I'm sitting on this buffalo and he is starting to come to and I'm in the middle of him. That was quite an experience; it was just like sitting on a big, powerful engine that was idling. Maybe it was my imagination, but I had the feeling it was slowly picking up steam as I was sitting there. Cars are going by. About all I get to do is wave at the people and say, "Oh, hi," like it was a perfectly normal activity. Sitting on the buffalo, we do it all the time up here.

Got him into the trailer, finally. That was a job in itself. He is getting more and more lively as time goes on. They brought him back and put him in the corral. Michael got him back, doctored him, and looked him over; then he got pneumonia or he had a twisted intestine and he got sick. It can happen sometimes, if you roll them over. Michael did everything anybody could possibly do, but the little devil hauled off and died. I think he did it just to spite Michael. I think he had this real, real enmity toward Michael. I saw him about ten or fifteen minutes before he finally flopped over. He was still doing that false charge where all of the hair stands up along their spine and the chaps on their forelegs turn outward, and he is making these false charges up to the time that he keeled over. I just thought, "Jimminy Christmas, what a valiant picture he made." Michael, by that time, had pretty well decided that he probably wouldn't make it. They came over and said he was dead.

Michael said, "Well, would you like me to skin him?"

I said, "No, I think he earned his robe." They buried him out in the field. Someday somebody'll dig it up! "What is this doing here? Well, weren't there reports of occasional buffalo clear over in the Willamette Valley?"

Well, after he had been dead for nearly two weeks, we were getting reports he had been seen here and he had been seen there. All over the place here, ridiculous places, saying they had seen a buffalo running through the woods, or through the neighborhood. I knew right where he was because there was a big mound of dirt there! Yeah, people are really peculiar sometimes in what they can imagine they see.

9 / A Family Complex

ost people associate the coasthouses, the A-frame museum, and the gallery at Ariel, Washington, with the Lelooska family. For Don and his family, those same structures were never separate from the people who created and used them, from what the larger family did and had become at Ariel. Indeed, the family and the buildings contributed mightily to Don's success as an individual artist.

The same forces that generated success—individual expertise, a family identity infused with "being Indian," and a historical period in which non-Indians became increasingly desirous of "things Indian"—also created stresses. Within the family, individuals understandably tried to define themselves separately from Don, who cast a large, long shadow. Dick and Jay, Don's brother and nephew, respectively, joined in the artistic enterprise for several years, only to break away from it altogether. Patty, as Don recounts in chapter 3, "Family across the Generations," tried to expand the gallery beyond the family complex at Ariel. With each of these incidents, Don felt the pebbles that his grandfather and granduncle had pressed into his hands slipping from his grasp. It bothered him that he could not keep everyone happy and secure. He also knew that families have problems, but hoped that his would find its way through such difficult times and come back together. For Don, as with most of us, some complications of life are never resolved.

Alongside any internal struggles, by the late 1980s and early 1990s external forces threatened the family's abilities to pursue the art and programs that its members had embraced for at least three decades. The same strains of exclusive definitions of what an "Indian" is, which fed beliefs that "a Cherokee *certainly* could not do anything of quality," from so many years before reemerged in the form of the 1990 Indian Arts and Crafts Act. These trends deeply troubled Don, who sought solace in his own sense of his Indian-ness, his family, and, as so often before, through assistance from a broad and strong network of friends.

ARIEL EXPANSIONS

We kind of balance each other.

We built the A-frame museum in '72. We decided on the A-frame style because of economics and logistics. It was the best way to get *a lot* of space using materials that were fairly readily available. I talked to Ralph Bozarth* about it. I was thinking of something rather modest in scope. Ralph likes challenges. So it kind of got bigger and bigger. Ralph went out with his boat and his outboard motor and towed a lot of the big timbers, the uprights, in from the Columbia River, dragged them up on the beach, and got his boat trailer and hauled them in here and stacked them up. He also got a timber sale from the Forest Service and had lumber sawed. The *cost* was minimal in building it. But it did maximize the space and, interestingly enough, climate-wise, it seems to have been very good for the things that have been in there—pretty constant temperature. If I really have to do a big, big project like a big totem pole or something, we just stick it down the middle of the building and it just becomes part of the stuff to be seen.

The bats moved in and they take care of our moth problem. Boy, I thought those rugs were goners. They hadn't had any care for about five or six years. When I got them down, they were just pristine. You just have to attribute it to those bats in there because they eat a tremendous amount. Then the squirrels moved in. So I sort of made a mental pact where they were con-

* Ralph Bozarth is a family friend who provided invaluable help in the construction of nearly every building at Ariel.

cerned: if they didn't eat the baskets, I wouldn't poison them. So far they've been good! All in all, I suppose we're environmentally correct on most of it. Smitty used to like to go up and shoot the bats with twenty-two shot shells. That is why we have some daylight coming through, but no water so far. Eventually, I would like to put a metal roof on it because it is a little more fireproof that way and a little tighter.*

The other A-frame was built not long after that, and Patty incorporated it into the dwelling house when she decided to expand. Her jewelry business was burgeoning, so she expanded the house and built the gallery. Patty's much more bold than I am. She has got two speeds, flat-out *charge* and stop! She is much more optimistic than I am, which is good. I suppose we kind of balance one another a little bit. For Patty, everything is doable or "It'll be all right" or "Things take care of themselves." And my sense of responsibilities sort of rebel sometimes at that! So sometimes it ends up that things work out because everyone is running themselves crazy to make it happen!

That was about when I thought it would be nice to have a big New Year's party and invite all the customers and friends. It would be great for business. Patty had an eye on that. And it *certainly was.* We used to have champagne and wine. Harlow, Smitty, couple of other friends, and I mixed up some fur-trade high wines.† I think I've still got the keg up there in the A-frame that we mixed it up in. It was cheap wine and pure grain alcohol, even some gunpowder, I think! But those parties just got so big, it was frightening.

Then the gallery opened in '76, '77. The original gallery was a place to display and sell our work. But everybody was so busy making a living, nobody really had time to run it. We never did a whole lot of advertising on it. It worked, and then Patty wanted to open the one down in the Yamhill Marketplace, which was a total disaster and just really messed up everything for a while. That closed, but the new concept of inviting other artists in and doing shows, and doing more advertising and all, seems to really be paying off. So in a way, we were both right, which is nice! This time she was *righter,* if that is a correct word, than I was!

---

* The family put on a new metal roof after Don's death.

† This usually contained pure grain alcohol, low-quality wine, sugar, gun powder, and potent spices—not a particularly palatable concoction.

We were down in Scottsdale, Arizona, about two years ago. She always catches me when I'm kind of mellowed out. I'm tired and I've just been fed and things are going rather nicely. Then she moves in with these little suggestions. I'm sitting there, feeling very mellow, and it has been nice to see a lot of our friends down there. Show is going pretty well. She says, "What would you think if I asked you to let me open up the gallery again? Just a small effort; we could have our work in there and the work of some of our friends who are artists and some of the young artists who can't get shown in major galleries because they don't have any kind of a résumé or anything." And she said, "I'd be totally responsible for the finances."

I was very mellow about the whole thing. I said, "Well, all right. Well, if you want to, you try it, but you'll be totally responsible for it."

"Oh, I will. I will. It is just going to be little, nothing to worry about."

Opened up. Right away, it filled up the gallery space we had, then it expanded into the hallway between the gallery and Patty's house, then it expanded into the house! It seems to be working very, very well. I'm really surprised and of course pleased immensely. It would be kind of nice if the gallery would take care of a lot of the stuff so we don't have to go and do a show here and a show there; have to fly there, ship the pieces, and insure everything. Besides, you make 50 percent more on anything you sell here, which is not to be ignored. So if Patty keeps all of her bookkeeping and everything straight, I don't see any reason why it shouldn't be a rousing success. I'm optimistic and that is *unusual* for me, because I'm usually the one to put the brakes on. I think it is going to work out pretty nicely, if everybody keeps cooperating and I don't panic too badly.

The thing is to learn "enough," and lots of Indians thought about this. I know my grandfather used to say, "The white people in their teachings don't seem to have anything about 'enough.'" That is, you have enough for your family, your needs, and some of your wants. Nobody ever has enough for all their wants, but you have a few more important ones. Then you must always have something that you have to share with somebody who doesn't. Mom is fanatical on that subject, but you know somewhere along the line, something has to be inside you to tell you "enough." Enough cars, enough TVs, enough stuff. So it makes life a little more pleasant and also casts a little different light on existence.

TRYING TO KEEP YOUR BALANCE

You walk down this little narrow road.

In spite of the fact that each of the buildings at Ariel served a different purpose and had a different meaning for those who built and used them, they made up a larger whole that was the Lelooska family complex. Don's identity was like those buildings. He was a modern American who wore store-bought clothes and was influenced by consumer culture. Don also saw himself as Indian, as Cherokee, and as Kwakiutl. These were not mutually exclusive but were simply a part of who he was. That people can have divergent and simultaneously existing points of identification is only recently recognized by much of the scholarly world. Rather than type-cast people, it is more productive to see that identity is a reflection of the complexities of being human. Identities shift and change, given the situations in which people find themselves and given the relationships they establish with individuals or groups.[1] This does not mean that identity is a façade, a disingenuous mask donned for the convenience of the moment. For Don, who he was grew out of the family into which he was born, what people thought about him, and the choices he made. During some periods of Don's life, negotiating the complicated labyrinth of identity was more difficult than other periods were. Still, kith and kin remained fixed points on his mental horizons, some distant and some nearby, helping him navigate. These associations were always a part of who Don was.

Being Indian means pride in the heritage and all. I probably would've become very insular like a lot of people who are focused purely on their own tribe and their own traditions if it hadn't been for my grandpa. He had *so* many friends and *so* many interests, was *so* fascinated. He was really quite a scholar in his own right. Because of him, I never really doubted I'm Cherokee. My source of pride was that we had these people—the Cherokee chiefs in those black broadcloth suits. They look like a board of directors. I'm always very proud of the fact that our people, the Cherokees, intellectually and politically were very adroit, but I'm also very, very proud that the Kwakiutl, one of the great lineages, was willing to accept our whole family as part of theirs, which was an immense compliment. So I probably feel . . . today more Kwak-iutl, more part of Jimmy Sewid's family than part of Oklahoma, which is far away. The memories of a kid, the hot summers, powwows, and people who were more interested in the oil business and the cattle business than they were in tribal politics and in preserving the culture. It is hard for me because I love them all. Particularly I love Jimmy's family. I would like to see things go well for them. Like any great house, they have their traditional enemies, which, I'm proud to say, are my enemies too!

I was proud of both sides of my family, but because of my grandfather, the Indian sort of dominated. I was crossing tribal barriers as a kid so much, and my grandfather did it *so* well, that it just seems so natural. I remember the first time I saw him dance with some of the old Lakota. He had his moc-casins, bells, just a breechcloth, a headdress—his honor bonnet they had given him; it is up in the collection—and of course all of his wounds. His old friends came and painted all of his old wounds, even the parade-ground saber scar on his cheek by his eye and the one on his leg, numerous bullet holes that he had, and knife marks and things on him! Boy, he looked *great.* I mean, I was so proud of him! The old guys, "moldy old varmints" as Grandma called them, called him Plenty Stripes because he had been a sergeant-major in the cavalry.

You would talk in Lakota about Plenty Stripes, all the blood he had shed in honor and defense of his people, defense of the country. That is another thing that always kind of got me. Here are these people who had suffered so much at the hands of the American government and yet they were *so loyal* and the flag meant *so* much to them—America, being *an American.* You go off to the army and you support your country. Of course, America may have been a metaphor for the earth. I've thought about that, too, but they were always *so proud,* and of course the warrior societies came back to life after World War II.[2] The young men who had gone and fought were respected again. Why, their warriors came in and carried the flag. My uncle and my grandfather went down there to volunteer the Monday after Decem-ber 7, 1941,* at the recruiting office. It got to me in a very special way. I understand it and, yet, I don't *quite* understand how they can do it.

My grandfather's family were still at war over the fact that some of them

---

* The date of the attack on Pearl Harbor.

went with Stand Watie* and fought with the South in the Civil War. Old C.V. ["Clem"] Rogers was one of the guys who went. So there was a schism there and I think that was part of the reason that Grandpa decided that going to Wyoming would be good. He didn't see any future for his grand-children, never wanted them to go to Indian school. He was just adamant about that. He didn't really want them raised on a reservation. His thing was: get your own land, hold it, compete, and don't apologize to anybody. He felt that certainly they had the intelligence and strength to do it, but it was just a matter of getting them "off the dole," as he put it.

Of course his first hitch in the cavalry turned him a lot against Indian schools. The government was taking the Apache kids and sending them off to school, and their parents were mutilating them and killing them, which they thought was better than putting them in the hands of these people who had hunted and killed them for generations.[3] He very, very definitely did not want his kids to experience what some of those Apache kids did when they were taken off in the trains. He would have to go out and bring them in. Put him in an awful bind, too. I mean, there was the oath and the flag and all that stuff, and he was in the middle. He came out of it vowing that no grandchild of his was going to be a reservation Indian. He was kind of critical of the Osage. Wasn't the fact, he thought, that they were rich, it was the fact that their wealth made them invalid. All they did was amuse themselves. He thought they should be getting their young people into law schools and things like that, learning to fight with the white man's weapons and preserve their culture. Otherwise, people were just going to keep exploit-ing them and taking it away from them.

It is tough. You . . . you walk down this little narrow road and you just try to keep your balance; you don't fall off on one side or the other. My grandfather and Jim Sewid *both* believed that you needed to take the best from both cultures. Both cultures are flawed. It is that way with all peoples. But you have to take the best of both and build your life on that; other-wise you end up just being *torn apart,* or *constantly* in conflict. It has been pretty hard. Looking back on it, I don't know why more of it hasn't both-ered me.

* Watie (1806–1871) was a Confederate general during the Civil War. Cherokees split over which side to support in the war.

SUCCESS CAN BE A TOUGH THING

It wasn't right in my face.

There are many Indians and Indian experiences. It makes a difference if a person grows up amid the cultural wealth but economic poverty of a reservation. It makes a difference if a person is affiliated with a tribe or not, "mixed-blood" or "full-blood," successful as a "compassionate trickster" or not.* Being Indian means struggling with oppression not only by non-Indians but by other Indians as well. Strength of character is not easy to maintain in a world that fosters self-doubt. Don's abilities to obtain some measure of success, then, are due to his own sense of self, the security and encouragement his family provided, and the sheer accidents, good and bad, that life spun in his direction.

Growing up off reservation had its advantages. It wasn't right in my face, this peer group of the jealous and the angry, like in any ghetto situation. Let's face it; that was what reservations were at that time. They were rural ghettos. So growing up off reservation made it easy in some ways; of course, there may have been some problems in other ways. I think that is why a lot of the people who are making it have moved out of the Indian community. I can think of a couple of Pueblo potters who're geniuses who did that. I think their work a hundred years from now, two hundred years from now, will be admired with the finest Oriental ceramics and things. I think they're doing *great* work and *new* work. They're breaking new ground, but they're carrying enough of the *old* thing that it still has the lifeblood of the art.

But it is tough for young artists. It is a tough row to hoe. I think the jealousy is the hardest thing for them to handle. But a lot of them get the big head, everyone tells them how wonderful they are. Boy, I tell you, growing up, Mom and my grandfather, my uncles, my grandmother, and a lot of the old friends tell you, "That is poison. Never believe it."

In a way, worst thing that can happen to you in an Indian community is to become a success or become prominent and get a lot of publicity. I've seen this just ruin the likes of some artists, especially those who were still

---

* For a definition of "compassionate trickster," see the introduction to chapter 5, "A Kind of Hunger."

living on the reservation. I can think of one promising Plains painter who got so much persecution from the jealous do-nothings that he committed suicide. So a lot of times, they have to move off the reservation and get away from that kind of backbiting and petty jealousy. There're always the groups and families that have old scores to settle. A lot of times this comes out, and for some reason it is kind of like the Japanese saying about when a nail sticks up, you pound it down. Well, on reservations this happens. Success can really be a tough thing!

You go through life a learner. There *are* no experts. You learn. You walk a ways, but you know there are always these hills. You go over the hill. You climb one hill and you think, "Oh boy, look, I made it." Then you look and here is a bigger hill over here and you just have to keep climbing and climbing. You never are going to have all of the answers. You must never pretend to. *Humility;* in some tribes, you have this tradition of humility. In others, arrogance and self-aggrandizement are accepted socially and expected of a man. So there is that to be considered, too. But a lot of artists suffer from getting a big head early on because there are all these fawning people and these nice white ladies telling you "how wonderful" and everything. You always need that good trusted little cadre of *sincere* critics, not the ones who want to cut you down out of jealousy, but the ones who want to see you do your best.

My best critics, surely the most merciless, have been within the family— Grandfather, my granduncles, my grandmother, and Mom, definitely. Quality is a big, big deal with her. She is very good and she is still at it. She had this pumped into her. She pumped it into me. I tried to give it to Smit. I did some kind of mean things to Smitty somewhere along the line! He was making stuff just to get his motorcycle parts and things! As a kid, he had to get this idea of "quality was first." You weren't going to knock out this stuff just to get your motorcycle parts or your ammunition or whatever you needed. That was the only reason he did that stuff for a long time. If I could keep that motorcycle broke down, why, Smitty was going to work! Now, I think, certainly, Smitty has these values.

The best critics were in the family. Then there were those wonderful, wonderful friends—the old people. They have a very good way of shrinking you up and getting you into shape because about the time you begin to think you know something, they come up with something that just—"My God," you think, "where has this been? Why didn't I see this?" or "Why didn't I know this?" or "I should've understood that." They're very good at that. But it happens so *smoothly* and so adroitly. Mom has kind of the rock-in-the-sock approach.

BEING A CERTIFIED INDIAN

Now you have to have a roll number.

In 1990, Congress passed the Indian Arts and Crafts Act, which required anyone producing art labeled as Indian or Native American to be an enrolled member of a federally recognized tribe or to be registered with one. The sale of "Indian" art mass-produced in places like the Philippines helped create the impetus for the act, but a struggle several decades old over who could claim to be an "authentic" or "real" Indian emerged in the debate.

Such determinations of authenticity are tied to political determinations scarcely a century old at best. It began to matter who was counted as "Indian" with the beginning of the reservation system and then the 1887 Allotment Act, because both tied being Indian to "privileges" doled out by the federal government. Federal legislation ranging from the 1934 Indian Reorganization Act, the Indian Claims Commission, and even the infamous Termination policy steadily laid a greater and greater emphasis not only on who was or was not Indian but also on what limited rewards might accrue to individuals so designated. Moderately successful court battles to secure treaty rights in the twentieth century and the minimal but important channeling of federal dollars to reservations since the 1960s have raised the stakes of being an official Indian.

The higher stakes have given some people the erroneous notion that Indians benefit from "special privileges." That, combined with the infusion of New Age mysticism into American popular culture, has led to huge increases in those claiming to be "Indian." In this context, the exclusiveness of the 1990 Indian Arts and Crafts Act makes sense, but looking at it from Don's perspective, from the position of someone who "paid his dues," mild though they may have been in comparative terms, suggests the problems inherent in such simple attempts to legislate identity. Don was painfully aware of these problems and indignant to have had to demonstrate that he was "Indian."

I feel, like a lot of the Indians, it is God and your grandparents who make you an Indian, not the federal government! Now you have a roll number or have to be recognized by a tribe as a person because of the 1990 Indian Arts and Crafts Act.[4] It grew out of the fact that the Indian art business has become *so* lucrative. There is an awful lot of jealousy. That is one of the things that has cut the Indians down in accomplishing so many things. A lot of the finest jewelers and beadworkers and all are not registered. They don't belong to any band. They're people who sort of did what we did. We went back and searched for a lot of the information on the art and ceremony.

My family has been off reservation for so long, the connections had been pretty well severed. They're still there, but Mom is reluctant to dig them up. Having met a few of the relatives in my younger days, I can see why she might feel that way. Steve Beckham was a big help, though. He is still trying to run down some parts of the family, our grandpa's people. Steve was the one who got the Cow Creek Band to come forward and give some assistance, that certification.* My niece Lee'll never be happy until she gets her card. To me it is irrelevant because, like I say, it is God and your grandparents. That fuss seems to have died down and the tribes seem to be taking other directions now, getting recognized and getting a casino. If you haven't got a tribal museum and a casino, you're nobody!

* Stephen Dow Beckham is a professor of history at Lewis and Clark College in Portland, Oregon. Beckham helped the Lelooska family obtain certification through the Cow Creek Band of Umpqua Tribe of Indians in order to meet the requirements of the 1990 act.

10 / New Foes, Old Friends

The last three years of Don's life were filled with uncertainty. His mortal illness, despite the fact that neither he, those in his family, nor his friends wanted to confront it, stared him in the face. The uneasiness that the Indian Arts and Crafts Act of 1990 had injected into his life waned in comparison to the diagnosis of colon cancer midway through 1993, his various treatments and surgery later that year, and recurrent health problems for most of the next year. By 1995, it seemed that Don was back in full swing, carving, going to shows, and enjoying his time in the back room with family. He was quieter, less energetic, and more reflective than I had known him to be, but he had gone through no small trauma. It seemed to most of us that Don had recovered from the surgery, that his cancer was in remission. We held our collective breath, hoping that if it came back, it would not be for years. As for Don, he could hardly speak of his colon cancer, almost always referring to it as "this" or "this thing," and to his medication as "those little pills." All of us, I believe, were in denial, not wanting to see that Don was really in decline, refusing to recognize the little signs that would add up to large problems— the chronic "bad cold," sleepless nights, and increased pain. Each came in such small increments that they seemed easy to explain away at the time.

I visited Don on New Year's Day in 1996 to give him a copy of the transcripts of the interviews we had done to that point. He seemed pleased to get the transcripts and to talk a bit more. He had been having problems with a persistent ailment, something akin to bronchitis, most of the fall and into the holiday season. In spite of that, he was still carving madly, happy to be back at it.

During our conversation, I let the tape recorder run while Don told me of his hospital stay and some of the visions he had there. We laughed about some of the visions and marveled at others. I cannot help but think that the bloody grizzly-bear vision Don had was of himself. It seemed as if Don was looking in a mirror. After all, the combination of cancer, medications, and surgery had altered his body dramatically. Don had lost much weight, though he was still a large man. His face showed a gauntness and a pallor new to him. I kept thinking, as he described the vision to me, of the name Grandfather Hinkle had given to Don as a child—Yana, "Bear."

Don was particularly touched by how wonderful people had been to him. He was astonished at the outpouring of sympathy and good wishes from many people who had been to the shows at Ariel. He always knew how impressionable children were, how much they looked up to him. However, the extent of his influence did not dawn on him until his illness made him slow down and consider it and his audiences began to recognize his mortality. Both of us were surprised at how deeply their sentiments touched Don. While the tape captured our laughter during the session, it did not record the hard swallows and welling tears that came to both of us now and then.

In what would be the final year of his life, Don's focus had narrowed almost entirely to his art and family. For more than a half-century, he had carved and worked with his hands on a daily basis. If nothing else, that habit kept him going. It also kept him vital, for he continued to think and dream about what he might do.

Don thought much, too, about those pebbles that his grandfather and granduncle had placed in his hand so many years ago. As much as health and stamina allowed, he spent time with his family, especially the youngest generation. Don's grandniece Jamie, niece Lottie, and grandnephew Dustin could often be found in the back room with him watching TV or scooting around the obstacles of the work area during the day. Just being around them, oblivious as they may have been to Don's condition, made Don happy. He tried to tell Patty, Smitty, Jay, Lee Ann, and Mariah all those things he wanted them to know, but that job would never end. Don also thought about James Sewid—"Jimmy," he always called him—and his daughters Dora and Daisy. Haunting visions of a mask he wanted to make for Jimmy cut through the increasing fog of pain and sleeplessness that troubled Don. He went into great detail about that mask, and I am pleased that he did, for it "lives" in its own way in these pages as Don's tribute to Jimmy and as my way of honoring both of them.

KWÉNKWENXWELIGI

. . . something I've got to do.

Images and icons surrounding Native Americans, such as teepees, horses, and certain beings such as Thunderbird, abound in the twentieth century. They have been misconstrued, misused, and trivialized by those who denigrate Native American belief systems or who seek to undermine the continued viability of Indian lives. In stark contrast, Don offered a glimpse into the deeper meanings of his own spirituality and a sense of Native peoples' cosmological ordering of the universe in his discussion about Kwénkwenxweligi,[1] a Kwakiutl supernatural being sometimes translated into English as Thunderbird.[2] Among the Kwakiutl, and throughout much of the Northwest Coast culture area more generally, four planes of existence or "worlds"—earth, undersea, underworld, sky world—structure the universe. Each realm has its own beings with particular powers. Beings from each realm, including humans, can cross over into the others but only in extraordinary circumstances. Earth contains humans, plants, and animals of land and sea. The undersea world is not literally the sea. Usually beings from the undersea come from great depths, from the unfathomable, and have fantastic powers. The underworld is not a place of the damned, though it is a place that most earthly beings wish to avoid. It is a mirror opposite of the earthly world and a place in which the beings, who are often much like people, have essence, not substance. Giant powerful beings, often great birds, and even the Supreme Being for some groups, inhabit the sky world.[3]

Jimmy Sewid gave Don and his family the rights to K̲ulus, the "baby" Thunderbird, who, in spite of his youth, still embodies tremendous power.

After Jimmy died, Don began to think about the beings represented in his lineage and wanted to do something for Jimmy. In one of the last interviews Don and I did before he went to surgery, Don described to me the Thunderbird mask he wanted to create in Jimmy's honor. Sitting there in that dark, cramped back room with the eerie glow of the big-screen TV providing most of the light, Don took me on a mental journey to see his visions of Kwénkwenxweligi. In doing so, he also wanted to tell me and those who would hear the tapes and read the narrative about his immense respect for Jimmy Sewid as well as for Jimmy's daughters, Dora Sewid-Cook and Daisy Sewid-Smith.

I'm currently trying to go through the process of building the thing in my mind, that Kwénkwenxweligi, that Thunderbird. That is going to haunt me. These ideas get inside you and somehow you just have to purge it. The only way you can purge it is to do it. That one is really going to bother me, because this is something intensely personal for me. I remember standing there on the porch at Jimmy's the day of his funeral. We went there before they closed the casket. I was talking to Bobby,* and he was telling me what the man who was in the bed next to Jimmy at the hospital had said that Jimmy said—and Dora and Daisy know about this, too—that Jimmy said something about the Thunderbird.

So you begin to think about the Thunderbird. You think about the stories—his personality in the myths and things, his position. This isn't second brother, this isn't third brother, this is *the Great Thunderbird*, Kwénkwenxweligi. This is the one who makes the terrible storms and darkens the sky. He is *terribly* powerful. If you were to even come *near* him, why, the heat from his body is so great you would be incinerated before you got an arm's length from him. You begin to build a mental picture of him. This is where you draw on the original source, I feel, which is the mythology. Then you begin, once you have this vision of him: the great curving beak with the big bulging eyes, because that is what makes the lightning, and the horns curving back over his head, because these are all mentioned in the stories. You think of this in gigantic terms. This is really a huge, dreaded, but sometimes benevolent creature. So you begin with that.

* Harold Robert Sewid, born ca. 1933, is James Sewid's son and roughly Don's age.

Then you begin to put it into practical terms. Now, if this is going to be done right, it is going to have to work. Making an opening mask that would work—aye, there's the rub! It has to work because if it doesn't, that is a terrible disgrace to the carver, to the family, to everyone, and it costs a lot of money because you have to *pay* your witnesses to forget about the whole thing. Literally, you close their mouths with wealth. This is done in a lot of cases.

You're putting all this together and you think about your hinges. Leather hinges are going to sag eventually. They're more *old-time* but if you're going to use this mask a lot and want to not have to repair it, then you use metal hinges of the simple kind that came on those Chinese tea chests. They used to use a lot of those on old masks. You would be surprised. I sometimes wonder how many tea chests were destroyed for their brass tacks, strips of brass, and hinges. Pretty early on, they were getting good metal hinges.* So you're going to opt for metal hinges.

Length: the longer the mask gets, the harder it is on the neck. Somewhere between twenty-four and thirty inches seems to be about as much as the human neck can stand and make the mask work.

Balance: you need to think about that. Is it going to be a two-way, where the face is just split down the middle and pops out to the sides? Is it going to be a three-way, where the jaw will drop down and the sides open out? Or is it going to be four pieces, top raising up, bottom part down, and the sides out, you see, so you get this *explosion* from the center? That is the one I like best, like our K̲ulus. So then I think about the K̲ulus. K̲ulus: Now, K̲ulus is semi-benevolent because he is a baby. He is an immature thunderbird. He has this downy body with just the pinfeathers. On the inside, you want to use Sisiutł, which is usually shown as kind of a belt. I think the Sisiutł should be inside the mask on either side as we did with K̲ulus.

This is when you begin to think about design. Now, we're going to make it something like K̲ulus, only he is going to have horns rather than the swept-back feathers and he is going to be more fierce. I'll probably give him copper teeth in addition to the curving beak so he is really fierce. Great curving brows, beetling down, the more fierce the better.

---

* The tea chests look much like a small steamer trunk or footlocker. Those and the metal hinges came in during the nineteenth-century fur-trade era.

Then he turns into a man. So now we're going to deal with the *inner* mask. That is the part that you'll make first, the inner mask, because that is going to determine the size of the outer mask, because you have to have so much room in clearances. (About six o'clock in the morning when I'm getting some pain, I wake up and start to construct this, then I doze off and go to sleep, and then as I come back and wake up, I think about it some more.) I'm going to have a human face, and I probably would have hands. I would like to do something different with the hands, maybe like the hands would raise up on either side of the face with its fingers pointing up, or the arms inside, or something inside. Wealth is always important, so coppers would be great to have because this is the symbol of wealth, power, and chieftaincy.

So we'll probably have a four-way explosive, *ferocious* Thunderbird. The human inside should be in the position of being in a supernatural state. Now, there are a couple ways to approach this. One is, you push the lips forward. That is the way the Cannibal Dancer, the Hamatsa, pushes his lips forward, like Tsonoquah,* too. That is because she eats children. She is uttering her cry, "oooh, hum, hum, hum." So you might want to push the lips slightly forward to indicate that. There should also be the red cedar bark. This man has power. Hamatsa is part of privilege,† so this is kind of a little nod in that direction; the Tseḵa,‡ the Hamatsa dances and all, those are, too. So it is just a little statement for the knowledgeable.

I just keep thinking and keep it jelling, throwing out this and putting in that. Smitty said you might even be able to have legs and arms, almost like a puppet body in this thing. Another thing you can do is put one of those canvas folded concertina-things in it, like the big sun that I'm making in the other room. You just begin in this way. It just gets inside your head and goes round and round and round.

When you think you have it figured out, then you sit down and begin to draw it. Now, how much drawing they did in the old days I don't know.

---

* Wild Woman of the Woods. For further explanation, see chapter 1, "A Life (Un)masked: Placing Personal Narrative."

† Privileges are generally passed down through lineages and publicly sanctioned at potlatches.

‡ This is the Winter Dance or Cedar Bark Dance Ceremony in which the Hamatsa danced. See chapter 6, "Openings to New Worlds," for further explanation.

I need to do it because a lot of times things have to be a specific size. Particularly when we're going to use the masks, you have to keep the brakes on somewhere. If you make the face very large, when you make the backboard part, why, then you would have to make everything else big enough to enclose it. I like to make a drawing. Drawing it lets me play with ideas, too. Whether or not the old carvers did this much, I'm not sure. But it saves a lot of cedar, and cedar is going to be harder and harder to get. I like to be careful. Even in the old days, to get a good piece of cedar, you had to go down to the beach and hunt or you had to pay to have one felled.

This mask is something I've got to do. Whether we keep it in our possession or I just send it home to Jimmy's family, I don't know. Kulus can be summoned any time. Tsonoquah can be summoned by the family. This is a right.[4] That Tsonoquah mask has been to a lot of big potlatches. At one of the big dos up there in Canada, Jimmy put about $8,000 dollars in small bills in the basket on Tsonoquah's back and Smitty danced the mask with someone just handing out the money behind him; that was so funny!

Now, we've got another choice coming up. So, you know, I'm going to have to confer with Daisy and Dora, who are our *best* authorities right now. Do we put a magnificent button blanket with a thunderbird on the dancer to conceal him? Do we make big taloned feet and scale armor, wooden feathers? That last one has to be considered full costume. A great mask with a magnificent button blanket to conceal the dancer would look more like a human or a transformed thunderbird, with a button blanket like a human would wear, rather than just showing a human face within the head and still having the big bird's body.

These are all things Smitty and I'll hash out. I'll make a drawing. I'll probably talk to Dora and Daisy and get their vision of it. They'll probably talk to some of the old folks who are around, who were dancers in their youth or who may have seen the original mask. Now, that is a possibility. If they could find somebody who saw the mask, that'll help. Because a lot of times their memories are *great* when you go to do these things. And they'll remember some little detail that makes a heck of a difference. But it'll just kind of grow and grow; it'll go away and it'll come back and it'll go away, but it is always there, I can't get it out of my head now! I just want to get the damn operation out of the way.

SINCE I'VE HAD THIS THING

I just would kind of like to keep on doing what I'm doing forever.

My grandparents, the old-timers, really knew how impermanent we are in this existence. Since I've had this thing [colon cancer], I've been on kind of an interesting voyage of my own—my own beliefs and all. You ever read any of Charlie Russell's* letters? Charlie Russell was sick. He wrote a friend of his and he says, "Anytime I cash in now, I win!" I kind of feel that way. I've had a heck of a life. I mean, I've known people and seen things that in this century a lot of people would never, never even believe. I've been terribly blessed. So I can't kick much about the whole thing. Besides, one of the tenets of a lot of tribes is, you do not pray for yourself. You pray for others, and in doing this, you make yourself worthy of the fact that others will pray for you. So that is how you deal with this stuff. I don't find an awfully great chasm between traditional beliefs and what we call Christianity. If Christ was God made man, then the Indians' concept of the Great Creator of All Things is not really so far-fetched. And if we have saints, there're spirits, the powers of nature and all. The more I put the two together, I see less distance between the two.

My life just seemed to flow along so naturally; the whole thing in some ways has been a kind of a déjà vu experience. It feels so natural. I can't imagine how it would've gone any other way, I suppose. I could've gone for a profession or something, but this is always what I enjoyed. I was always able to make about the amount of money that I thought I needed or the family needed at the time. So it is very comfortable for me.

I never realized, until this happened—what with the phone calls, the letters, and the things that have happened—really how many lives the little program and our work has touched. I suppose what I've done in my life has touched a lot of lives in the end. Frankly, at this juncture, I feel better about what I do than I think I ever have! So many nice things are happening to me. Well, if it wasn't for my little problem here facing me, I would feel very, very, very good. Life, the challenges, and things I want to do. I just would kind of like to keep on doing what I'm doing forever. Because I do enjoy it. I would pay to do it if I didn't make a good living at it.

---

* Charles Marion Russell (1864–1926) was a well-known artist of Western Americana.

I recently started doing some painting. I can't really carve after the surgery. Well, I don't want to sound mystical because that is getting to be something that is overdone; the loon is a healer and there are loon traditions in Jimmy's family. So there I am, I can't sit very long and I'm bored and disgusted. So got to thinking about loons and I started drawing loons; I made some drawings and finally I made a painting of the myth of the young man who was healed by the loons. I decided I would paint a loon, and when you do something like that, it is a form of magic. You think about it and the tradition is turned over in your mind while you do it. You sing the song that belongs to that particular entity and it is a form of magic, I suppose. It just pleased me to do it. I took this long, shallow "S" form of a loon and it was going to be a loon with a figure on his back, because in several of the stories, the loon takes you away in order to heal you, sometimes dives into the water and things like that. So I was thinking of those traditional stories and then all of a sudden without even really thinking about it, I did the circle and here is the loon. The loon is going up; he is not going down, he is not diving.* Then all of a sudden it begins to come back into my mind. That design just sort of happened. It just sort of fell out. I found the sicker I got, the more Indian I was becoming, frankly! A lot of strange stuff happened. That is what started it.

It was kind of fun and took my mind off of things. So after the loon thing, I had been thinking about puffins and a puffin story, and about the dragonfly and the frog; it is a story that ends when the stomach speaks, the heart is silent, and the frog swallows the dragonfly, his lady love. I did a painting of the ant and the bear story and another one or two. Lot of stories began to come back to me that I didn't even know I had collected. They were just back in my brain someplace. I had them around and I thought, "Well, maybe we'll just put them away. Maybe we'll get some prints made or something." They looked pretty good at the time, but I wasn't trusting my own judgment at that moment.

Mary Ann Normandin† shanghaied them and got them photographed. She was looking ahead to a children's book of the folktales, the ones they

---

* Loons are generally portrayed moving downward.

† Mary Ann Normandin is a longtime friend of the family and was an administrator at Lewis and Clark College in Portland, Oregon.

usually tell the kids. She talked to John Nicholas, a columnist at the *Oregonian*. Lo and behold, somebody tells me that John Nicholas's column reported that I was recovering from cancer surgery and working on a children's book while I was recovering. Mary Ann, on the basis of that, takes it to a publisher and gets it accepted. Well, Mary Ann is just great. She is such a help to everybody in the family. I did one painting for Mary Ann, because she really appreciated the drawings and thought they had a place. I did Salmon Boy for her.

The publisher seemed to get real excited, according to Mary Ann, and they thought they would like to try a book; they needed about twelve stories illustrated with the drawings. You're dealing with children, and the classic northern flat design is cold, formal, and sometimes so abstract that it is very hard for people to get anything out of it. So I kind of drew on the Kwakiutl tradition of taking something from the north and sort of "Kwakiutlizing" it. I used the "U" shapes and joints and things like that.[5] That is where the Kwakiutl element comes in, and you begin to loosen up. They borrowed the things from the north that pleased them and adapted it to their own style, which was probably very like the Nootka[6] in very ancient time. I'm worried about a lot of them because some of them were just *too cute!* At least I thought so. But actually, they were coming out like paintings of carvings in a lot of ways, which gave them that stiff, flat look that I think they needed.

It was a lot of fun and I taped the stories. It worked its way up to about twelve stories.[7] By that time, it is like eating peanut M&M's. Nobody can eat one peanut M&M. I ended up with eighteen or twenty paintings. It was fun to take it from the oral tradition, which is what I grew up in, and put it into print. It is a whole new thing. I would like to continue to experiment with it on kind of an ongoing basis. We'll see. But it is hard to take the text from an oral version into a printed version and keep it what you want it to be. So much of the myths and legends that you read, that are available to teachers, have been so trimmed and polished and turned into new Western-concepts stories that it kind of spoils them. Everybody wants to tinker with them. When they teach you to tell stories, you don't do that. That is not good. Make yourself sick if you deliberately do that. The mere telling of stories carries a blessing with it; the old storytellers were good because they did a lot of it and they understood the boundaries. For the children's book,

I would like to get written down some of the different stories I've collected and told, so the teachers will have them.

After I felt better, after the surgery and all, I made that big sea otter bowl, the mother sea otter, a huge one. That was just mostly to see whether I could do it. I've been making a lot of smaller things, for which there is a really good market that I hadn't thought about. I do a lot more of the alder things than I had for years. It is a better wood than cedar for smaller things like frontlets, rattles, those elegant little feast dishes, and those big ladles that they used to fill with eulachon oil and present to a chief. Then he was expected to guzzle down the whole big ladle full of eulachon grease. Some of the ladles, I swear, would hold a gallon. I tell you, that much of anything, standing with a big audience of your peers, waiting for you to goof or throw up or something, must've been something.

The smaller pieces aren't as taxing physically for me. I had made a lot of the rattles and frontlets and things for years, but I've been doing mostly the big mechanical masks and opening masks and boxes. You work at something to master the technique and eventually after you've done that, well, the major portion of the fun is gone out of it: the adventure and experimentation and *really* being able to put yourself in the place of the guys who were building them a long time ago. Doing the big pieces finally impressed me as being more of a carpentry job than what I like to do, the theatrical sorts of carvings and things.

I had forgotten how much fun it was to carve alder. I rediscovered that. I made a lot of alder pieces. In fact, I took quite a few up to Seattle for the show. It worked out very nicely. I hadn't looked for it to, because Seattle is sort of overrun by the Canadian carvers and all the rest of them. One guy bought all the show, save the Puffin Rock, which I kind of wanted to keep for a while. That was taking the painting and turning it into a sculpture. It was a kind of fun experiment.

I have got to get the pole in the carport finished someday.* It is essentially done. It just needs the wings and the arms carved and then to be painted. Kulus and Tsonoquah, the family crests, are on it. When we had it about halfway finished, we had a potlatch, had everybody down from Canada

---

* Don's younger brother Smitty completed the pole for Don's memorial potlatch. It now stands in front of the museum at Ariel.

[about 1977]. Patty had a huge number of those little salmon that she does in ivory cast into silver and we gave them to the people who had positions: some were tie clips, some were on chains. So the pole is pretty well paid for. There would have to be another potlatch when we raise it. I just haven't been able to get around to it. It is certainly well seasoned!

You know, when I was in the hospital recovering from surgery, I was in La-la Land! I wonder where these things come from sometimes. The Indian explanation is the one I like best. These things have connections to the past and to the future and could be beneficial—warnings and things like that. Yeah, I had some doozies. It was the grizzly bear coming through the ceiling. His face was bloody. He looked like he had been wounded. His head, shoulders, and one arm were in the ceiling up there and he was looking down at me. He was around a couple of nights. Then, off to the side, kind of out of the corner of the eye, was this thing, it sort of looked like a prison cell and there was an Oriental guy, an old Chinese, who was in this cell—only saw him once. He was just there. Bear, he didn't have anything to say other than he was a rather big bear. I wasn't afraid of him because he was bloody from something. You see, at this point in the old days, you dream something like that, then you take the pipe and you go to somebody who is knowledgeable in interpreting dreams and visions. You learn the secret that it contains.

The one, really, that I have a hard time coping with—it doesn't really bother me, but it is a little haunting in a way. Old Mary, Mom's grandma, was a healer with herbs and things like that. I can't remember having ever seen her, but she is very vivid to me because Mom talks so much about her. Grandpa used to talk all about her. Other people have told me about her and how she would sit in her rocking chair, rock and smoke her pipe. Oh, when I had a really bad infection here quite a few years ago, I was running a fever of about 105. The night before it broke and the fever disappeared, on the wall was this shadow. It was a rocking chair accompanied by sound effects: *squeak, squeak, squeak, squeak.* There was this image of this apparently old woman, and she has a little pipe in her mouth and she was just rocking back and forth, back and forth. Been there a long time and I think finally I dozed off or something. I thought, "Well, I was delirious." What I had seen was my mind's image of Old Mary and the fact she was a healer. The next morning, I was going to go to the doctor, why, kaboom, the fever broke and my temperature went down, and just everything resolved itself very quickly.

Well, she showed up at the hospital. She was on the wall there—*squeak, squeak, squeak, squeak.* I heard it before I looked, and there she was, *squeak, squeak, squeak, squeak.* Man, I just had a very good feeling after that. I figured, "Well, this is going to be all right. She has come to look after me." Then, of course, there are those white genes that say, "Of course, you were whacked out on that stuff they were giving you." The bear and the old Chinese could've been that, but the other one was such a perfect reprint of the other experience—that is the one that kind of haunts me. I can understand how they saw and interpreted things in very different ways from the way people do today.

Old Dawson, one of the old Kwakiutl fellows in British Columbia, called. I had either just had the operation, or they had just heard about it. We weren't really bosom buddies; he was always really a lot of fun—he kidded me and would always come and sit down a while. But the phone rang and I picked it up.

He said, "It's me, it's Dawson. Well, I hear you got cancer pretty bad."

And I say, "Yeah, yeah, I think I'll probably be okay."

"Well," he says, "we have ways of doing those things. Have you fed the people?" He meant, "Have you given a feast?"

I said, "Well, oddly enough, yes." We had had some kind of do. We had that birthday party, my sixtieth, which made the *Oregonian* society page!

And he says, "Oh, that's good. Have you picked your successor?"

I said, "Well, I suppose, in a way. Smitty's a good carver."

He said, "Yeah, he'll do fine." He went on, couple other things. Says, "You been telling your story to someone?"

"Yes," I says, "I've been doing that, too."

"Good." And then he says, "You got one of them blankets, don't you? I says, "You mean a Chilkat blanket?"*

He says, "Yeah, *ya'yak'sum.*[8] Yeah, well, you know, you put that over

---

* Weaving for robes and basketry was widespread in the Northwest Coast culture area. Chilkat blankets, woven among the Tlingit peoples of southeast Alaska, remain among the most highly desired and respected.

your box, and then your successor takes that off and puts it on and then he's the boss!"

"Yeah," I says, "done all that."[9]

He says, "Well, it looks like you're doing everything just right." Says, "You know, it's going to be a *damn* shame when you don't die!"

That is characteristic of Old Dawson's humor. He'll go on at great length on something. I've seen him suck people in—students, museum people, and all. He goes along, along, along and in the end, ka-bing, it suddenly dawns on you that he has been yanking your leg. That is classic Indian humor. It just has all of those elements.

When I was taking that radiation therapy, some of it got pretty miserable while they were setting up the exact places and everything to project the radiation. I had on one of those little hospital shirts, if you can imagine one of those *stupid shirts*. They were pumping all this stuff through the rectum so it would light up in the pictures. I was there, just sort of wishing the whole damn thing would go away. Then this nurse came over and bent over and kissed me on the forehead, which is kind of strange, I thought. She said, "That's for all the children!" Apparently her kids had been, or she had been, or she knew somebody who had been to the school programs. I thought that was the strangest thing, and I never got to see her face. So I wouldn't recognize her if I saw her. I don't know if I'll get back to the school programs or not. I would *like* to.

It is amazing the number of people I run into who tell me they were here when they were kids and their kids had been up. It just sort of goes on and on and on. Now we have these people who come to the program and they've got their kids along. They say, "We were here when we were kids, so we wanted to bring our kids." I guess I'll have to figure when I'm really getting old because there'll be a grandparent here with the grandkids.

Ran into one of the rangers from down at Fort Vancouver Park a few weeks ago. It was when the first of the governmental shutdowns took place.* The park closed and the rangers had to cancel their school programs for the kids who were coming to the fort. He was saying that this woman had called

---

* These happened in fall 1996, when neither President Clinton nor Congress could agree on a budget.

Don's work area at Ariel, Washington, in the spring of 1996. Photo by the author.

him. It was kind of busy, I guess, because teachers were calling in to see whether they were going to be able to do their tour of the fort, who was going to be doing it, and all that. He told this one teacher that the school programs had all been canceled because the government had shut down all of the national monuments. She was *really* mad. So she sort of squawked around and pretty soon, she says, "Well, first of all, Chief Lelooska dies on us and now they've shut the fort down. What are our children supposed to do?" It is like old Mark Twain: "The reports of my demise have been greatly exaggerated!"

I think this thing put me back into more attention to old ways of doing things and more traditional ways of thinking. Sort of unplugging things that get to you. Just sort of, "Don't sweat the little stuff." Yeah, it made me think about a lot of things. It makes you appreciate every day and every thing that goes on. So I take time to kind of enjoy some things that I didn't before. I take a little time to sit where it is quiet, look at things like the humming-birds, squirrels, and things around here in the spring. I really enjoyed them. It's the first time that I've really gone out and sat still for a couple of hours and just watched things going on. And realizing what the old people believe, that it is a living earth, that there are practically no inanimate objects. I've found myself more into that way of thinking. I believed that pretty strongly when I was a kid. I was around the old people so much. Yeah, I appreciate things more. So many nice things are happening to me. I wonder if I'm being prepared for an exit or something.

EPILOGUE

We strained against the weight and uneven path.

Eight of us sat a little apart from the family during the funeral in the coast-house. The raw cedar coffin was directly in front of us. Many of the people who were central in Don's life were there, including Father Powell, Dora Sewid-Cook, and Daisy Sewid-Smith. As the service came to a close, we stood and waited. The large extended "family" contingent[10] filed by to view Don one last time.

As one of the pallbearers, I waited for the crowd to pass. One by one, they approached the coffin. Some spoke quietly to Don. Others turned away as if not wanting to see him in this state. After the last person filed past, we went forward and took hold of the casket's thick cedar rails. Getting it out of the coasthouse, down the gravel trail, and then over the slick wooden steps to the hearse waiting in the parking lot was an ungainly process. As we strained against the weight and uneven path, it seemed fitting to me. That voyage was as graceful as cancer and death had been.

A long line of cars followed the hearse ten miles to the Yale Valley Cemetery near Smitty and and his wife Julia's house. Once there, the crowd reassembled at the gravesite. A drenching September rain fell, and each drop that struck the cedar casket exploded into a spicy-sweet puff as Father Powell said a brief prayer. Then the ceremony ended and most of the crowd left. It was to have been a small family gathering, and by Lelooska standards it was, with only 150 to 200 people there. Finally, when only a handful of people remained, I unpinned from my lapel the sprig of cedar the family had given me and put it on Don's coffin alongside several others.

As I drove back down to the gallery for the post-funeral dinner, I thought about spring 1996 and the last set of evening programs in which Don had participated. I had made certain my children went to one. Even if they did not remember it clearly, I wanted them to see the performance.

I knew if they did, they would have memories of Don as the powerful figure he cut in my own childhood. I am glad I did not wait. Although the programs that spring had gone well, by early summer 1996 it was clear to all that the end was very, very near. The cancer was spreading rapidly through his body. The doctors gave him weeks to live, and treatments were no longer an option. Keeping Don comfortable and engaged in life emerged as the first order of business.

Don kept up a good front through his sixty-third birthday celebration that summer, but by late August he was in great pain. Cancer had spread into his shoulders and arms, making it impossible for him to draw or paint, much less to carve. He had begun to lose his voice, too, which gradually diminished to a harsh and crackling whisper. I visited Don then. His emotional pain matched his physical discomfort. Carving and speaking—those sustaining elements of his adult life—were no longer open to him. We chatted briefly. I worried about overtaxing him and intruding. I thanked him for telling me his story and let him know I had been sharing some of it with my history classes. He was pleased, but talking was a strain for both of us at that point. We parted quietly, not wanting to say much at all about the obvious.

That visit was just a day or two before Don went into a drastic decline and not more than two weeks before he died. His family was there with him when he finally just stopped breathing and ceased to be.

Conclusion

Many people have mourned Don Lelooska Smith's passing, whether they knew him as an artist, a storyteller and performer, a friend, or a family member. No doubt a great number celebrate Don's exceptional achievements. They look to his career as a consummate carver. His art and sculptural forms grace numerous homes of private collectors and hang on many corporate walls. The Oregon Historical Society portrays his work prominently in its entryways and halls, even using it in some of its advertising. Museums around the country continue to display his work, and art galleries still sell it.

The powerful connections Don made to Makah and Kwakiutl individuals were as exceptional as his artistic attainments. During his life, tribes such as the Makah and Kwakiutl used his creations as a means to express and celebrate their cultures. Many Makah saw their powerful and vital essence represented in the Cha'chik figure he carved during one of the Indian Arts and Crafts Board demonstrations at Neah Bay. They saw a kindred spirit in Don as they told him whaling stories and shared private glimpses of a grand whaling canoe and its associated paraphernalia. These events took place more than forty years after Makahs had ceased their whaling activities, but the deep meaning of whaling for them had not abated. Although Don did not trigger a renaissance in Makah whaling culture, his presence and activities confirmed what was already taking place. His stories about that experience offer compelling evidence that whaling was never "dead" for many Makahs, a point of great significance during the whaling controversies of the mid- and late 1990s.

Don also connected in intimate and personal ways with the prominent Kwakiutl Sewid family. Don and Jimmy developed a fraternal bond that sustained a friendship born of mutual respect and even need. Don needed Jimmy to provide legitimacy to and authority for the production of Northwest Coast masks and their use in performances. Without that sanction, Don would still have been an artist, but would have suffered from nagging doubts about trespassing on others' territories. For Jimmy's part, adopting Don and conferring rights and privileges on him gave Jimmy access to a skilled carver; it kept certain names, rights, and privileges within his family's domain; and it fit into a larger Kwakiutl pattern of the deliberate, public, and very political performance of culture.

The programs at Ariel matched Don's artistic achievements and his successful relations with certain Indian tribes. The programs were a curious mix of entrepreneurial activity and sincere educational outreach. Don was open about the ways that ticket sales filled in slack times. He was also explicit about how the programs brought in potential customers. In the shows, however, no member of the family ever pitched their art explicitly. It was there for all to view, to see in action. If audience members spent money at the family gallery or put in orders for masks, poles, or jewelry, it was of their own initiative. Had Don done the evening shows only for adults and families, one could be more suspicious of his motives. The fact that he and the family did shows for thousands of schoolchildren each year for decades generated ticket sales, but, more importantly, it educated people about Native Americans. Don was such a powerful raconteur that these performances may well stand as his most lasting legacy. People remember him and the stories he told.

In all these aspects, Don was clearly exceptional, but it is useful to see his life in the context of twentieth-century developments for Native Americans as well as for Native American art. At critical moments, paths opened up for Don that he chose to take, and that made all the difference. Don came of age during an era of resurgent tribal power, and he was not immune to it. Don, and apparently his grandfather, worried about "vanishing" cultures of Native American tribes. In the first half of the twentieth century, such notions were ubiquitous. Indians and non-Indians alike believed that the knowledge of older generations was passing away before their eyes. Anthropologists took great pains to "salvage" these cultures before they were lost. In a sense, Don and his grandfather did the same as they conducted their own ethnographies during their many meetings with Enoch Hinkle's friends, or later in Don's life as he ran his "mental tape recorder" during his conversations with Native people from many different tribal backgrounds.

The fallacy of the belief that Native cultures were disappearing is more obvious with hindsight. Beginning in the second half of the twentieth century, students of Native Americans have confirmed the vitality of Indian cultures. If anything, those earlier ethnographers not only documented the flexibility of the cultures with which they interacted, but they also participated in the changes themselves. Partly through them, Native Americans realized that they had a cultural capital that was possible to wield to their advantage outside their own tribal boundaries. Thus, when the Makah set up their cultural museum or the Kwakiutl began hosting public potlatches and feasts, those events not only confirmed the importance of specific cultural patterns to individual tribes, they also announced the potency of the respective culture to any viewers who happened that way.[1]

Likewise, Tommy and Flora Thompson of Celilo Falls realized that their presence in the halls of Oregon's capitol building or the state historical society only enhanced the power of their treaty in gaining some settlement for their people when dam construction inundated the falls. The people who participated in the Indian encampment at the Pendleton Round-Up found in that setting not only a place where they were the object of what some might characterize as the "colonizers' gaze," but also a site at which they could articulate what it meant to be Indian. It was a vital connection to the past, the present, and each other. Like Don and the members of his family who identified as Indian, Native Americans during the twentieth century employed the materials available to sustain their cultures and themselves. As Morris Foster points out in his study of the Comanche, what it meant to "be Comanche" shifted over time, but in no single epoch were people any more or less Comanche.[2]

The twentieth century was about much more than just tribal identity for Native Americans. During the century, a broad identity among Native Americans as "Indians" emerged. It had many sources. Some came from confronting a racist society that cast all Native groups and individuals together in one fictitious "racial" category. Another came from federal policy that sought to regularize government control over these people with whom earlier generations of officials had negotiated treaties. Racism and "Indian" policies alone did not make Indians. Intertribal connections, intermarriages, off-reservation life, and a realization that the oppression and discrimination they shared gave them a common "enemy" convinced many individuals that they could adopt an identity as Indian without losing a tribal and family affiliation.[3] Don's life off reservation and tribal rolls did not exclude him from identifying as Indian in spite of the federal government's refusal to recognize him as such. He and others like him have depended on living family connections, tribal traditions, and modern circumstances (including various levels of cultural performances) to build identity.[4]

Don's identity was not one of pure imagination. He did not wake up one morning with the determination to make himself an Indian. He was born into it, suffered discrimination because of it, and triumphed by embracing it actively. Accepting that identity, even without federal recognition of it, was as burdensome as it was enlightening. He suffered from charges that he was not "really" Indian, that he was the "wrong kind" of Indian at the same time that he benefited from being Indian, from being Cherokee, and even from being Kwakiutl. His is a predicament in which many have found themselves in the twentieth century, but Indians have always known who they were. If one can accept that being Indian means that individuals and groups do not have to be categorized as authentic or inauthentic or forced into some static and abstract definitions of "traditional" culture, the ways in which Don formed his identity stand as the most significant aspect of his life. Don's life experiences counter those who argue that modern urban consumer culture strips away traditional culture. All cultures change, and Don's life reveals the creative hybridity that embodies being Indian for so many people in the twentieth century.[5]

Focusing only on identity, however, neglects the areas in which Don had his greatest direct impact—his art and performances. The shifts in American perceptions of Indian art made possible Don's lifelong voyage into Northwest Coast art—the strongest manifestation of his hybridity. The early-twentieth-century rise in demand for mass-produced Indian curios made a livelihood in arts and crafts possible for Don.[6] Choosing that alternative meant that he spent many hours producing items for sale to tourists who expected certain stereotypical Indian or Western features to appear, a situation immediately recognizable to many Indians similarly engaged in the trade.[7] In spite of those pressures, Don found ways to make some of the items meet the needs of his Indian customers.

The mid-twentieth-century broadening of definitions of art to include newly produced items made Don's transition from the curio trade to Northwest Coast art possible.[8] Others of Don's generation made similar transitions, though they followed different paths. Some did so through academic patronage of their work and expertise. The University of British Columbia, the University of Washington, and the museums associated with them played particularly strong supporting roles for some artists. Don never gained full entry at those institutions, though he had no lack of supporters elsewhere. Other artists had ready tribal affiliations by birth upon which to draw. Their hard work and skills carried them into the ranks of the famous, but they had an advantage that Don could not claim. All had in common a growing market and an increasingly knowledgeable and appreciative audience for their works. They were not confined to producing only for specific tribes or simply reproducing items for museum dioramas.

Producing that art—some for markets, some for museums, and some for Native use and performances—was like the programs in Don's life. All are cultural displays wrought with multiple meanings. How they are read depends on delivery and audience as well as the contexts in which they are created and employed. Don's art and performances match Indian participation in Wild West shows, rodeos, powwows, and potlatches. All are complicated cultural displays.

Timing and context are critical. Don entered into the fray when the art world was cautious about but still open to a man of mixed Cherokee and "white" ancestry producing Northwest Coast art. His various performances were similarly timed. From the 1970s into the 1990s, tribal calls for self-determination and sovereignty combined with federal legislation to restrict who could sell their works as "Indian art." Don managed to negotiate a path through that morass, but had he arrived on the scene earlier or later, one can only imagine that breaking into the ranks of well-known artists and public figures would have been difficult, if not impossible. Don was an exceptional man, but one whose choices were bounded by the time in which he lived. His narrative reveals as much about his time as it does about his life.

Don led a complicated life. My understanding of it has grown with each interview session, each editing of the transcripts, and each draft of this narrative. I recall after the first set of interviews with Don that I went to the Museum of Anthropology at the University of British Columbia in Vancouver. My long talks with Don gave me a greater level of interest and expertise than I had had on my previous visits. I was curious about the various poles and especially the two Haida-style coasthouses standing outside the museum. Finding the entrance to the houses locked, I circled each several times, stopping periodically to look through any available gaps between the wide cedar planks.

As I did so, I remembered the countless times during my teens when I helped the Lelooska family with evening shows. I spent a good portion of the time looking through the peephole in the carved screen that separates the staging area from the dance floor. Sometimes I did it in order to time some sound effect appropriately. Other times I pressed my eye to the hole just to watch. There were other viewpoints, too, and each of us involved in the programs had a favorite vantage point from which we preferred to catch glimpses of the program. Although we good-naturedly argued about which was best or playfully jostled for prime positions, each spot was problematic. We could make out the dancers and masks as they swept past, but no matter which crack or knothole we chose, some portion of the performance was always just out of view. Sometimes we guessed what was happening by listening to the sounds of the performance, but our perspectives were always partial. Looking into Don's life through his narrative is like looking into the coasthouse through those gaps, like watching the Tsonoquah transformation mask danced in the program. Understanding a life is always incomplete, a glimpse into just a part of a whole. We construct our stories from the pieces before us.

NOTES

PREFACE

1. The essays in Judith Okely and Helen Callaway, eds., *Anthropology and Autobiography* (London: Routledge, 1992), stridently offer such a call. Greg Sarris, *Mabel McKay, Weaving the Dream* (Berkeley: University of California Press, 1994), offers a much more powerful and subtle model. Sarris, who grew up around McKay, tells his readers about himself while he illuminates McKay's life. The mixed voices create a beautifully rich, complementary text.

NOTE TO THE READER

1. For excellent examples of how tribes and bands shift and change over time, as well as the problematics of essentializing "tribe," see Frederick E. Hoxie, *Parading Through History: The Making of the Crow Nation in America, 1805–1935* (New York: Cambridge University Press, 1995); Thomas Biolsi, *Organizing the Lakota: The Political Economy of the New Deal on the Pine Ridge and Rosebud Reservations* (Tucson: University of Arizona Press, 1992); Morris W. Foster, *Being Comanche: A Social History of an American Indian Community* (Tucson: University of Arizona Press, 1991); and Alexandra Harmon, *Indians in the Making: Ethnic Relations and Indian Identities Around Puget Sound* (Berkeley: University of California Press, 1999).

2. See Helen Codere, "Kwakiutl: Traditional Culture," in *Northwest Coast,* vol. 7,

Handbook of North American Indians, ed. Wayne Suttles (Washington, D.C.: Smithsonian Institution, 1990), 359–77.

1 / A LIFE (UN)MASKED

1. Sometimes spelled Tsunuqua or Dzōnoqwa. See Note to the Reader for further explanation of variant spellings.

2. Sometimes spelled Hauhauk or Hoh-hox. See "The more you learn, the more ignorant you feel" in chapter 7, "Producing Art," for further explanation of Huxwhukw and the Hamatsa Society, one of the most prominent and powerful to which Kwakiutl men belong.

3. Harry Assu with Joy Inglis, *Assu of Cape Mudge: Recollections of a Coastal Indian Chief* (Vancouver: University of British Columbia Press, 1989), 128n.8, provide a concise and helpful description of the Hamatsa Society and ritualized cannibalism. See also Wilson Duff, "The Killer Whale Copper: A Chief's Memorial to His Son," in *The World Is as Sharp as a Knife: An Anthology in Honour of Wilson Duff,* ed. Donald N. Abbot (Victoria: British Columbia Provincial Museum, 1981), 153–56.

4. For descriptions of blankets, rattles, and head rings, see Doreen Jensen and Polly Sargent, *Robes of Power: Totem Poles on Cloth* (Vancouver: University of British Columbia Press and University of British Columbia Museum of Anthropology, 1986), and Allen Wardwell, *Tangible Visions: Northwest Coast Indian Shamanism and Its Art* (New York: Monacelli Press, 1996).

5. Chinook Jargon is a trade language widely used by peoples of the Northwest. Its origins are obscure, but it included words from many Native American languages as well as those of the different European Americans who came to the region as explorers and fur traders.

6. In the early 1970s, newspaper estimates placed the annual attendance at approximately 15,000. By the time of his death, similar reports placed the annual number at 25,000 to 30,000 visitors. For examples, see Suzanne Richards, "Lelooska Always Has Time for Visitors," *Oregon Journal,* Dec. 2, 1971, sect. 2, p. 1; and Leverett Richards, "Lelooska, Indian Artist and Cultural Treasure, Dies at 63," *Oregonian,* Sept. 6, 1996, B9.

7. In its vertical files, the Oregon Historical Society has a fairly representative set of Portland, Oregon, and Vancouver, Washington, area newspaper and magazine clippings from 1959 to 1996 on Don and the Lelooska family. See also Randolf Falk, *Lelooska* (Millbrae, Calif.: Celestial Arts, 1976); Pasadena Museum of

Modern Art, *Lelooska, Shona-ha, Tsunagi, Patty Fawn* (Pasadena, Calif.: Design World Productions, 1974); Douglas Congdon-Martin, *Lelooska: The Traditional Art of the Mask—Carving a Transformation Mask* (Atglen, Penn.: Schiffer Publishers, 1996); Wink Blair, "Lelooska," *American Indian Art Magazine* 1:2 (1976), 82–85; Larry Glosh, "Symposium: The Future of Indian Art," *American Indian Art Magazine* 3:1 (1977), 25–27, 93–96; Wendy Gordon and Brenda Buratti, "Lelooska," *Four Winds* 1:4 (1980), 33–40; and Darwin Goodey, *Lelooska: Myths, Masks, Magic* (Ellensburg, Wash.: Central Washington University, 1996), videorecording produced by Chris Smart that is primarily a reconstruction of one of the shows, but contains several stories told by Don.

8. For several good examples, see Julie Cruikshank, *Life Lived Like a Story: Life Stories of Three Yukon Native Elders* (Lincoln: University of Nebraska Press, 1990), and Virginia Yans-McLaughlin, "Metaphors of Self in History: Subjectivity, Oral Narrative, and Immigration Studies," in *Immigration Reconsidered: History, Sociology, and Politics,* ed. Virginia Yans-McLaughlin (New York: Oxford University Press, 1990). It is essential to distinguish personal narratives from Indian oral histories or oral traditions. The former can be highly variable depending upon the situation in which the narrative is told. The latter, origin stories and stories of various beings and historical figures, are frequently bound by protocols and are not particularly malleable. Within a given group, audiences know the context in which the stories should be told and understood. These "oral histories" are markedly different from personal narratives.

9. Noel Dyck and James B. Waldram, "An Introduction to the Issues," in *Anthropology, Public Policy, and Native Peoples in Canada,* ed. Noel Dyck and James B. Waldram (Montreal: McGill-Queen's University Press, 1993), 3–38; Rosalind C. Morris, *New Worlds from Fragments: Film, Ethnography, and the Representation of Northwest Coast Cultures* (Boulder, Colo.: Westview Press, 1994); Arnold Krupat, *Ethnocriticism: Ethnography, History, Literature* (Berkeley: University of California Press, 1992); and James Clifford, *The Predicament of Culture: Twentieth-Century Ethnography, Literature, and Art* (Cambridge: Harvard University Press, 1988).

10. For these issues among Native Americans, see Gerald Vizenor, *Earthdivers: Tribal Narratives on Mixed Descent* (Minneapolis: University of Minnesota Press, 1981); Arnold Krupat, *The Voice in the Margin: Native American Literature and the Canon* (Berkeley: University of California Press, 1989), esp. 14–17, 133–201; and James Ruppert, *Mediation in Contemporary Native American Fiction* (Norman: University of Oklahoma Press, 1995), esp. 3–35. These issues are central for many now studying identities;

see Stuart Hall, "Introduction: Who Needs 'Identity'?" in *Questions of Cultural Identity,* ed. Stuart Hall and Paul Du Gay (London: Sage Publications, 1996), 4; Lawrence Grossberg, "Identity and Cultural Studies: Is That All There is?" in *Questions of Cultural Identity,* 88–90; and Kathleen Neils Conzen, David A. Gerber, Ewa Morawska, and George E. Pozzetta, "The Invention of Ethnicity: A Perspective from the U.S.A.," *Journal of American Ethnic History* 12:1 (1992), 3–41. For a discussion of the "racialized state," see Michael Omi and Howard Winant, *Racial Formation in the United States from the 1960s to the 1990s,* 2d ed. (New York: Routledge, 1994).

11. Ruppert, *Mediation in Contemporary Native American Fiction,* 3–35.

12. Unless otherwise indicated, all quotes from Don are from our taped interviews. Copies of the tapes and a transcript are located at the Center for Pacific Northwest Studies, Western Washington University, Bellingham, Washington.

13. See Patricia C. Albers, "From Legend to Land and Labor: Changing Perspectives on Native American Work," in *Native American Wage Labor: Ethnohistorical Perspectives,* eds. Alice Littlefield and Martha C. Knack (Norman: University of Oklahoma Press, 1996), esp. 247–51, as well as repeated references in the other essays in that same volume; and Victoria Wyatt, "Alaskan Indian Wage Earners in the 19th Century: Economic Choices and Ethnic Identity on Southeast Alaska's Frontier," *Pacific Northwest Quarterly* 78:1–2 (1987), 43–50.

14. For a good, succinct discussion of the broader developments, see Bruce Bernstein, "Contexts for the Growth and Development of the Indian Art World in the 1960s and 1970s," in *Native American Art in the Twentieth Century,* ed. W. Jackson Rushing III (London: Routledge, 1999), 57–58. For an in-depth discussion of circumstances in the Southwest, see David W. Penney and Lisa Roberts, "America's Pueblo Artists: Encounters on the Borderlands," in *Native American Art in the Twentieth Century,* 21–38.

15. For one of the best and most concise discussions of the history and contemporary meanings of Indian participation in rodeos as well as Indian rodeos available, see Peter Iverson, *Riders of the West: Portraits from Indian Rodeo* (Seattle: University of Washington Press; Vancouver, B.C.: Greystone, 1999). The photos by Linda MacGannell demonstrate how Indians have made rodeos their own in very powerful ways. For discussions on the history of powwows, see Robert Desjarlait, "The Contest Powwow versus the Traditional Powwow and the Role of the Native American Community," *Wicazo Sa Review* 12:1 (1977), 115–27, and Benjamin R. Kracht, "Kiowa Powwows: Continuity in Ritual Practice," *American Indian Quarterly* 18:3 (1994), 321–48.

16. Jeff Zucker, Kay Hummel, and Bob Høgfoss, *Oregon Indians: Culture, History, and Current Affairs, an Atlas and Introduction* (Portland: Oregon Historical Society, 1983), 98, 102, 116–21.

17. Historians usually portray the twentieth-century phenomenon of pan-Indianism, or the development and acceptance of an "Indian" identity by Native North Americans, in political terms by focusing on organizations such as the National Congress of American Indians (established in 1944). Attention given to national politics has overshadowed examination of the cultural and social origins of pan-Indianism at the grass roots.

18. In the twentieth century, particularly given the governmental bans on ritual and ceremonial practices, many Northwest Coast carvers have at various times leaned heavily on copying styles of older items in museum and photographic collections. See Margaret B. Blackman and Edwin S. Hall Jr., "The Afterimage and Image After: Visual Documents and the Renaissance in Northwest Coast Art," *American Indian Art Magazine,* spring 1982, pp. 30–39. Blackman and Hall argue that these images and existing pieces provide "a rich legacy upon which to draw when personal memory has little to tap" but they tend to exist as "'works of art,' devoid of the activity and context in which they were once enmeshed" (36). Similarly, the confiscation of masks and other regalia meant that copying was "an accepted way of learning" but distinguishes the "art" produced since the mid-1970s as "inescapably part of a present cultural politics" of anti-colonialism; see Charlotte Townsend-Gault, "Northwest Coast Art: The Culture of Land Claims," *American Indian Quarterly* 18:4 (1994), 445–67.

19. Bernstein, "Growth and Development of the Indian Art World," 57–58; Penney and Roberts, "America's Pueblo Artists," 21–38.

20. Ira Jacknis, "Repatriation as Social Drama: The Kwakiutl Indians of Southern British Columbia, 1922–1980," *American Indian Quarterly* 20:2 (1996), 274–86; Judith Ostrowitz, "Privileging the Past: A Case Study in Contemporary Kwakwa̲ka'wakw Performance Art," *American Indian Art Magazine* 20:1 (1994), 54–61; and Townsend-Gault, "Northwest Coast Art." For a recent discussion about the politics of Native American studies, which includes references to the politics of art and of "mixed-blood," see the special issue edited by Devon A. Mihesuah, "Writing About (Writing About) American Indians," *American Indian Quarterly* 20:1 (1996).

21. Clarence Burke (1889–1987) from the Umatilla Reservation was Round-Up Chief at Pendleton from the 1940s through the 1960s. Tommy Kuni Thompson

(ca. 1855–1959) and Flora Thompson (ca. 1901–1979) were key figures among the Wyam at Celilo Falls. Tommy and Flora gained much attention when slack water created by the completion of The Dalles Dam inundated the vital Native fisheries at the falls in 1957.

22. Gail K. Sheffield, *The Arbitrary Indian: The Indian Arts and Crafts Act of 1990* (Norman: University of Oklahoma Press, 1997), 80–101, provides a useful overview of the "identity" literature relative to arts, and issues of being Cherokee (105–115).

23. For a discussion of essentialism in the context of Native American studies, see Mihesuah, ed., "Writing About (Writing About) American Indians." Those who use blood quantum to determine who is "Indian" and who is not (frequently tribes use this measure to determine eligibility for enrollment, as does the federal government in disbursing money) find themselves oddly aligned with eugenicists and racists who embrace the biological determinism of "blood lines." This runs counter to contemporary social science and humanities focuses on cultural formations as the determining factor in identity.

24. For a call for scholars to engage complicated models, see John L. Comaroff, "Ethnicity, Nationalism, and the Politics of Difference in an Age of Revolution," in *The Politics of Difference: Ethnic Premises in a World of Power,* eds. Edwin N. Wilmsen and Patrick McAllister (Chicago: University of Chicago Press, 1996), 162–83. Other scholars have repeatedly and publicly asked for more straightforward, engaging prose unburdened by jargon; see Patricia Nelson Limerick, "Dancing with Professors: The Trouble with Academic Prose," *New York Times Book Review,* Oct. 31, 1993, p. 73.

25. John Purdy, "Comment: Native Americans, Cultural Production, and the State, 1930s and 1960s," unpublished remarks presented at the Pacific Northwest History Conference, Tacoma, Washington, 1997.

26. For a useful discussion of the issues, see Sherry B. Ornter, "Resistance and the Problem of Ethnographic Refusal," *Comparative Study of Society and History* 51:1 (1995), 173–93.

27. James Sewid had rights to Tsonoquah from his mother's lineage. It is the crest of the Temltemlels clan. See Bill Holm, *Smoky-Top: The Art and Times of Willie Seaweed* (Seattle: University of Washington Press, 1983), 42.

28. Jacknis, "Repatriation as Social Drama"; Ostrowitz, "Privileging the Past"; and Dyck and Waldram, "An Introduction to the Issues," 11–23.

2 / GROWING UP INDIAN

1. For a compelling collection of autobiographical and loosely fictionalized auto-biographical childhood stories that illustrate the range of experiences, see Patricia Riley, ed., *Growing Up Native American: An Anthology* (New York: William Morrow and Company, 1993).

2. Janet Hale Campbell provides evidence of that continuity; in spite of tremendous dislocation in her life, she continues to think of the Coeur d'Alene reservation as home. See her *Bloodlines: The Odyssey of a Native Daughter* (New York: Harper and Row, 1993).

3. Some Mexican Americans claim indigenous origins and rights to places in North America. See Jack D. Forbes, comp., *Aztecas del Norte: The Chicanos of Aztlán* (Greenwich, Conn.: Fawcett Publications, 1973); James Diego Vigil, *From Indians to Chicanos: The Dynamics of Mexican American Culture* (Prospect Heights, Ill.: Waveland Press, 1984); Rodolfo Acuña, ed., *Occupied America: A History of Chicanos,* 3d ed. (New York: Harper and Row, 1988); and Rudolpho A. Anaya and Francisco A. Lomeli, eds., *Aztlán: Essays on the Chicano Homeland* (Albuquerque: University of New Mexico Press, 1989).

4. For an introduction to the issues of population decline, see Russell Thornton, *American Indian Holocaust and Survival: A Population History Since 1492* (Norman: University of Oklahoma Press, 1987).

5. Inés Hernandez, "Foreword: Reflections on Identity and Culture," in *Growing Up Native American,* 7–9; Patricia Riley, "Introduction," in *Growing Up Native American,* 21.

6. Studies of Native American childhood experiences and their impact on identity, like those of children in general, remain understudied. For some treatment, see Riley, ed., *Growing Up Native American,* and N. Ray Hiner and Joseph M. Hawes, eds., *Growing Up in America: Children in Historical Perspective* (Urbana: University of Illinois Press, 1985), esp. 169–70. For a review and provocative statement regarding Indian boarding-school experiences, which receive more attention than any other portion of Native American childhood experiences, see Michael C. Coleman, *American Indian Children at School, 1850–1930* (Jackson: University Press of Mississippi, 1993), esp. 3–59. See, too, Elliot West, *Growing Up in Twentieth-Century America: A History and Reference Guide* (Westport, Conn.: Greenwood Press, 1996).

7. For good beginning points and discussions of federal Indian policy, see Don-

ald Parman, *Indians and the American West in the Twentieth Century* (Bloomington: Indiana University Press, 1994), and Donald Fixico, *Termination and Relocation: Federal Indian Policy, 1945–1960* (Albuquerque: University of New Mexico Press, 1986).

8. Paul C. Rosier, "'The old system is no success': The Blackfeet Nation's Desire to Adopt the Indian Reorganization Act of 1934," *American Indian Culture and Research Journal*, 23:1 (1999), 1–37, demonstrates in this focused case just how complicated the results of the IRA were. Ultimately, the IRA contributed to much factionalism as different groups on reservations struggled to gain positions of power relative to each other.

9. Frederick E. Hoxie, *A Final Promise: The Campaign to Assimilate the Indians, 1880–1920* (Lincoln: University of Nebraska Press, 1984).

10. The Osage, originally on the Atlantic seaboard, migrated to Missouri and then Kansas before their removal to Oklahoma.

11. The 1868–1869 Winter Campaign was part of the U.S. Army's attack on tribes when they were least mobile. In November 1868, Lt. Col. George Armstrong Custer led the Seventh Cavalry in a devastating attack on the Cheyenne, which was his first major engagement with Native Americans. The Cheyenne were part of the forces massed against Custer in 1876 at the Little Bighorn.

12. In historic and contemporary times, popular culture is replete with problematic images and representations of Native Americans, as noted nearly two decades ago by Gretchen Bataille, "Education and the Images of the American Indian," *Explorations in Ethnic Studies* 1:1 (1978), 37–49. See the various essays in S. Elizabeth Bird, ed., *Dressing in Feathers: The Construction of the Indian in American Popular Culture* (Boulder, Colo.: Westview Press, 1996).

13. Gender roles among Native Americans varied significantly and changed dramatically, though not all was merely a result of contact with European Americans. For example, for attention to earlier transformations see Carolyn Garret Pool, "Reservation Policy and the Economic Position of Wichita Women," *Great Plains Quarterly* 8:3 (1988), 158–71, and Susan M. Hartmann, "Women's Work among the Plains Indians," *Gateway Heritage* 3:4 (1983), 2–9.

14. In the winter of 1890, U.S. troops massed around Sioux gathered at Wounded Knee (South Dakota) because of the threat of uprisings supposedly fueled by the prophecies and practices of the Ghost Dance. With only the slightest provocation, soldiers opened fire on the Sioux. The official death count stands at 153, but some estimates more than double that number. The incident remains not only

a symbol of the brutality practiced against Native Americans, but also a point of resistance when American Indian Movement activists occupied the place again in 1973.

15. U.S. troops found four babies under the bodies of their dead mothers but only one, a girl, survived. A non-Indian military family adopted and raised her. Whether Sioux families found other babies after the incident or this is an instance of personal narratives not meshing exactly with recorded history remains unclear. See James Mooney, "The Ghost Dance Religion and the Sioux Outbreak of 1890," *Fourteenth Annual Report of the Bureau of Ethnology,* part 2 (Washington, D.C.: Government Printing Office, 1896), 876–80.

16. Patricia C. Albers, "From Legend to Land and Labor: Changing Perspectives on Native American Work," in *Native American Wage Labor: Ethnohistorical Perspectives,* eds. Alice Littlefield and Martha C. Knack (Norman: University of Oklahoma Press, 1996), esp. 247–51, as well as repeated references in the other essays in the same volume.

17. The Ponca originally migrated from the Atlantic to the upper Midwest and then onto the Plains. An 1865 treaty promised them reservation lands in the Dakotas, but the Sioux displaced them. They fled to eastern Nebraska seeking sanctuary among the Omaha, but the U.S. government resettled them in Oklahoma in the late nineteenth century.

18. The federal government undertook significant military building projects in Alaska during World War II. Many Native Americans found employment for the federal government more easily than with private employers, though much segregation remained even there.

19. An archetype of the rough-and-tumble woman of the mythic gun-slinging, dance-hall Old West in Texas, Starr, born Myra Belle Shirley in 1848, lived a hard, bawdy life. Challenging the confines of the gender roles of her day, she passed rapidly through a succession of lovers until her unsolved murder in 1889. Starr has been the subject of at least fifty books, three movies, and one off-Broadway play. The first of those movies came out in the 1940s, when Don probably saw it in the theaters.

3 / FAMILY ACROSS THE GENERATIONS

1. For the best general discussion of the topic, see Peter Iverson, *When Indians Became Cowboys: Native Peoples and Cattle Ranching in the American West* (Norman: University of Oklahoma Press, 1994). Important case studies are found in Alice

Littlefield and Martha C. Knack, eds., *Native Americans and Wage Labor: Ethnohistorical Perspectives* (Norman: University of Oklahoma Press, 1996).

2. I have retained Don's use of racial epithets, not to demonstrate any racist tendency, but to capture the very historical labeling that those names connote.

3. Pendleton had a relatively large Chinese population because of mining and agricultural work in the area. For a list of companies operated by Chinese (seven general merchandise companies, but no tailors), see Margaret Willson and Jeffrey L. MacDonald, "International Chinese Business Directory for the Year 1913:" Introduction [and Reprint]," *The Annals of the Chinese Historical Society of the Pacific Northwest* 3 (1985–1986), 85.

4. The 1887 Dawes Act, in part intended to make farmers of Indians on reservations, broke up tribal lands, assigned them to individuals, and led to the sale or leasing of much reservation land to non-Indians. While the 1934 Indian Reorganization Act ended the allotment of reservation lands, Native Americans continued leasing lands even after that date.

5. Gretchen M. Bataille, *Native American Women: A Biographical Dictionary* (New York: Garland, 1993), xiii.

6. For an explanation of how some Blackfeet played the Great Northern's tourism to their advantage, but also how those who were not favored by the railroad company suffered in dire poverty, see William E. Farr, *The Reservation Blackfeet, 1882–1945: A Photographic History of Cultural Survival* (Seattle: University of Washington Press, 1984), 191–92.

7. For a discussion of the lodges with photos from the early 1940s when Don most likely saw them, see John C. Ewers, *Blackfeet Crafts,* Indian Handicrafts no. 9 (Washington, D.C.: U.S. Indian Service, 1945), 24–27.

8. Enoch may well have been visiting the C. Chan Herb Company and the Chinese Tea Garden, listed as the only establishments in Salem at the time, and taken Don along; see The People's Foreign Relations Association of China, *Meiguo Huaqiao Nianji* [Handbook of Chinese in America] (New York: The People's Foreign Relations Association of China, 1946), 607–8.

4 / LEARNING FROM PEOPLE

1. Jeff Zucker, Kay Hummel, and Bob Høgfoss, *Oregon Indians: Culture, History, and Current Affairs, an Atlas and Introduction* (Portland: Oregon Historical Society, 1983), 98, 102, 116–21.

2. Much the same is noted in Henry B. Zenk, "Kalapuyans," in *Northwest Coast*, vol. 7, *Handbook of North American Indians*, ed. Wayne Suttles (Washington, D.C.: Smithsonian Institution, 1990), 547–53.

3. Born circa 1862, Ishi, a Yana Yahi, spent most of his life trying to avoid contact with whites in California, but in 1911 finally let himself be "found." Known widely as "the last wild Indian," Ishi lived and worked at the University of California Museum of Anthropology until his death of tuberculosis in 1916. For more details, see Theodora Kroeber, *Ishi in Two Worlds: A Biography of the Last Wild Indian in North America* (Berkeley: University of California Press, 1961), 97, 162–63.

4. For example, the Klaskino were included as part of the Kwakiutl, and Franz Boas's studies were cited as the only major source on the group, by Helen Codere, "Kwakiutl: Traditional Culture," in *Northwest Coast*, vol. 7, *Handbook of North American Indians*, ed. Wayne Suttles (Washington, D.C.: Smithsonian Institution, 1990), 359–77.

5. Also sometimes known as the "Longhouse Religion," the teachings of this faith by various prophets speak to world renewal through a general rejection of European American lifeways. Smohallah, "the Dreamer," was one of the better-known prophets. Born circa 1815 to 1820, he became very influential by the 1850s and continued to be so until his death in 1895. See Robert H. Ruby and John A. Brown, *Dreamer-prophets of the Columbia Plateau: Smohalla and Skolaskin* (Norman: University of Oklahoma Press, 1989).

6. The Middle Oregon Treaty, signed in 1855 and ratified by Congress in 1859, relocated most of the Indians of the central Oregon area to the Warm Springs Reservation, which had originally been Paiute territory. In 1929, a federal statute set aside lands at Celilo Falls for a village. In 1958, the villagers and people at the Warm Springs Reservation won $4 million in a settlement for the flooding of the village. Most of the money remained in a tribal fund that went toward the establishment of the Kah-Nee-Tah resort in the early 1970s.

7. Among the best of the more recent studies are David Wallace Adams, *Education for Extinction: American Indians and the Boarding School Experience, 1875–1928* (Lawrence: University Press of Kansas, 1995); Clyde Ellis, *To Change Them Forever: Indian Education at the Rainy Mountain Boarding School, 1893–1920* (Norman: University of Oklahoma Press, 1996); and K. Tsianina Lomawaima, *They Called It Prairie Light: The Story of Chilocco Indian School* (Lincoln: University of Nebraska Press, 1994). Others argue that Indian families did not seek to avoid the schools as much as some authors have suggested; see Michael C. Coleman, *American Indian Chil-*

dren at School, 1850–1930 (Jackson: University Press of Mississippi, 1993). One of the few historical studies of Indian education after the boarding schools ended is by Margaret Connell Szasz, *Education and the American Indian: The Road to Self-determination Since 1928* (Albuquerque: University of New Mexico Press, 1977). For works produced at the beginning of the transition to self-determination, see Herbert A. Aurbach, ed., *National Research Conference on American Indian Education* (Kalamazoo, Mich.: Society for the Study of Social Problems, 1967), and U.S. Dept. of Health, Education, and Welfare, *The Indian Education Act: Reformation in Progress* (Washington, D.C.: Government Printing Office, 1976).

8. Contemporary contest powwows emerged out of the dances and other intertribal ceremonies at rodeos and fairs beginning in the 1940s and 1950s, but expanded dramatically after the 1960s. Few debate the meteoric rise of the contemporary contest powwow, but the degree of homogenization brought by the apparent adoption of Plains-style dances is hotly contested. For good coverage of the debates, see Robert Desjarlait, "The Contest Powwow versus the Traditional Powwow and the Role of the Native American Community," *Wicazo Sa Review* 12:1 (1977), 115–27; Mark Matten, "The Powwow as a Public Arena for Negotiating Unity and Diversity in American Indian Life," *American Indian Culture and Research Journal* 20:4 (1996), 183–201; and Benjamin R. Kracht, "Kiowa Powwows: Continuity in Ritual Practice," *American Indian Quarterly* 18:3 (1994), 321–48.

9. The Pendleton Round-Up Collection at Oregon Historical Society in Portland, Oregon, as well as the clippings file on the Round-Up there, abundantly illustrate the ways in which the Pendleton Round-Up Association used Indians.

10. Because of Burke's position as Round-Up Chief, the press often referred to him as the "most photographed Indian in Western America." The fact that he had posed for one picture with John F. Kennedy and Jacqueline Kennedy during the 1960 presidential campaign added to his fame.

11. In the context of pushing for the application of treaty rights and other claims in the 1950s, this story must have carried much political poignancy.

12. For a stinging critique, see Rayna Green, "The Tribe Called Wannabee: Playing Indian in America and Europe," *Folklore* 99:1 (1988), 30–55.

13. Carrie A. Lyford, *The Quill and Beadwork of the Western Sioux*, Indian Handicrafts no. 1 (Lawrence, Kans.: Haskell Institute, 1940).

14. This probably refers to modern tribal and intertribal dances more than the contemporary powwow dances. For a general overview of the historic transformations, see Desjarlait, "The Contest Powwow versus the Traditional Powwow."

15. See L. G. Moses, *Wild West Shows and the Images of American Indians, 1883–1933* (Albuquerque: University of New Mexico Press, 1996).

16. Between the 1880s and 1930s, George T. Emmons collected thousands of pieces that went into museum collections in New York, Chicago, and Denver as well as the Smithsonian Institution. Don may be referring to the materials collected by George Dorsey for the Field Museum in 1897. Franz Boas held Emmons in disdain because of his "free market tactics." See E. S. Lohse and Frances Sundt, "History of Research: Museum Collections," in *Northwest Coast*, vol. 7, *Handbook of North American Indians*, ed. Wayne Suttles (Washington, D.C.: Smithsonian Institution, 1990), 90; Douglas Cole, *Captured Heritage: The Scramble for Northwest Coast Artifacts* (Norman: University of Oklahoma Press, 1995), 151–53, 169–71.

17. I have rendered the words and names in these stories phonetically, based on how they might have been written using Chinook Jargon.

18. Speelyai is a regional spelling and rendition of the name for Coyote.

5 / "A KIND OF HUNGER"

1. Gerald Vizenor, *Earthdivers: Tribal Narratives on Mixed Descent* (Minneapolis: University of Minnesota Press, 1981).

2. Much work in Native American literature and criticism calls for broader views of Native Americans. For examples, see Arnold Krupat, *Ethnocriticism: Ethnography, History, Literature* (Berkeley: University of California Press, 1992); Arnold Krupat, *The Voice in the Margin: Native American Literature and the Canon* (Berkeley: University of California Press, 1989), esp. 14–17, 133–201; and James Ruppert, *Mediation in Contemporary Native American Fiction* (Norman: University of Oklahoma Press, 1995), 19–20. Historians of Native America and other fields have also called for broader views of group identities. Some good examples are found in David Rich Lewis, "Reservation Leadership and the Progressive-Traditional Dichotomy: William Wash and the Northern Utes, 1865–1928," *Ethnohistory* 38 (1990), 124–42, and George J. Sanchez, *Becoming Mexican American: Ethnicity, Culture, and Identity in Chicano Los Angeles, 1900–1945* (New York: Oxford University Press, 1993).

3. One's legal status as an "Indian" depends upon the ability to prove enrollment in a federally recognized tribe. Many people fall outside this narrow definition of Indian for a wide variety of reasons. See the special issue edited by Devon A. Mihesuah, "Writing About (Writing About) American Indians," *American Indian Quarterly* 20:1 (1996). For a careful consideration of the problems of "Indian" iden-

tity and politics in the recent era, see Joane Nagel, *American Indian Ethnic Renewal: Red Power and the Resurgence of Identity and Culture* (New York: Oxford University Press, 1996).

4. The number of people claiming a newfound or rediscovered Indian ancestry has risen dramatically in the past two decades, in part because of the impression that money and benefits are readily available. Such views are not only erroneous, but also quite harmful to federally recognized Indians, whose economic well-being on reservations hangs by a thread at best. When combined with a New Age co-optation of Native mysticism and the popularity of "playing Indian," the levels of misunderstanding are only compounded. For a stinging critique, see the final two chapters of Philip J. Deloria, *Playing Indian* (New Haven, Conn.: Yale University Press, 1998).

5. For two fine examples of the reexamination of the American Indian Movement in this vein, see Paul Chaat Smith and Robert Allen Warrior, *Like a Hurricane: The Indian Movement from Alcatraz to Wounded Knee* (New York: New Press, 1996), and Troy R. Johnson, *The Occupation of Alcatraz Island: Indian Self-determination and the Rise of Indian Activism* (Urbana: University of Illinois Press, 1996). A less political but equally compelling explanation of how being Indian, tribal, and urban can coexist is offered by Joan Weibel-Orlando, *Indian Country, L.A.: Maintaining Ethnic Community in Complex Society* (Urbana: University of Illinois Press, 1991).

6. In the early 1960s, Feder was also the curator of American Indian art at the Denver Museum of Art in Colorado.

7. The term "Chinook" is a general linguistic designation for the many bands of Native people living in densely packed villages along the Columbia River from its mouth to The Dalles.

8. The Oregon Museum of Science and Industry is in Portland. In the late 1950s and early 1960s, OMSI sent groups of school-age children on educational field trips to Longview, Washington, by train and then bused them back to Portland. The OMSI buses began stopping at Kalama to visit with Don and the family. Those stopovers jump-started the Lelooska family's daytime programs and gave them much exposure in the greater Portland area.

9. For a prime example of how critics and the general public began to view the production of utilitarian items as a respectable craft, but did not readily accept it as art—and an examination of the ways in which crafts remain largely the province of women—see Elizabeth Hawkins, *Indian Weaving, Knitting, Basketry of the Northwest* (Vancouver, B.C.: Hancock House Publishers, 1978).

10. Established in 1937 to promote the sales of Indian-made crafts, the Indian Arts and Crafts Board (IACB) languished in the late 1940s and 1950s. In the 1960s, interest in Native American arts revived the IACB. In this context, anthropologist Edward Malin negotiated with the IACB to be its consultant for the Pacific Northwest excluding Alaska, which had a regularly appointed official. Malin had done graduate work with Frederica de Laguna on the Tlingit of southeast Alaska as well as among the Kwakiutl of British Columbia, and found that his association with the IACB was a means to stay engaged in the field outside academe.

11. For example, a work that focuses on carvings to the near exclusion of most utilitarian items is Edward Malin, *Indian Art of the Northwest Coast: The Cultural Background of the Art,* with collection notes by Norman Feder (Denver: Denver Art Museum, 1962). For a general discussion, see Bruce Bernstein, "Contexts for the Growth and Development of the Indian Art World in the 1960s and 1970s," in *Native American Art in the Twentieth Century,* ed. W. Jackson Rushing III (London: Routledge, 1999), 57–58.

12. Later in the interview, Don was careful to add that Makah cultural production was also hidden from outsiders. Those outsiders then attributed the apparent lack of certain types of art as a loss. Moreover, Makah art is in the Westcoast style, a more geometric and two-dimensional style than the better-known art of the people to the north.

13. In 1922, Indian Agents at Neah Bay forced the Makah to cease their whaling activities. At the time of this interview with Don, the Makah had not begun their efforts to reestablish whaling, which is guaranteed by treaty. I have no doubt that Don would have been delighted with the Makah success in securing those rights and in taking their first whale in spring 1999.

14. Spelling and definitions from George Gibbs, *A Dictionary of the Chinook Jargon or Trade Language of Oregon* (Washington, D.C.: Smithsonian Institution, 1863).

15. Malin wrote an unsigned feature article for the Indian Arts and Crafts Board magazine with a picture of the Cha'chik carving and a general overview of Don's work and Northwest Coast art. See "Lelooska," *Smoke Signals* 49 (summer 1966), 3–17, esp. 15.

16. About five centuries ago, a large mudslide buried five houses at Ozette, near Cape Alava on the Pacific Coast. Since the 1970s, excavations have yielded more than 50,000 items, including pieces of the houses and other organic materials preserved in the mud. For further information, see Ruth Kirk and Richard D. Daugh-

erty, *Exploring Washington Archaeology* (Seattle: University of Washington Press, 1978), and Ann M. Reuker and Erna Gunther, "Makah," in *Northwest Coast,* vol. 7, *Handbook of North American Indians,* ed. Wayne Suttles (Washington, D.C.: Smithsonian Institution, 1990), 429.

17. The Makah Cultural and Research Center opened in 1979 and was one of the first tribally controlled museums in the country, marking a significant departure from non-Indian–administered institutions.

6 / OPENINGS TO NEW WORLDS

1. A classic on the subject, originally published in 1977, is by Robin Fisher, *Contact and Conflict: Indian–European Relations in British Columbia, 1774–1890,* 2d ed. (Vancouver: University of British Columbia Press, 1992), 45–46.

2. In spite of the repression, Native arts continued to flourish until the 1920s. See Fisher, *Contact and Conflict,* 119–45.

3. For the best explanations of what these seizures meant to the families involved, see Daisy (My-yah-nelth) Sewid-Smith, *Prosecution or Persecution* (Cape Mudge, B.C.: Nu-Yum-Baleess Society, 1979), and Harry Assu with Joy Inglis, *Assu of Cape Mudge: Recollections of a Coastal Indian Chief* (Vancouver: University of British Columbia Press, 1989), esp. 103–21. An excellent study of the topic is provided by Douglas Cole, *An Iron Hand Upon the People: The Law Against the Potlatch on the Northwest Coast* (Seattle: University of Washington Press for Douglas & McIntyre, 1990).

4. See Sewid-Smith, *Prosecution or Persecution,* 2–5, and Assu and Inglis, *Assu of Cape Mudge,* 104–5. For an insightful discussion of the politics of the museums that compares them to more standard museums, see James Clifford, "Four Northwest Coast Museums: Travel Reflections," in *Exhibiting Cultures: The Poetics and Politics of Museum Display,* eds. Ivan Karp and Steven D. Lavine (Washington, D.C.: Smithsonian Institution, 1991), 212–54.

5. James P. Spradley, ed., *Guests Never Leave Hungry: The Autobiography of James Sewid, a Kwakiutl Indian* (New Haven, Conn.: Yale University Press, 1969).

6. The University of British Columbia and the British Columbia Provincial Museum gave government sponsorship to the revitalization of Northwest Coast art. In 1947, the University of British Columbia invited well-known carver Mungo Martin to direct work on pole restorations and to carve new poles for Totem Park. Shortly thereafter, he began working for the British Columbia Provincial Museum in Victoria. Martin took on Henry Hunt and his son Tony as apprentices there.

Between 1959 and 1963, Douglas Cranmer and Bill Reid began carving projects sponsored by the university. See E. S. Lohse and Frances Sundt, "History of Research: Museum Collections," in *Northwest Coast*, vol. 7, *Handbook of North American Indians*, ed. Wayne Suttles (Washington D.C.: Smithsonian Institution, 1990), 93–94.

7. Building the coasthouse provided space for private functions as well as an arena for public performances that were, in essence, political statements about the vitality of Kwakiutl culture to non-Indians in Canada.

8. Chief James Knox "of Fort Rupert" in 1965 held the potlatch so that his step-son Peter Knox (son of Dave Martin, who had died long before) could become a Hamatsa. The event was one of the first in the new community house sponsored by the Kwak'wala Arts and Crafts Organization. It also coincided with British Columbia's Centennial Year and with Sports Day at Alert Bay, so there was an extraordinarily big crowd. For a good description of the potlatch, see Spradley, *Guests Never Leave Hungry*, 245–48.

9. Franz Boas, "The Social Organization and Secret Societies of the Kwakiutl Indians," in *Report of the U.S. National Museum for 1895* (Washington, D.C.: Smithsonian Institution, 1897).

10. Because rights are passed from father-in-law to son-in-law or his family among the Kwakiutl, that ceremony requires some of the largest potlatches. Protocol demands that the father-in-law and son-in-law host alternate potlatches in which the bride "price" is paid and then returned. The potlatch is thus a recognition and assertion of the rights and privileges passed on through the daughter/wife.

11. Along the Northwest Coast, the social organization of various bands and tribes is quite complex. Social organization, politics, and economics historically hinged upon a person's membership in a particular exogamous moiety. Clans, lineages, and house groups then subdivided the moieties. Among the Kwakiutl, various bands or tribes each had several "houses" or numayms (also 'Na'mima) with different supernatural ancestral origins. Each house also claimed titles, crests, and property, all of which figured into the ranking system. The Kwakiutl used the flexibility of the house system to overcome depopulation and other changes wrought by Canadian colonization. For a discussion of Kawkiutl social organization and the house system, see "The 'Na'mima System," *U'mista News*, accessed December 2000, www.rescol.ca/aboriginal/umistweb/art14-e.html, and Helen Codere, "Kwakiutl: Traditional Culture," in *Northwest Coast*, 366–68. For Tlingit social organization, see Frederica de Laguna, "Tlingit," in *Northwest Coast*, vol. 7, *Handbook of North American Indians*, ed. Wayne Suttles (Washington, D.C.: Smithsonian Institution,

1990), 212–13; for Haida social organization, see Margaret B. Blackman, "Haida: Traditional Culture," in *Northwest Coast,* vol. 7, *Handbook of North American Indians,* ed. Wayne Suttles (Washington, D.C.: Smithsonian Institution, 1990), 248–52.

12. Tseḵa, a set of Kwakiutl ceremonies commonly known as the Winter Dance Ceremony (or the Cedar Bark Dance), was the one in which the Hamatsa danced. Tła'sala dances represent the transformation of people into supernatural beings or the acquisition by the dancer of some great power. Attendants and other dancers torment the person until he or she is forced to leave the house, but then the dancer returns, often transformed into one of the many supernatural beings. Potlatches and feasts, in contrast to the dance complexes, are occasional, not seasonal ceremonies. For scattered but helpful references to the historic and contemporary Tła'sula and Tseḵa dances, see Assu with Inglis, *Assu of Cape Mudge.* For more standard treatments, see Bill Holm, "Kwakiutl: Winter Ceremonies," in *Northwest Coast,* vol. 7, *Handbook of North American Indians,* ed. Wayne Suttles (Washington, D.C.: Smithsonian Institution, 1990), 378–86; Bill Holm, *Smoky-Top: The Art and Times of Willie Seaweed* (Seattle: University of Washington Press, 1983), 72; and Aldona Jonaitis, *Chiefly Feasts: The Enduring Kwakiutl Potlatch* (Seattle: University of Washington Press, 1991).

13. Potlatches are occasional ceremonies to mark specific events. The most essential element of a potlatch is the distribution of gifts, which publicly confirms or witnesses the event. The value of the gift typically corresponds to the importance of the event and the rank of the recipient as well as to the person or family hosting the potlatch. Scholars debate the origins and functions of potlatches, but it is clear that they are complex and variable in their function historically as well as in the present day. The best, concise review of theories about the potlatch is provided in Wayne Suttles and Aldona Jonaitis, "History of Research in Ethnology," in *Northwest Coast,* vol. 7, *Handbook of North American Indians,* ed. Wayne Suttles (Washington, D.C.: Smithsonian Institution, 1990), 84–86.

14. The traditional/progressive split can be too easily overemphasized. For example, Spradley in *Guests Never Leave Hungry* portrays Sewid as progressive, even assimilationist, but his actions surrounding the repatriation of artifacts and the public performances of ceremonies have led others to cast him as more "traditional." See also Ira Jacknis, "Repatriation as Social Drama: The Kwakiutl Indians of Southern British Columbia, 1922–1980," *American Indian Quarterly* 20:2 (1996), 274–86, and Judith Ostrowitz, "Privileging the Past: A Case Study in Contemporary Kwakwaḵa'wakw Performance Art," *American Indian Art Magazine* 20:1 (winter 1994),

54–61. Like other Indian leaders, Sewid's actions did not fall into neat categories. See David Rich Lewis, "Reservation Leadership and the Progressive-Traditional Dichotomy: William Wash and the Northern Utes, 1865–1928," *Ethnohistory* 38 (1990), 124–42.

15. Spradley, *Guests Never Leave Hungry,* 47–48, 113–14.

16. Malin had been associated with the Denver Art Museum and Norman Feder for some time. He wrote a piece for the *Denver Art Museum Quarterly* (winter 1962), which he revised and reprinted as *Indian Art of the Northwest Coast: The Cultural Background of the Art,* with collection notes by Norman Feder (Denver: Denver Art Museum, 1962), based on the museum's collection and his fieldwork on the Northwest Coast between 1946 and 1949 plus other trips to the region.

17. Rolf Knight, *Indians at Work: An Informal History of Native Indian Labour in British Columbia, 1858–1930* (Vancouver, B.C.: New Star Books, 1978).

18. Douglas E. Cranmer, Robert Davidson, Bill Holm, Henry Hunt, Bill Reid, and Don Lelooska Smith participated in the exhibit held at the Vancouver Art Gallery, June 15 to September 24, 1967. See Wilson Duff, *Arts of the Raven: Master Works by the Northwest Coast Indian* (Vancouver, B.C.: Vancouver Art Gallery, 1967).

19. George Simpson was governor of Rupert's Land when the Northwest Company merged with the Hudson's Bay Company in 1821, and then in 1826 became governor-in-chief of HBC North American territories. On *The Beaver,* see Charles W. McCain, *The History of the S.S. Beaver* (Vancouver, B.C.: Evans and Hastings, 1894). Aemilius Simpson was its captain; he died on September 21, 1831, near the Nass and Skeena Rivers in British Columbia. See also Harold A. Innis, *The Fur Trade in Canada: An Introduction to Canadian Economic History* (New Haven, Conn.: Yale University Press, 1962).

20. "Minor terrorisms" most likely refers to the wave of Native protests that followed the Canadian government's issue of *The Statement of the Government on Indian Policy, 1969.* This "white paper" proposed the termination of federal responsibility for and separate legal status of Native peoples and spurred vigorous political protests among Natives, particularly the Métis peoples who, because of mixed ancestry, had an ambiguous legal status in Canada. The 1982 Constitutional Act helped resolve much of the debate when it reconfirmed Native aboriginal and treaty rights and defined the Métis as an aboriginal population.

21. Willie Seaweed's formal names were Hiłamas, X̱andzas̱amudy or Yakuɫala ("All Bad"), and Mukwitalasuu ("Four Men Come to Fight"). See Holm, *Smoky-Top,* 7.

22. Jimmy Sewid describes their marriage at age fifteen in Spradley, *Guests Never Leave Hungry*, 66–71.

23. The Sisiutł, usually represented as a giant double-headed serpent, was a warrior's animal. Looking at it causes death. Its blood hardens the skin. Its scales can be used as arrowheads and one of its eyes, if thrown from a sling, will destroy all in its path. It can be used to represent supernatural power or as a crest. See Holm, *Smoky-Top*, 57 and 59. Chief Tom Dawson of Kingcome Inlet told Jimmy Sewid that Sisiutł "represents the strength of the Kwakiutl people" according to Spradley, *Guests Never Leave Hungry*, 214–15.

24. Doris and Clint Gruber were longtime customers and friends of the Lelooska family. Doris was a television journalist for Channel 6, the CBS affiliate station in Portland, Oregon. Clint worked at the Oregon Museum of Science and Industry (OMSI), through which Don made many connections to build up the educational daytime programs at Ariel, Washington, as well as the evening programs geared more to adults and potential customers.

25. Sewid-Smith, *Prosecution or Persecution*.

7 / PRODUCING ART

1. Researchers have established a high correlation between prolonged exposure to plicatic acid, common in many types of cedar, to allergic reactions, respiratory ailments, and the lowering of immune systems in humans and animals. See the online essay by a doctoral candidate in epidemiology at the University of North Carolina at Chapel Hill, Jeff Johnston, "A review of the biomedical literature from 1986 through 1995" (November 1998), http://www.trifl.org/cedar.html.

2. Holm is the recognized authority on the form and style of Northwest Coast art. Born in 1925, Holm attended the University of Washington, taught in the Seattle Public Schools system, and then earned an appointment at the Burke Museum and the School of Art at the University of Washington. Holm retired in 1985 but has remained active in his research and writing about Northwest Coast art.

3. Bill Holm speaks of how Willie Seaweed used a compass to create perfect circles for parts of the eye design; see Holm, *Smoky-Top: The Art and Times of Willie Seaweed* (Seattle: University of Washington Press, 1983), 49. For documentation of a variety of techniques, from the use of pencils and compasses to sketchbooks and slide collections, that Northwest Coast artists use to check designs, see also

Patricia Cosgrove-Smith, "Smoky-Top: The Art and Times of Willie Seaweed," *American Indian Art Magazine* (autumn 1983), 65–69; Margaret B. Blackman and Edwin S. Hall Jr., "The Afterimage and After: Visual Documents and the Renaissance in Northwest Coast Art," *American Indian Art Magazine* (spring 1982), 30–39; and Steven C. Brown, "Formlines Changing Form: Northwest Coast Art as an Evolving Tradition," *American Indian Art Magazine* (spring 1997), 62–73 and ff.

4. *Oplopanax horridum* is known as devil's club. Its roots and succulent stems are eaten in Alaska. *Fatsia horridia,* devil's walking stick, is used among the Crow and Cheyenne with tobacco and is called "stinking medicine." It is also used by shamans in incantations. See Elias Yanovsky, "Food Plants of the North American Indians," U.S. Department of Agriculture misc. pub. 237 (1936), in *An Ethnobotany Source Book: The Uses of Plants and Animals by American Indians,* ed. Richard I. Ford (New York: Garland, 1986), 12, 47.

5. The Animal Kingdom Dance is a dance of many masks, which the Sewid family owned as part of its cultural property. A brief version of the story is that a woman got into an argument with her husband and ran off into the woods. While there, she happened to surprise all the animals, who had taken on human forms while gathered in a secret cave. The woman thus shamed the animals into giving her the rights to their masks, dances, and songs. These origin narratives exist in great variety, but the basic story line of ancestors who spy on the animals in some supernatural setting and thereby gain their powers is ubiquitous in the region, according to Holm, *Smoky-Top,* 126–41.

6. I saw it performed at Cape Mudge, B.C., during a 1979 potlatch to commemorate the 100th anniversary of the church there. Don had done a number of the masks for the dance and had given them to the Sewid family. For a description of the Kwiksutainuk version of the ceremonies, see Spradley, *Guests Never Leave Hungry,* 39–41.

7. Willie Seaweed was one of the earlier artists to use white backgrounds. See Holm, *Smoky-Top,* and Cosgrove-Smith, "Art and Times of Willie Seaweed."

8. This probably refers to the period beginning in the late 1860s that followed the establishment of Fort Rupert in 1849 on the northeast portion of Vancouver Island and the destruction of the village there in 1865 by the British navy. This halted the expansion of Kwakiutl bands as well as Bella Coola from the north, resulting in an era of relative "peace."

9. One of the great cannibal birds danced by initiates of the Hamatsa Society,

the most prominent and powerful of the societies among Kwakiutl. The bird's long beak reaches up to five and a half feet in length and distinguishes the mask. The cannibal birds—Hu̱xwhukw, Crooked Beak (Galokwudzuwis), and Raven (GwāwēsEml)—come from the home of Baxwbakwalanuksiwe ("Cannibal-at-the-north-end-of-world," the many-mouthed flesh-eating spirit) searching for food. The Hamatsa dancer meets these birds in the forest, where he takes on their terrible powers, returns to his house, and is eventually reined in by dance attendants.

10. During the arrests that followed the Cranmer potlatch, Indian Agent William M. Halliday was to have shipped the seized pieces to Ottawa, but an unspecified number of items never made the trip, having been removed or purchased by collectors. Axel Rasmussen, superintendent of schools in Wrangell and Skagway, collected numerous artifacts from southeast Alaska and British Columbia between the 1920s and 1940s. The Portland Art Museum first acquired his collection in the late 1940s. See E. S. Lohse and Frances Sundt, "History of Research: Museum Collections," in *Northwest Coast,* vol. 7, *Handbook of North American Indians,* ed. Wayne Suttles (Washington D.C.: Smithsonian Institution, 1990), 90–91.

11. T. F. McIlwraith, *The Bella Coola Indians* (Toronto: University of Toronto Press, 1948).

12. Some scholars tend to see Kwakiutl art as more conservative than others because of continuation of performance and the politics of it. See Judith Ostrowitz, "Privileging the Past: A Case Study in Contemporary Kwakwa̱ka'wakw Performance Art," *American Indian Art Magazine* 20:1 (winter 1994), 54–61.

13. The historical evolution of the potlatch is a part of the cultural dynamics of the Northwest Coast generally and the Kwakiutl in particular. Helen Codere, *Fighting With Property: A Study of Kwakiutl Potlatching and Warfare, 1792–1930* (New York: J. J. Augustin, 1950), and Codere, "Kwakiutl: Traditional Culture," in *Northwest Coast,* 359–77, offer this explanation for the potlatch.

14. Sometimes this is rendered as "The Great Killer Whale."

15. Martin bought it in 1942 for $2,100 and later broke it at his son David's induction into the Hamatsa Society. Martin later broke it again to shame those who questioned his son's right to do that. Martin continued to use it by displaying it at important functions, and its last ritual appearance was as a "coffin" for his son. In 1960, Martin donated it to the British Columbia Provincial Museum. Willie Seaweed painted the killer whale design on the surface. See Codere, "Kwakiutl: Traditional Culture," in *Northwest Coast,* 370, and Holm, *Smoky-Top,* 61–68.

16. Anthropologist Wilson Duff wrote and taught extensively about the Indi-

ans of the Northwest Coast. From 1950 to 1965 he was curator of ethnology at the British Columbia Provincial Museum and was a professor at the University of British Columbia until his death in 1976. Duff testified in land cases for Native people and was active in a host of other issues relevant to the cultural and political renaissance of British Columbia's First People in the 1950s and 1960s.

17. Michael M. Ames, "A Note on the Contributions of Wilson Duff to Northwest Coast Ethnology and Art," in *The World Is as Sharp as a Knife: An Anthology in Honour of Wilson Duff,* ed. Donald N. Abbot (Victoria: British Columbia Provincial Museum, 1981), 17–21.

18. A well-rounded description of a copper, described as a "shield-like symbol of wealth" that can "shield against injury by rivals" and can be "broken (cut) to shame a rival," can be found in Holm, *Smoky-Top,* 61–68, who further notes its shape may also be a metaphor for the human body.

8 / LEARNING FROM EXPERIENCE

1. The St. Augustine's Indian Center was established in the early 1960s to assist Indians relocated to Chicago by the Bureau of Indian Affairs and those who came of their own accord. It has one of the largest caseloads of any Indian center in the country.

2. Father Peter J. Powell, born in 1928, began ethnographic work as a teenager and was eventually adopted by the Cheyenne for his assiduous work in capturing their heritage in his published work. Aside from his work at St. Augustine's Indian Center, Father Powell, an Episcopal priest, is also a research associate at the Newberry Library.

3. Peter J. Powell, *Sweet Medicine: The Continuing Role of the Sacred Arrows, the Sun Dance, and the Sacred Buffalo Hat in Northern Cheyenne History,* 2 vols. (Norman: University of Oklahoma Press, 1969).

4. Born in 1915 in eastern Washington, Rev. Wilfred P. Schoenberg, S.J., did much of his primary, secondary, and graduate schooling at Gonzaga, in Spokane, Washington. From the end of World War II to the mid-1960s, interrupted only by his seminary studies and ordination, he taught history at the secondary and collegiate levels at Gonzaga. Having gained some training as an archivist, in the mid-1950s he actively began to collect materials related to the history of Catholicism in the Pacific Northwest. This led him to Indian missions and ultimately to the founding of the Museum of Native American Cultures, in 1965. He oversaw

the museum until he left. Since that time Schoenberg has transferred to Portland, Oregon, and has published several books, including *A History of the Catholic Church in the Pacific Northwest, 1743–1983* (Washington, D.C.: The Pastoral Press, 1987). Some of the items were repatriated and the remainder transferred to the Northwest Museum of Arts and Culture, in Spokane.

9 / A FAMILY COMPLEX

1. Stuart Hall, "Introduction: Who Needs 'Identity'?" in *Questions of Cultural Identity,* eds. Stuart Hall and Paul Du Gay (London: Sage Publications, 1996), 4; Lawrence Grossberg, "Identity and Cultural Studies: Is That All There is?" in *Questions of Cultural Identity,* eds. Hall and Du Gay, 88–90; and Kathleen Neils Conzen, David A. Gerber, Ewa Morawska, and George E. Pozzetta, "The Invention of Ethnicity: A Perspective from the U.S.A.," *Journal of American Ethnic History* 12:1 (1992), 3–41.

2. For a discussion on the topic, which deserves much more attention than it has garnered, see Alison R. Bernstein, *American Indians and World War II: Toward a New Era in Indian Affairs* (Norman: University of Oklahoma Press, 1991), 131–58.

3. For more than three decades, Don spoke about how this coercion of the Kiowa Comanche Apache Reservation affected his grandfather; see Leverett Richards, "Hubbard Indian Achieves Fame as Carver, Expert on Tribal Lore," *Oregonian,* Jan. 4, 1959. Published literature on the reservation hints at such coercion but does not provide much detail. See Morris W. Foster, *Being Comanche: A Social History of an American Indian Community* (Tucson: University of Arizona Press, 1991), and Thomas W. Kavanagh, *Comanche Political History: An Ethnohistorical Perspective, 1706–1875* (Lincoln: University of Nebraska Press, 1996).

4. The first book-length treatment of the topic is by Gail K. Sheffield, *The Arbitrary Indian: The Indian Arts and Crafts Act of 1990* (Norman: University of Oklahoma Press, 1997).

10 / NEW FOES, OLD FRIENDS

1. *Kwénkwenxweligi* has been spelled a number of ways, including *Kwankwankwaligi* and *Ku'unkunxulig'a.* Don's pronunciation led me to render it as I have.

2. Stories of Thunderbird are available in Franz Boas and George Hunt, *Kwakiutl Texts* (Leiden: E. J. Brill/New York: G. E. Stechert, 1905), 295–312.

3. For discussions of the cosmology, see Franz Boas, "The Social Organization

and Secret Societies of the Kwakiutl Indians," *Report of the U.S. National Museum for 1895* (Washington, D.C.: Smithsonian Institution, 1897), and Edward Malin, *A World of Faces: Masks of the Northwest Coast Indians* (Portland, Ore.: Timber Press, 1978), esp. 41–51. The relationship between art and cosmology is revealed in Bill Holm, *Smoky-Top: The Art and Times of Willie Seaweed* (Seattle: University of Washington Press, 1965), esp. 122; a sweeping discussion of Native American architecture in North America, including the Northwest Coast, with a focus on Haida cosmology, is provided by Peter Nabokov and Robert Eastman, *Native American Architecture* (New York: Oxford University Press, 1989).

4. This refers to those rights and privileges given to Don and the Lelooska family by James Sewid for the songs and ceremonies. Since Jimmy Sewid granted Don and the family rights and privileges, they traveled many times to potlatches and feasts given in British Columbia, especially at Cape Mudge. At potlatches, money and material goods are given away to repay debts as well as to confirm a person's or family's rank in the social order.

5. For a discussion of this, see Bill Holm, *Northwest Coast Indian Art: An Analysis of Form* (Seattle: University of Washington Press, 1965), 41–43.

6. Nootka (Nuu-chah-nulth), or Westcoast, art is strikingly different from that of northerly neighbors in its concentration on painted designs on flat surfaces rather than shallow or deep relief carving.

7. Christine Normandin, ed., *Echoes of the Elders: The Stories and Paintings of Chief Lelooska* (New York: Callaway Editions, 1997), and Normandin, ed., *Spirit of the Cedar People: More Stories and Paintings of Chief Lelooska* (New York: DK Ink, Callaway Editions, 1998).

8. James Sewid discusses his use of a Chilkat blanket (*ya'yak'sum*) in Doreen Jensen and Polly Sargent, *Robes of Power: Totem Poles on Cloth* (Vancouver: University of British Columbia Press and University of British Columbia Museum of Anthropology, 1986), 58. Regarding Chilkat blankets and Northwest Coast weaving more generally, see Cheryl Samuel, *The Raven's Tail* (Vancouver: University of British Columbia Press, 1987).

9. Don had already named his brother Smitty as his successor and had talked about the Chilkat blanket among the family. At Don's funeral, Dora and Daisy placed Don's blanket on Smitty's shoulders, pledging to continue their relationship with the Lelooska family and renewing the family's rights and privileges.

10. Of Don's immediate family, only his brother Dick and his nephew Jay were

not present. Several dozen people sat in the family section, from cousins to friends of long association, my mother among them.

CONCLUSION

1. Ira Jacknis, "Repatriation as Social Drama: The Kwakiutl Indians of Southern British Columbia, 1922–1980," *American Indian Quarterly* 20:2 (1996), 274–86; Judith Ostrowitz, "Privileging the Past: A Case Study in Contemporary Kwakwa̱ka'wakw Performance Art," *American Indian Art Magazine* 20:1 (winter 1994), 54–61; Judith Ostrowitz, *Privileging the Past: Reconstructing History in Northwest Coast Art* (Seattle: University of Washington Press, 1999); and Charlotte Townsend-Gault, "Northwest Coast Art: The Culture of Land Claims," *American Indian Quarterly* 18:4 (1994), 445–67.

2. Morris W. Foster, *Being Comanche: A Social History of an American Indian Community* (Tucson: University of Arizona Press, 1991).

3. Larry W. Burt, *Tribalism in Crisis: Federal Indian Policy, 1953–1961* (Albuquerque: University of New Mexico Press, 1982), 58; Donald Fixico, *Termination and Relocation: Federal Indian Policy, 1945–1960* (Albuquerque: University of New Mexico Press, 1986); and Inés Hernandez, "Foreword: Reflections on Identity and Culture," in *Growing Up Native American: An Anthology,* ed. Patricia Riley (New York: William Morrow and Co., 1993), 8–10.

4. Helpful reviews and statements can be found in Joane Nagel, *American Indian Ethnic Renewal: Red Power and the Resurgence of Identity and Culture* (New York: Oxford University Press, 1996), 83–105, and Michael Omi and Howard Winant, *Racial Formation in the United States from the 1960s to the 1990s,* 2d ed. (New York: Routledge, 1994).

5. Mixed-blood peoples are spoken of as "cultural tricksters" in a positive sense by Gerald Vizenor, *Earthdivers: Tribal Narratives on Mixed Descent* (Minneapolis: University of Minnesota Press, 1981), but other scholars speak less highly of the focus on mixed-blood peoples, in some cases labeling it as misleading and unproductive to consider those lives much further. Those who hold this position argue that studies of cultural creativity detract from a focus on politics. For a recent discussion about the politics of Native American studies, which includes references to the politics of art and of "mixed blood," see the special issue edited by Devon A. Mihesuah, "Writing About (Writing About) American Indians," *American Indian Quarterly* 20:1 (1996).

6. Native American interactions with cultural tourism have been explored more thoroughly in the Southwest than anywhere else. For example, see Nancy Peake, "'If it came from Wright's, You bought it right': Charles A. Wright, Proprietor, Wright's Trading Post," *New Mexico Historical Review* 66:3 (1991), 261–86. There was a strong tradition of this trade, too, in the Pacific Northwest. See Frank Norris, "Showing Off Alaska: The Northern Tourist Trade, 1878–1941," *Alaska History* 2:2 (1987), 1–18. The debate among scholars over cultural tourism and Native Americans hinges around the degree to which the activity significantly undermines and demeans Native cultures or the degree to which it reinforces existing patterns. For examples of the former, see Peter Whiteley, "The End of Anthropology (at Hopi)?" *Journal of the Southwest* 35:2 (1993), 125–57, and Patricia Jasen, "Native People and the Tourist Industry in Nineteenth-Century Ontario," *Journal of Canadian Studies* 28:4 (1993–1994), 5–27. For examples of the latter, see Robert Jarvenpa, "Commodification versus Cultural Integration: Tourism and Image Building in the Klondike," *Arctic Anthropology* 31:1 (1994), 26–46, and Carol Chiago Lujan, "A Sociological View of Tourism in an American Indian Community: Maintaining Cultural Integrity at Taos Pueblo," *American Indian Culture and Research Journal* 17:3 (1993), 101–20. Because of the great variety of local and historical circumstances, generalizations cast as either commodification or cultural integration tend to break down on close examination. Moreover, Don's experiences suggest that the production of his pieces could simultaneously exist as commodities for some, as objects of art for others, and as ritual paraphernalia for still others. A piece could even pass through those different "states" in its life. Therefore, the context of the production, exchange, and use of the piece had much to do with its role.

7. Alice Littlefield and Martha C. Knack, eds., *Native Americans and Wage Labor: Ethnohistorical Perspectives* (Norman: University of Oklahoma Press, 1996).

8. The 1939 Golden Gate International Exposition in San Francisco was really among the first instances in which Northwest Coast art was presented as art (Erna Gunther was in charge of the exhibit), and the general public had only recently accepted it as such just prior to her writing *Art in the Life of the Northwest Coast Indians* (Portland, Ore.: Portland Art Museum, 1966), vii–viii. It is ironic, though, that Gunther argues "Northwest Coast cultures [have] lost their identity, and their arts[,] their raison d'être. Not that it is too late; they are highly treasured and coveted by museums and collectors."

BIBLIOGRAPHY

Acuña, Rodolfo, ed. *Occupied America: A History of Chicanos*. 3d ed. New York: Harper and Row, 1988.

Adams, David Wallace. *Education for Extinction: American Indians and the Boarding School Experience, 1875–1928*. Lawrence: University Press of Kansas, 1995.

Albers, Patricia C. "From Legend to Land and Labor: Changing Perspectives on Native American Work." In *Native American Wage Labor: Ethnohistorical Perspectives*, edited by Alice Littlefield and Martha C. Knack. Norman: University of Oklahoma Press, 1996, 245–73.

Ames, Michael M. "A Note on the Contributions of Wilson Duff to Northwest Coast Ethnology and Art." In *The World Is as Sharp as a Knife: An Anthology in Honour of Wilson Duff*, edited by Donald N. Abbot. Victoria: British Columbia Provincial Museum, 1981, 17–21.

Anaya, Rudolpho A., and Francisco A. Lomeli, eds. *Aztlán: Essays on the Chicano Homeland*. Albuquerque: University of New Mexico Press, 1989.

Assu, Harry, with Joy Inglis. *Assu of Cape Mudge: Recollections of a Coastal Indian Chief*. Vancouver: University of British Columbia Press, 1989.

Aurbach, Herbert A., ed. *National Research Conference on American Indian Education*. Kalamazoo, Mich.: Society for the Study of Social Problems, 1967.

Bataille, Gretchen. "Education and the Images of the American Indian." *Explorations in Ethnic Studies* 1:1 (1978), 37–49.

———. *Native American Women: A Biographical Dictionary.* New York: Garland, 1993.

Bernstein, Alison R. *American Indians and World War II: Toward a New Era in Indian Affairs.* Norman: University of Oklahoma Press, 1991.

Bernstein, Bruce. "Contexts for the Growth and Development of the Indian Art World in the 1960s and 1970s." In *Native American Art in the Twentieth Century,* edited by W. Jackson Rushing III. London: Routledge, 1999, 57–74.

Biolsi, Thomas. *Organizing the Lakota: The Political Economy of the New Deal on the Pine Ridge and Rosebud Reservations.* Tucson: University of Arizona Press, 1992.

Bird, S. Elizabeth, ed. *Dressing in Feathers: The Construction of the Indian in American Popular Culture.* Boulder, Colo.: Westview Press, 1996.

Blackman, Margaret B. "Haida: Traditional Culture." In *Northwest Coast.* Vol. 7 of *Handbook of North American Indians,* edited by Wayne Suttles. Washington, D.C.: Smithsonian Institution, 1990, 240–60.

Blackman, Margaret B., and Edwin S. Hall Jr. "The Afterimage and Image After: Visual Documents and the Renaissance in Northwest Coast Art." *American Indian Art Magazine* (spring 1982), 30–39.

Blair, Wink. "Lelooska." *American Indian Art Magazine* 1:2 (1976), 82–85.

Boas, Franz. "The Social Organization and Secret Societies of the Kwakiutl Indians." *Report of the U.S. National Museum for 1895.* Washington, D.C.: Smithsonian Institution, 1897.

Boas, Franz, and George Hunt. *Kwakiutl Texts.* Leiden: E. J. Brill; New York: G. E. Stechert, 1905.

Brown, Steven C. "Formlines Changing Form: Northwest Coast Art as an Evolving Tradition." *American Indian Art Magazine* (spring 1997), 62–73 and ff.

Burt, Larry W. *Tribalism in Crisis: Federal Indian Policy, 1953–1961.* Albuquerque: University of New Mexico Press, 1982.

Campbell, Janet Hale. *Bloodlines: The Odyssey of a Native Daughter.* New York: Harper and Row, 1993.

Clifford, James. "Four Northwest Coast Museums: Travel Reflections." In *Exhibiting Cultures: The Poetics and Politics of Museum Display,* edited by Ivan Karp and Steven D. Lavine. Washington, D.C.: Smithsonian Institution, 1991, 212–54.

———. *The Predicament of Culture: Twentieth-Century Ethnography, Literature, and Art.* Cambridge: Harvard University Press, 1988.

Codere, Helen. *Fighting with Property: A Study of Kwakiutl Potlatching and Warfare, 1792–1930.* New York: J. J. Augustin, 1950.

———. "Kwakiutl: Traditional Culture." In *Northwest Coast.* Vol. 7 of *Handbook of*

North American Indians, edited by Wayne Suttles. Washington, D.C.: Smithsonian Institution, 1990, 359–77.

Cole, Douglas. *Captured Heritage: The Scramble for Northwest Coast Artifacts.* Norman: University of Oklahoma Press, 1995.

———. *An Iron Hand Upon the People: The Law Against the Potlatch on the Northwest Coast.* Seattle: University of Washington Press for Douglas & McIntyre, 1990.

Coleman, Michael C. *American Indian Children at School, 1850–1930.* Jackson: University Press of Mississippi, 1993.

Comaroff, John L. "Ethnicity, Nationalism, and the Politics of Difference in an Age of Revolution." In *The Politics of Difference: Ethnic Premises in a World of Power,* edited by Edwin N. Wilmsen and Patrick McAllister. Chicago: University of Chicago Press, 1996, 162–83.

Congdon-Martin, Douglas. *Lelooska: The Traditional Art of the Mask—Carving a Transformation Mask.* Atglen, Penn.: Schiffer Publishers, 1996.

Conzen, Kathleen Neils, David A. Gerber, Ewa Morawska, and George E. Pozzetta. "The Invention of Ethnicity: A Perspective from the U.S.A." *Journal of American Ethnic History* 12:1 (1992), 3–41.

Cosgrove-Smith, Patricia. "Smoky-Top: The Art and Times of Willie Seaweed." *American Indian Art Magazine* (autumn 1983), 65–69.

Cruikshank, Julie. *Life Lived Like a Story: Life Stories of Three Yukon Native Elders.* Lincoln: University of Nebraska Press, 1990.

de Laguna, Frederica. "Tlingit." In *Northwest Coast.* Vol. 7 of *Handbook of North American Indians,* edited by Wayne Suttles. Washington, D.C.: Smithsonian Institution, 1990, 203–29.

Deloria, Philip J. *Playing Indian.* New Haven, Conn.: Yale University Press, 1998.

Desjarlait, Robert. "The Contest Powwow versus the Traditional Powwow and the Role of the Native American Community." *Wicazo Sa Review* 12:1 (1977), 115–27.

Duff, Wilson. *Arts of the Raven: Master Works by the Northwest Coast Indian.* Vancouver, B.C.: Vancouver Art Gallery, 1967.

———. "The Killer Whale Copper: A Chief's Memorial to His Son." In *The World Is as Sharp as a Knife: An Anthology in Honour of Wilson Duff,* edited by Donald N. Abbot. Victoria: British Columbia Provincial Museum, 1981, 153–56.

Dyck, Noel, and James B. Waldram. "An Introduction to the Issues." In *Anthropology, Public Policy, and Native Peoples in Canada,* edited by Noel Dyck and James B. Waldram. Montreal: McGill-Queen's University Press, 1993, 3–38.

Ellis, Clyde. *To Change Them Forever: Indian Education at the Rainy Mountain Boarding School, 1893–1920*. Norman: University of Oklahoma Press, 1996.

Ewers, John C. *Blackfeet Crafts*, Indian Handicrafts no. 9. Washington, D.C.: U.S. Indian Service, 1945.

Falk, Randolf. *Lelooska*. Millbrae, Calif.: Celestial Arts, 1976.

Farr, William E. *The Reservation Blackfeet, 1882–1945: A Photographic History of Cultural Survival*. Seattle: University of Washington Press, 1984.

Fisher, Robin. *Contact and Conflict: Indian-European Relations in British Columbia, 1774–1890*. 2d ed. Vancouver: University of British Columbia Press, 1992.

Fixico, Donald. *Termination and Relocation: Federal Indian Policy, 1945–1960*. Albuquerque: University of New Mexico Press, 1986.

Forbes, Jack D., comp. *Aztecas del Norte: The Chicanos of Aztlán*. Greenwich, Conn.: Fawcett Publications, 1973.

Foster, Morris W. *Being Comanche: A Social History of an American Indian Community*. Tucson: University of Arizona Press, 1991.

Gibbs, George. *A Dictionary of the Chinook Jargon or Trade Language of Oregon*. Washington, D.C.: Smithsonian Institution, 1863.

Glosh, Larry. "Symposium: The Future of Indian Art." *American Indian Art Magazine* 3:1 (1977), 25–27, 93–96.

Goodey, Darwin. *Lelooska: Myths, Masks, Magic*. Ellensburg, Wash.: Central Washington University, 1996. Videorecording produced by Chris Smart.

Gordon, Wendy, and Brenda Buratti. "Lelooska." *Four Winds* 1:4 (1980), 33–40.

Green, Rayna. "The Tribe Called Wannabee: Playing Indian in America and Europe." *Folklore* 99:1 (1988), 30–55.

Grossberg, Lawrence. "Identity and Cultural Studies: Is That All There Is?" In *Questions of Cultural Identity*, edited by Stuart Hall and Paul Du Gay. London: Sage Publications, 1996, 87–109.

Gunther, Erna. *Art in the Life of the Northwest Coast Indians*. Portland, Ore.: Portland Art Museum, 1966.

Hall, Stuart. "Introduction: Who Needs 'Identity'?" In *Questions of Cultural Identity*, edited by Stuart Hall and Paul Du Gay. London: Sage Publications, 1996, 1–17.

Harmon, Alexandra. *Indians in the Making: Ethnic Relations and Indian Identities Around Puget Sound*. Berkeley: University of California Press, 1999.

Hartmann, Susan M. "Women's Work among the Plains Indians." *Gateway Heritage* 3:4 (1983), 2–9.

Hawkins, Elizabeth. *Indian Weaving, Knitting, Basketry of the Northwest.* Vancouver, B.C.: Hancock House Publishers, 1978.

Hernandez, Inés. "Foreword: Reflections on Identity and Culture." In *Growing Up Native American: An Anthology,* edited by Patricia Riley. New York: William Morrow and Co., 1993, 7–10.

Hiner, N. Ray, and Joseph M. Hawes, eds. *Growing Up in America: Children in Historical Perspective.* Urbana: University of Illinois Press, 1985.

Holm, Bill. "Kwakiutl: Winter Ceremonies." In *Northwest Coast.* Vol. 7 of *Handbook of North American Indians,* edited by Wayne Suttles. Washington, D.C.: Smithsonian Institution, 1990, 378–86.

———. *Northwest Coast Indian Art: An Analysis of Form.* Seattle: University of Washington Press, 1965.

———. *Smoky-Top: The Art and Times of Willie Seaweed.* Seattle: University of Washington Press, 1983.

Hoxie, Frederick E. *A Final Promise: The Campaign to Assimilate the Indians, 1880–1920.* Lincoln: University of Nebraska Press, 1984.

———. *Parading Through History: The Making of the Crow Nation in America, 1805–1935.* New York: Cambridge University Press, 1995.

Innis, Harold A. *The Fur Trade in Canada: An Introduction to Canadian Economic History.* New Haven, Conn.: Yale University Press, 1962.

Iverson, Peter. *Riders of the West: Portraits from Indian Rodeo.* Seattle: University of Washington Press; Vancouver, B.C.: Greystone, 1999.

———. *When Indians Became Cowboys: Native Peoples and Cattle Ranching in the American West.* Norman: University of Oklahoma Press, 1994.

Jacknis, Ira. "Repatriation as Social Drama: The Kwakiutl Indians of Southern British Columbia, 1922–1980." *American Indian Quarterly* 20:2 (1996), 274–86.

Jarvenpa, Robert. "Commodification versus Cultural Integration: Tourism and Image Building in the Klondike." *Arctic Anthropology* 31:1 (1994), 26–46.

Jasen, Patricia. "Native People and the Tourist Industry in Nineteenth-Century Ontario." *Journal of Canadian Studies* 28:4 (1993–1994), 5–27.

Jensen, Doreen, and Polly Sargent. *Robes of Power: Totem Poles on Cloth.* Vancouver: University of British Columbia Press and University of British Columbia Museum of Anthropology, 1986.

Johnson, Troy R. *The Occupation of Alcatraz Island: Indian Self-determination and the Rise of Indian Activism.* Urbana: University of Illinois Press, 1996.

Johnston, Jeff. "A Review of the Biomedical Literature from 1986 through 1995" (November 1998), http://www.trifl.org/cedar.html.

Jonaitis, Aldona. *Chiefly Feasts: The Enduring Kwakiutl Potlatch.* Seattle: University of Washington Press, 1991.

Kavanagh, Thomas W. *Comanche Political History: An Ethnohistorical Perspective, 1706–1875.* Lincoln: University of Nebraska Press, 1996.

Kirk, Ruth, and Richard D. Daugherty. *Exploring Washington Archaeology.* Seattle: University of Washington Press, 1978.

Knight, Rolf. *Indians at Work: An Informal History of Native Indian Labour in British Columbia, 1858–1930.* Vancouver, B.C.: New Star Books, 1978.

Kracht, Benjamin R. "Kiowa Powwows: Continuity in Ritual Practice." *American Indian Quarterly* 18:3 (1994), 321–48.

Kroeber, Theodora. *Ishi in Two Worlds: A Biography of the Last Wild Indian in North America.* Berkeley: University of California Press, 1961.

Krupat, Arnold. *Ethnocriticism: Ethnography, History, Literature.* Berkeley: University of California Press, 1992.

———. *The Voice in the Margin: Native American Literature and the Canon.* Berkeley: University of California Press, 1989.

"Lelooska." *Smoke Signals* 49 (summer 1966), 3–17.

Lewis, David Rich. "Reservation Leadership and the Progressive-Traditional Dichotomy: William Wash and the Northern Utes, 1865–1928." *Ethnohistory* 38 (1990), 124–42.

Limerick, Patricia Nelson. "Dancing with Professors: The Trouble with Academic Prose." *New York Times Book Review,* Oct. 31, 1993, 73.

Littlefield, Alice, and Martha C. Knack, eds. *Native Americans and Wage Labor: Ethnohistorical Perspectives.* Norman: University of Oklahoma Press, 1996.

Lohse, E. S., and Frances Sundt. "History of Research: Museum Collections." In *Northwest Coast.* Vol. 7 of *Handbook of North American Indians,* edited by Wayne Suttles. Washington, D.C.: Smithsonian Institution, 1990, 88–97.

Lomawaima, K. Tsianina. *They Called It Prairie Light: The Story of Chilocco Indian School.* Lincoln: University of Nebraska Press, 1994.

Lujan, Carol Chiago. "A Sociological View of Tourism in an American Indian Community: Maintaining Cultural Integrity at Taos Pueblo." *American Indian Culture and Research Journal* 17:3 (1993), 101–20.

Lyford, Carrie A. *The Quill and Beadwork of the Western Sioux.* Indian Handicrafts no. 1. Lawrence, Kans.: Haskell Institute, 1940.

Malin, Edward. *Indian Art of the Northwest Coast: The Cultural Background of the Art,* with collection notes by Norman Feder. Denver: Denver Art Museum, 1962.

———. *A World of Faces: Masks of the Northwest Coast Indians.* Portland, Ore.: Timber Press, 1978.

Matten, Mark. "The Powwow as a Public Arena for Negotiating Unity and Diversity in American Indian Life." *American Indian Culture and Research Journal* 20:4 (1996), 183–201.

McCain, Charles W. *The History of the S.S. "Beaver".* Vancouver, B.C.: Evans and Hastings, 1894.

McIlwraith, T. F. *The Bella Coola Indians.* Toronto: University of Toronto Press, 1948.

Mihesuah, Devon A., ed. "Writing About (Writing About) American Indians." *American Indian Quarterly* 20:1 (1996), special issue.

Mooney, James. "The Ghost Dance Religion and the Sioux Outbreak of 1890." In *Fourteenth Annual Report of the Bureau of Ethnology,* part 2. Washington, D.C.: Government Printing Office, 1896, 876–80.

Morris, Rosalind C. *New Worlds from Fragments: Film, Ethnography, and the Representation of Northwest Coast Cultures.* Boulder, Colo.: Westview Press, 1994.

Moses, L. G. *Wild West Shows and the Images of American Indians, 1883–1933.* Albuquerque: University of New Mexico Press, 1996.

Nabokov, Peter, and Robert Eastman. *Native American Architecture.* New York: Oxford University Press, 1989.

"The 'Na'mima System." *U'mista News* (December 2000), http://www.rescol.ca/aboriginal/umistweb/art14-e.html.

Nagel, Joane. *American Indian Ethnic Renewal: Red Power and the Resurgence of Identity and Culture.* New York: Oxford University Press, 1996.

Normandin, Christine, ed. *Echoes of the Elders: The Stories and Paintings of Chief Lelooska.* New York: Callaway Editions, 1997.

———, ed. *Spirit of the Cedar People: More Stories and Paintings of Chief Lelooska.* New York: DK Ink, Callaway Editions, 1998.

Norris, Frank. "Showing Off Alaska: The Northern Tourist Trade, 1878–1941." *Alaska History* 2:2 (1987), 1–18.

Okely, Judith, and Helen Callaway, eds. *Anthropology and Autobiography.* London: Routledge, 1992.

Omi, Michael, and Howard Winant. *Racial Formation in the United States from the 1960s to the 1990s.* 2d ed. New York: Routledge, 1994.

Ornter, Sherry B. "Resistance and the Problem of Ethnographic Refusal." *Comparative Study of Society and History* 51:1 (1995), 173–93.

Ostrowitz, Judith. "Privileging the Past: A Case Study in Contemporary Kwakwa̱ka̱'wakw Performance Art." *American Indian Art Magazine* 20:1 (winter 1994), 54–61.

———. *Privileging the Past: Reconstructing History in Northwest Coast Art.* Seattle: University of Washington Press, 1999.

Parman, Donald. *Indians and the American West in the Twentieth Century.* Bloomington: Indiana University Press, 1994.

Pasadena Museum of Modern Art. *Lelooska, Shona-ha, Tsunagi, Patty Fawn.* Pasadena, Calif.: Design World Productions, 1974.

Peake, Nancy. "'If it came from Wright's, You bought it right': Charles A. Wright, Proprietor, Wright's Trading Post." *New Mexico Historical Review* 66:3 (1991), 261–86.

Penney, David W., and Lisa Roberts. "America's Pueblo Artists: Encounters on the Borderlands." In *Native American Art in the Twentieth Century,* edited by W. Jackson Rushing III. London: Routledge, 1999, 21–38.

The People's Foreign Relations Association of China. *Meiguo Huaqiao Nianji* (Handbook of Chinese in America). New York: The People's Foreign Relations Association of China, 1946.

Pool, Carolyn Garret. "Reservation Policy and the Economic Position of Wichita Women." *Great Plains Quarterly* 8:3 (1988), 158–71.

Powell, Peter J. *Sweet Medicine: The Continuing Role of the Sacred Arrows, the Sun Dance, and the Sacred Buffalo Hat in Northern Cheyenne History.* 2 vols. Norman: University of Oklahoma Press, 1969.

Purdy, John. "Comment: Native Americans, Cultural Production, and the State, 1930s and 1960s." Remarks. Tacoma, Wash.: Pacific Northwest History Conference, 1997.

Reuker, Ann M., and Erna Gunther. "Makah." In *Northwest Coast.* Vol. 7 of *Handbook of North American Indians,* edited by Wayne Suttles. Washington, D.C.: Smithsonian Institution, 1990, 422–30.

Richards, Leverett. "Hubbard Indian Achieves Fame as Carver, Expert on Tribal Lore." *Oregonian,* Jan. 4, 1959 [no page number available].

———. "Lelooska, Indian Artist and Cultural Treasure, Dies at 63." *Oregonian,* Sept. 6, 1996, B9.

Richards, Suzanne. "Lelooska Always Has Time for Visitors." *Oregon Journal,* Dec. 2, 1971, sect. 2, p. 1.

Riley, Patricia, ed. *Growing Up Native American: An Anthology.* New York: William Morrow and Company, 1993.

Rosier, Paul C. "'The old system is no success': The Blackfeet Nation's Desire to Adopt the Indian Reorganization Act of 1934." *American Indian Culture and Research Journal* 23:1 (1999), 1–37.

Ruby, Robert H., and John A. Brown. *Dreamer-prophets of the Columbia Plateau: Smohalla and Skolaskin.* Norman: University of Oklahoma Press, 1989.

Ruppert, James. *Mediation in Contemporary Native American Fiction.* Norman: University of Oklahoma Press, 1995.

Samuel, Cheryl. *The Raven's Tail.* Vancouver, B.C.: University of British Columbia Press, 1987.

Sanchez, George J. *Becoming Mexican American: Ethnicity, Culture, and Identity in Chicano Los Angeles, 1900–1945.* New York: Oxford University Press, 1993.

Sarris, Greg. *Mabel McKay, Weaving the Dream.* Berkeley: University of California Press, 1994.

Schoenberg, Rev. Wilfred P., S.J. *A History of the Catholic Church in the Pacific Northwest, 1743–1983.* Washington, D.C.: The Pastoral Press, 1987.

Sewid-Smith, Daisy (My-yah-nelth). *Prosecution or Persecution.* Cape Mudge, B.C.: Nu-Yum-Baleess Society, 1979.

Sheffield, Gail K. *The Arbitrary Indian: The Indian Arts and Crafts Act of 1990.* Norman: University of Oklahoma Press, 1997.

Smith, Paul Chaat, and Robert Allen Warrior. *Like a Hurricane: The Indian Movement from Alcatraz to Wounded Knee.* New York: New Press, 1996.

Spradley, James P., ed. *Guests Never Leave Hungry: The Autobiography of James Sewid, a Kwakiutl Indian.* New Haven, Conn.: Yale University Press, 1969.

Suttles, Wayne. "History of Research: Early Sources." In *Northwest Coast.* Vol. 7 of *Handbook of North American Indians,* edited by Wayne Suttles. Washington, D.C.: Smithsonian Institution, 1990, 70–72.

Suttles, Wayne, and Aldona Jonaitis. "History of Research in Ethnology." In *Northwest Coast.* Vol. 7 of *Handbook of North American Indians,* edited by Wayne Suttles. Washington, D.C.: Smithsonian Institution, 1990, 73–87.

Szasz, Margaret Connell. *Education and the American Indian: The Road to Self-Determination Since 1928.* Albuquerque: University of New Mexico Press, 1977.

Thornton, Russell. *American Indian Holocaust and Survival: A Population History Since 1492.* Norman: University of Oklahoma Press, 1987.

Townsend-Gault, Charlotte. "Northwest Coast Art: The Culture of Land Claims." *American Indian Quarterly* 18:4 (1994), 445–67.

U.S. Dept. of Health, Education, and Welfare. *The Indian Education Act: Reformation in Progress*. Washington, D.C.: Government Printing Office, 1976.

Vigil, James Diego. *From Indians to Chicanos: The Dynamics of Mexican American Culture*. Prospect Heights, Ill.: Waveland Press, 1984.

Vizenor, Gerald. *Earthdivers: Tribal Narratives on Mixed Descent*. Minneapolis: University of Minnesota Press, 1981.

Wardwell, Allen. *Tangible Visions: Northwest Coast Indian Shamanism and Its Art*. New York: Monacelli Press, 1996.

Weibel-Orlando, Joan. *Indian Country, L.A.: Maintaining Ethnic Community in Complex Society*. Urbana: University of Illinois Press, 1991.

West, Elliot. *Growing Up in Twentieth-Century America: A History and Reference Guide*. Westport, Conn.: Greenwood Press, 1996.

Whiteley, Peter. "The End of Anthropology (at Hopi)?" *Journal of the Southwest* 35:2 (1993), 125–57.

Willson, Margaret, and Jeffrey L. MacDonald. "International Chinese Business Directory for the Year 1913: Introduction [and Reprint]." *The Annals of the Chinese Historical Society of the Pacific Northwest* 3 (1985–1986), 70–85.

Wyatt, Victoria. "Alaskan Indian Wage Earners in the 19th Century: Economic Choices and Ethnic Identity on Southeast Alaska's Frontier." *Pacific Northwest Quarterly* 78:1–2 (1987), 43–50.

Yanovsky, Elias. "Food Plants of the North American Indians," U.S. Department of Agriculture misc. pub. 237 (1936). In *An Ethnobotany Source Book: The Uses of Plants and Animals by American Indians*, edited by Richard I. Ford. New York: Garland, 1986.

Yans-McLaughlin, Virginia. "Metaphors of Self in History: Subjectivity, Oral Narrative, and Immigration Studies." In *Immigration Reconsidered: History, Sociology, and Politics*, edited by Virginia Yans-McLaughlin. New York: Oxford University Press, 1990, 254–92.

Zenk, Henry B. "Kalapuyans." In *Northwest Coast*. Vol. 7 of *Handbook of North American Indians*, edited by Wayne Suttles. Washington, D.C.: Smithsonian Institution, 1990, 547–53.

Zucker, Jeff, Kay Hummel, and Bob Høgfoss. *Oregon Indians: Culture, History, and Current Affairs, an Atlas and Introduction*. Portland: Oregon Historical Society, 1983.

INDEX

LIBRARY OF CONGRESS CATALOGING-IN-PUBLICATION DATA

Friday, Chris

Lelooska : the life of a northwest coast artist / Chris Friday.

p.   cm.

Includes bibliographical references and index.

ISBN 0-295-98324-8 (alk. paper)

1. Lelooska, 1933—1996.

2. Indians of North America—Northwest Coast of North America—Biography.

3. Indian artists—Northwest Coast of North America—Biography.

I. Title.

E78.N78F75 2003   700'.92—dc21   [B] 2003040287